# WHAT MAMMAL IS THAT?

# WHAT MAMMAL IS THAT?

*by*

RONALD STRAHAN

*with the magnificent illustrations of Neville W. Cayley*
*and*
*additional illustrations by Peter Schouten*

ANGUS
& ROBERTSON
PUBLISHERS

The Publishers wish to thank the
Australian Museum for allowing
the reproduction of the illustrations
in the section Australian Mammals:
Words and Pictures.

ANGUS & ROBERTSON PUBLISHERS

Unit 4, Eden Park, 31 Waterloo Road,
North Ryde, NSW, Australia 2113, and
16 Golden Square, London W1R 4BN,
United Kingdom

First published in Australia
by Angus & Robertson Publishers in 1987

Illustrations by Neville W. Cayley
© Angus & Robertson Publishers 1987
Text by Ronald Strahan
© Angus & Robertson Publishers 1987
Illustrations by Peter Schouten
© Angus & Robertson Publishers 1987

National Library of Australia
Cataloguing-in-publication data.

Cayley, Neville W. (Neville William), 1887–1950.
  What mammal is that?

  Includes index.
  ISBN 0 207 15325 6.

  1. Mammals — Australia — Identification. 2. Mammals —
  Australia — Pictorial works. I. Strahan, Ronald,
  1922- . II. Schouten, Peter. I. Title.
599.0994

Typeset in 12pt Bem by Midland Typesetters
Printed in Singapore

# CONTENTS

# FOREWORD

This book is primarily a celebration of the art of Neville W. Cayley, illustrator of the two most widely used reference books in the history of Australian zoology. *What Bird is That?*, of which he was both author and illustrator, has passed through 38 printings since its publication in 1931 and may be regarded as the Australian birdwatcher's Bible (albeit, like the Gospels, obscure in certain passages). In common with hundreds of thousands of other readers I used it when young as my first source of information on Australian avifauna and, like all who used the book, I was often frustrated by the tiny, crowded illustrations. Several years ago, Cayley's original plates came to light in the archives of the publishers, Angus & Robertson, who decided to issue a revised edition in a larger format and with separate marginal illustrations of each species. The task of revision, and of making new illustrations of the species of which Cayley was not aware, fell to my colleague, Terence Lindsey, scientific editor in the Australian Museum's National Photographic Index of Australian Wildlife. The enthusiastic reception of his beautiful volume stimulated the publishers to dig deeper, to unearth Cayley's original illustrations for Ellis Troughton's *Furred Animals of Australia*, and to commission me to produce this companion volume.

Whereas *What Bird is That?* became one of a plethora of books on Australian birds, *Furred Animals of Australia* remained virtually the only general account of Australian mammals for a considerable part of the twentieth century. Gould's magnificent *The Mammals of Australia*, published between 1845 and 1863, was a work of surprising accuracy and insight but has always been rare and expensive. *The Animals of Australia* by A. H. S. Lucas and W. H. D. Le Souef (1909) had a useful section on Australian mammals, including some original observations but, like *The Wild Animals of Australia* by A. S. Le Souef and Harry Burrell (1926), much of the text was lifted, with very little alteration, from the *Catalogue of Marsupialia and*

*Monotremata in the Collection of the British Museum (Natural History)* by Oldfield Thomas (1888). Interestingly, the section on bats in Le Souef and Burrell's book was written by Troughton, then 33 years old and Curator of Mammals and Skeletons in the Australian Museum: it was obviously based on his original researches.

Five years later, in 1931, Troughton's own book (originally to have been called *What Mammal is That?*) was published. Until the appearance of W. D. L. Ride's *A Guide to the Native Mammals of Australia* in 1970, it provided the only available systematic treatment of the Australian mammals and, inasmuch as Ride's treatment of most species was restricted to essential diagnostic characters, *Furred Animals* can be said to have remained the basic reference until the multi-authored *Australian Museum Complete Book of Australian Mammals* which I had the honour to edit and bring to fruition in 1983.

In short, Troughton's work had no rival for half a century, a period which saw the emergence of Australian mammalogy as a vigorous scientific discipline. His book has served its purpose and there would be little point in re-issuing it. I have therefore chosen to write a new text in a skeletal, telegraphic style similar to *What Bird is That?*. It lacks Troughton's interesting digressions and manifest humanity but, by attempting to give the same emphasis to each species, I have tried to show what we know about their basic ways of life and, equally significantly, to show where information is so sparse that little can be said.

The text is derived from the published work of numerous authors, boiled down to bare essentials. I have drawn heavily upon *The Australian Museum Complete Book of Australian Mammals* (1983); C. H. S. Watts and C. Aslin's *The Rodents of Australia* (1981); *Carnivorous Marsupials*, edited by M. Archer (1982); *Possums and Gliders*, edited by A. Smith and I. Hume (1984); and Judith E. King's *Seals of the World*

(1983), but it must be emphasised that I bear responsibility for any errors or misinterpretations.

I remarked at the outset that this book has its origin in Cayley's illustrations. In my opinion, Cayley was a technically competent portrayer of birds but, in comparison with many other practitioners of the craft, his paintings are flat and rather lifeless. Much the same can be said of his mammal paintings: they are inferior to those made jointly by Gould and Richter 70 to 100 years earlier but they comprise the only other reasonably comprehensive set. For this reason alone they deserve re-publication in a larger format. However, the set is incomplete. Even in 1931, *The Furred Animals of Australia* did not include illustrations of every known species and, since then, more species have been recognised—either by discovery or as the result of reassessment of earlier classifications. When I began to count the gaps, it became clear that Cayley's work covered only about two-thirds of the species that are currently recognised.

Peter Schouten, whose sense of animal form has been well demonstrated in his reconstructions of Australian fossil animals, was commissioned by the publishers to fill these substantial gaps. Advisedly, he did not attempt to mimic Cayley's style but developed his own technique—which may well be unique—using fine-pointed coloured pencils. Whereas Cayley worked from skins and mounted specimens, Schouten has relied mainly upon photographs in the extensive collections of the National Photographic Index of Australian Wildlife.

In a sense, this book is comparable with the apocryphal axe used to decapitate King Charles— regarded as authentic despite replacement of the head and the handle. Troughton's *Furred Animals* reappears here under his original title but with a new text and a substantial proportion of new illustrations. I do not know whether the shade of my old friend is currently measuring the wingspans of cherubim or the tail-lengths of demons, but I hope that, if he becomes aware of this metamorphosis, his great sense of humour will enable him to share the joke with me.

Long before wildlife conservation became fashionable, Ellis Troughton was one of a few voices raised on behalf of native animals. As an outcome of European settlement and the introduction of a number of exotic animals, the nineteenth century witnessed the extermination of about a dozen mammalian species and a catastrophic decline in the distribution of some two dozen others. By the 1930s, when Troughton began writing, the situation had stabilised somewhat, inasmuch as little arable land remained uncleared and sheep, cattle, cats, foxes, pigs, brumbies, goats,

donkeys and camels had spread into virtually every part of Australia in which they could survive. Yet threats persisted: the remaining rainforests and eucalypt forests were (and still are) diminishing and demands for agricultural land were (and still are) leading to the clearing of the last of the mallee and brigalow scrubs. There were virtually no programmes for the protection or management of rare or endangered species, or for the dedication of areas of land specifically to provide secure habitats for these species (most national parks having been established for their scenic values).

What Troughton felt in his heart was blisteringly documented by A. J. Marshall in *The Great Extermination*, published in 1966. With hard facts and figures, Marshall painted a picture of pillage, waste and rape, of ignorance, apathy and cupidity, which was designed to shock and shame Australians into a sense of collective responsibility for the fauna and flora of their country. Many readers were influenced by him but, as is so often the case, attitudes in Australia were shaped less by indigenous influences than by those emanating from the USA. In the late 1950s conservation had achieved respectability in America and by the mid-1960s the urban middle class of Australia followed suit. In 1967 Australia's first National Parks and Wildlife Service was established in New South Wales, followed rapidly by similar organisations in each State and in the federal Territories.

By this time, too, research on native mammals had achieved a solid base in universities and the CSIRO Division of Wildlife Research. What may be called the modern phase of research on Australian mammals (physiology, ecology, genetics, behaviour) began in 1948 when Horace Waring arrived from England to take up the chair of zoology in the University of Western Australia. Ten years later, the volume of research and number of research workers was sufficient to justify the formation of the Australian Mammal Society and, some 20 years later, universities were able to provide the young graduates required to establish wildlife services on a sound scientific footing.

*Australian Mammalogy*, the thriving journal of the Australian Mammal Society, was founded in 1972. Its fourth issue, in 1975, subtitled the "Ellis Troughton Memorial Number", included an obituary by his friend and colleague, J. H. Calaby. Calaby refers to Troughton's entering the employ of the Australian Museum in 1908 at the tender age of 14 and to his continuance in that institution—apart from two years' service as a stretcher-bearer in France in 1917 and 1918—until his retirement in 1958. (He did not mention—as I feel compelled to—that young Ellis appeared for his interview in a "Little Lord Fauntleroy" suit of velvet knickerbockers—perhaps presaging his lifelong predilection for things theatrical.)

On his return from war service in 1919, Troughton was promoted to curator and remained in charge of the mammal department of the Museum for the remainder of his working life. His research was almost exclusively on the taxonomy and nomenclature of Australian mammals but, lacking any formal training in zoology, he could not communicate well with the new wave of mammalogists, who disregarded many of his calliper-based definitions. I was one of his critics and, in my *Dictionary of Australian Mammal Names* (1981) I remarked that, "unfortunately, the nine new genera [of bats] that he proposed . . . are no longer recognised". It is interesting, however, that two of these genera have recently been resurrected and that his support for the division of the quolls into three genera, *Dasyurus*, *Dasyurops* and *Satanellus*, is again fashionable. Younger workers are finding that Troughton was sometimes right, but for what they may regard as the wrong reasons.

Troughton was an Australian who maintained the traditions of nineteenth-century European classificatory zoology. His job, as he saw it, was primarily to define species and to describe their appearance. Consideration of their physiology, behaviour, population dynamics, etcetera, lay outside his purlieu and his published comments on the way of life of the species that he described are essentially anecdotal. To say this is not to decry his substantial contribution to Australian mammalogy but simply to observe that many developments passed him by, unheeded. Through all the reprintings and editions of *Furred Animals*, he added not a word about such exciting discoveries as ruminant digestion in kangaroos or delayed implantation of their embryos and he dismissed continental drift as no more than a "theory". He continued to fight battles that had raged in the early nineteenth century, such as whether kangaroos were born in the normal mammalian way or budded from their mothers' teats and whether platypuses laid eggs.

In respect of wildlife he was less a conservationist than a preservationist. He did not argue for active management of endangered animal populations, simply urging that we cease doing what seems to be injurious. His approach was essentially anthropomorphic and, although I regard it as inadequate as a programme of action, I must include his creed here as an indication of the deep emotion with which he approached the animals that he trapped and shot to further his researches.

A CREED FOR NATURE LOVERS

*I believe:*

*That, because the Australian continent fostered all the fascinating furred animals, birds and flowers that awaited the coming of civilization, our land must remain their everlasting sanctuary.*

*That, because the forests and trees supply food and shelter for the birds, and unique marsupials like the Koala, such forests should not be destroyed without adequate reason and due replacement.*

*That wild flowers should be gathered only with that appreciative care due to living things of exquisite scent and beauty.*

*That the nests of birds, built with such patient devotion, should never be destroyed in thoughtless curiosity; that their eggs should be left to bring forth lovely feathered songsters; that the rifling of their homes is no less a crime than is theft from our own.*

*That enjoyment of the living plants and animals will provide a more lasting and universal source of pleasure and education than collecting their remains, save in the cause of science, and for exhibitions which increase knowledge and the love of nature.*

*That we should not destroy living things that are harmless to us, as we hope to avoid harmful things ourselves; that even harmful creatures should be controlled with due regard for their zoological heritage and right to survive.*

*That any wholesale sacrificing of native animals for monetary gain, in a country so rich in resources of grain, stock, and minerals, is a confession of incompetence and wasteful greed, unworthy of the Australian Commonwealth.*

*That, because ancient Australian isolation evolved the gentlest and least harmful host of furred animals the world can ever know they must be conserved with benevolent care and receive adequate sanctuary for their future survival, subject only to the vital needs of man.*

*E. T., 1936*

He was kind, gentle and "a fellow of infinite jest". As a young man I was happy to sit at his feet. No longer young, I understand what it is like to be surrounded by brilliant young zoologists who regard one as old-fashioned, so it is with some fellow-feeling that I offer this echo of his book to an audience far more critical and well-informed than he faced in 1931.

Ronald Strahan,
NATIONAL PHOTOGRAPHIC INDEX OF
AUSTRALIAN WILDLIFE,
THE AUSTRALIAN MUSEUM
*January 1987*

# ARRANGEMENT OF TEXT

## COMMON NAME

Very well-known species usually have explicit common names (Koala, Red Kangaroo, Platypus) but the names of less familiar species may vary with the locality. Thus, what is known in New South Wales as the Mountain Brushtail Possum tends to be called the Bobuck in Victoria and what many Western Australians refer to as the Woylie is elsewhere known as the Brush-tailed Bettong. Unfortunately, most Australian mammals are unknown to the general public which has therefore felt no need to name them—except in a very general sense as possums, kangaroos, bandicoots and the extremely misnamed "marsupial mice" and "native cats".

The challenge to give vernacular names to Australian mammals has been accepted with enthusiasm by numerous authors over the past two centuries and, in the absence of any rules or guiding principles, the result has been bedlam. Some authors have simply translated the scientific names into English, some have created their own descriptive names and others have sought to use Aboriginal names (overlooking the fact that a widespread species may be known by vastly different names in the numerous Aboriginal languages and dialects). Until it becomes embedded in common usage, no common name can be regarded as "correct" but the Australian Mammal Society has attempted to establish some order by producing a list of recommended names. This forms the basis of the common nomenclature used in this book. Wherever practicable, the noun part of each common name corresponds with the genus (or a group of allied genera) and the adjective part refers to the appearance of the species or to its distribution.

## SCIENTIFIC NAME

The system of scientific nomenclature of animals and plants has been established for more than two centuries. Each species is given a name consisting of two words, the first being the generic name, which is a noun; the second being the specific name, effectively an adjective qualifying that noun. As a noun, the generic name can stand on its own: thus we may speak of the genus *Macropus* to include all the kangaroos and the larger wallabies, or *Petrogale* in reference to most of the rock-wallabies. Great care is taken to ensure that each generic name is unique.

Since a specific name is adjectival, it cannot be used in isolation. Such names as *australis* (southern), *longicaudata* (long-tailed), *maculata* (spotted), or *cinereus* (ashy-coloured) have been used in hundreds, perhaps thousands, of names and all occur at least twice in the names of Australian mammals. Quite clearly, one cannot refer to a species except by giving both parts of its scientific name: *Macropus rufus*, the Red Kangaroo; *Macropus giganteus*, the Eastern Grey Kangaroo; *Macropus fuliginosus*, the Western Grey Kangaroo; and so on. Since this takes up a lot of space, there is a convention that, once the name of a genus has been introduced into a passage, it can be referred to thereafter by its initial letter. Once we know that we are referring to *Macropus*, we can refer to its various species as *M. rufus, M. giganteus*, and so on.

In many instances we find that a widespread species comprises several recognisably different forms, each more or less geographically distinct. While these are capable of interbreeding, their isolation tends to make such interbreeding rather infrequent. Such forms are variously known as races or subspecies. The name of a subspecies consists of three words: the generic name, the specific name and the subspecific name. For example, the Common Brushtail Possum, *Trichosurus vulpecula*, has three distinct subspecies: one extending over most of the mainland, one restricted to north-eastern Queensland and one restricted to Tasmania. These are known respectively as *Trichosurus vulpecula vulpecula, Trichosurus vulpecula johnstoni* and *Trichosurus vulpecula fuliginosus*. These trinomials are extremely clumsy but, once the name of the species has been introduced, they may be shortened to *T. v. vulpecula, T. v. johnstoni*, and so on.

## CLASSIFICATION

Merely to be able to deal with the million or so species of animals that have already been described (there are probably at least another million yet to be named), we would need some system of categories. In fact, the ambitions of zoologists go further, for they attempt a classification that coincides with the course of evolution. By placing a number of species in the same genus, a zoologist expresses a considered opinion that these species evolved from a common ancestor. In grouping genera into a family, families into superfamilies and superfamilies into suborders or orders, similar judgments are made.

Yet each such judgment is limited by the evidence available at the time and the sagacity of the individual making the decision. As new evidence comes to hand or new lines of argument are brought to bear upon old evidence, our classification of animals is modified. There is no absolute guarantee that each successive modification brings our classification closer to a reconstruction of an evolutionary "tree" but, in general, this seems to be the case.

For example, in the three years between the publication of *The Australian Museum Complete Book of Australian Mammals* and the present volume, there have been a number of significant revisions of the relationship between certain marsupials. Differences between the quolls are seen to be so great that they are now distributed between three genera. What had been long regarded as a single family of ringtail possums is now classified as two families, the Pseudocheiridae and Petauridae, and the so-called pygmy-possums are here divided into "true" pygmy-possums (Burramyidae) and primarily gliding species (Acrobatidae). The component species of each group remain unchanged; what these changes indicate is that their common ancestors are more remote than was hitherto assumed. It would be very surprising if no further changes were made in the light of evidence yet to come.

## DERIVATION OF SCIENTIFIC NAMES

When a new species is named, the person conferring the name has almost infinite latitude. One can indicate what seems to be a significant difference from related species, a geographic locality, the name of the discoverer, the sponsor of an expedition or even one's spouse or sweetheart; a name may even be nonsensical. Virtually the only possibility ruled out (by good manners rather than impropriety) is naming a species after oneself. This is hardly necessary since, if one names enough species after one's colleagues, they can usually be relied upon to reciprocate.

The methodology of biological nomenclature was established at a time when most educated Europeans had a reasonable knowledge of Latin and at least an acquaintance with Greek. In naming an animal *Macropus fuliginosus*, a nineteenth-century author could be reasonably sure his reader would recognise its reference to a "sooty-coloured big-foot", that *Phascolarctos cinereus* was an "ash-coloured pouched-bear" and *Taphozous nudicluniatus* a "bare-buttocked tomb-dweller". Since few Australians now have much acquaintance with classical languages, I have included the barest indication of the derivation of the names of Australian mammals and of the families and higher categories that are relevant to their classification. More detailed explanations are given in my *Dictionary of Australian Mammal Names* (1981).

## PRONUNCIATION

One can seldom pronounce a zoological name intelligently without recognition of the roots from which it is derived. This point has escaped many of the current generation of Australian zoologists, who are meticulous in their pronunciation of phosphohexoisomerase, deoxyribonucleic acid or dihydroxyphenylpyruvate (where the component *chemical* roots are recognisable) but become unintelligible when pronouncing relatively simple biological names, the roots of which are unknown to them. I have heard respected Australian mammalogists (many of whom mistakenly refer to their discipline as "mam-ol'-o-jee") pronounce *Pseudomys*, as "sue-doh'-meez", *Dendrolagus* as "den-drol'-ah-gerz" and *Nycticeius* as "nik-tice'-ee-us". In my dictionary I provided a guide to pronunciation, based on the simple premise (happily accepted by chemists) that the pronunciation of a scientific name, designed to be international, is determined by the components from which it is constructed. Stubbornly, and however uphill the battle, I again provide the basis of a rational (and reasonably international) pronunciation of the names of Australian mammals, using a simpler phonetic system and a more restricted range of vowels than in the dictionary. This leads to an over-emphatic pronunciation but, given that

Australian usage will inevitably slur and mute any distinctions that I recommend, this is not inappropriate. The convention for vowel sounds is as follows:

| | | | |
|---|---|---|---|
| ay | as in *bay* | oh | as in *doe* |
| a | ,, ,, *bat* | o | ,, ,, *dot* |
| ah | ,, ,, *bah* | or | ,, ,, *for* |
| ee | ,, ,, *bee* | aw | ,, ,, *law* |
| e | ,, ,, *bet* | ue | ,, ,, *sue* |
| er | ,, ,, *fern* | u | ,, ,, *but* |
| ie | ,, ,, *die* | oo | ,, ,, *good* |
| i | ,, ,, *bit* | ow | ,, ,, *cow* |
| air | ,, ,, *fair* | oy | ,, ,, *boy* |

In some cases where a syllable ends in a consonant, the system has been modified: thus "sute" instead of "suet" and "dite" instead of "diet".

### LENGTH

Many separate measurements (lengths of head plus body, tail, hindfeet, forearm, etcetera) are used in the formal description and diagnosis of mammals. Here, we are concerned only to give an idea of the relative sizes of the species described; the measure chosen for this purpose is the total length, nose-tip to tail-tip. The illustration of each animal is reproduced in approximate real-life proportion to the other animals illustrated on the plate.

### HABITAT

The habitat of a terrestrial species is defined by a large number of factors, not least of which are the availability of water, the nature of the soil, the sunlight, temperature variations, rainfall, vegetation and age thereof, and presence of other species. In many instances, definition of the overall environment is without much significance, the survival of a species being dependent upon such factors as the microclimate within centimetres of the forest floor, the presence of nesting holes in old trees or access to humid caves.

In this book I have been able to do little more than indicate the broad parameters of the habitats of the species treated—often because we lack more detailed knowledge.

### NOTES

Here the information is limited essentially to the daily rhythm of activity of a species; food and how this is obtained; notable aspects of behaviour; and reproduction.

Where an entry is short, it may reasonably be inferred that the species has not been the subject of much research.

### STATUS

Judgments on the status of a species or subspecies have at least two components. One is an assessment of total numbers, which is seldom practicable except in the rarest species. Another is essentially a prognosis—whether its population is increasing, stable or decreasing—and the extent to which its habitat and associated life-support systems are becoming better or worse. For the majority of Australian mammals the weight of evidence is such that one can say either that they appear to be secure for the foreseeable future or that they appear to be endangered. Nevertheless, there remains a significant minority about which we have insufficient information to make a judgment. Some species that are here referred to as "vulnerable" fall into this category.

### DISTRIBUTION MAP

It must be emphasised that the blank areas of a distribution map are usually more informative than those that are shaded: there is a very high probability that a species will *not* be found in the blank area. The shaded area indicates the maximum known range of a species: it does not imply that it can be found throughout the area, merely that it is likely to occur *in appropriate habitats* within the defined area.

# AUSTRALIAN MAMMALS

As a consequence of its long isolation from the other continents, Australia has a very limited variety of native mammals: of the 22 major groups (orders) of mammals living in the world today, only five were represented on Australian soil prior to the arrival of humans some 50,000 years ago. These are the monotremes (platypus and echidna), two orders of marsupials, the bats and the rodents. A sixth group, the seals, includes several species that come ashore on parts of the coast, and a seventh, represented by the Dugong, enters tropical estuaries. On the other hand, Australia (and New Guinea, which is part of the same landmass) is unique in being the only part of the world with representation of the three subclasses of living mammals. The subclass Prototheria is represented by the monotremes, the subclass Metatheria by the marsupials, and the subclass Eutheria by the bats, rodents, seals and the Dugong.

Monotremes, which comprise only the Platypus and two species of echidnas (one restricted to New Guinea), differ considerably in appearance but have basically similar internal anatomy. They hatch their young from soft-shelled eggs and produce milk from numerous glands on the mother's belly, rather than through teats, as in other mammals. The considerable differences in the way of life of the Platypus and echidnas suggest that, in the past, there must have been a range of less specialised monotremes of more "ordinary" appearance, but the fossil record is so poor that no sign of these has yet been found. The subclass Prototheria is a large assemblage of extinct forms other than the monotremes, and we might well ask why it is that only the two contemporary species have survived. The answer seems to be that they are so specialised that they have no significant competitors. Apart from the Water-rat, the Platypus is the only aquatic mammal in Australia and there is virtually no overlap in the food needs of the two species. The Short-beaked Echidna is in an even more fortunate position, since no other Australian mammal feeds habitually on ants.

A characteristic of marsupials is that they give birth to very small young with incomplete hindlimbs (see p. 9). Another less familiar feature is that the first toe in the foot (the "big" toe) usually protrudes at a right angle to the other toes providing a strong grip when climbing. This toe has been lost in some marsupials which run or hop on the ground, but its presence in the less specialised species is a clear indication that the first marsupials were arboreal. Many still live in trees and some Australian species have a membrane between the fore- and hindlimbs which permits them to glide from one tree to another. Some, such as wombats and bilbies, make deep burrows; one, the Marsupial Mole, spends almost all of its time below the desert sand. Most will swim if it is necessary to do so but only one, the Yapok of South America, dives below the surface to find its food. Most marsupials run in the ordinary quadrupedal manner when on the ground, but the kangaroos and their kin have perfected a hopping gait which, interestingly, is more energy-efficient than galloping.

The first marsupials probably fed mainly upon insects, perhaps supplemented by soft fruits. Many of the modern marsupials are excellent predators but others have become generalised plant-eaters, while a few others such as the tree-kangaroos, Greater Glider and Koala, eat the leaves of trees. The Honey-possum, with its long tongue, is specialised for lapping nectar, and the Numbat, with its even longer tongue, feeds exclusively on termites. The Sugar Glider supplements its diet of insects by eating the gum of acacias and it also gouges grooves in the trunks of smooth-barked eucalypt trees to obtain sap. Kangaroos are the only marsupials able to subsist on grasses. Only one marsupial, the Numbat, is active throughout the day. All the others feed at night or around dusk and dawn, except sometimes in very cold weather.

Eutherians are the familiar mammals, comprising all those that are neither marsupials nor monotremes. Ranging from whales to bats and from elephants to mice, they are the dominant vertebrates of present times. Placental mammals differ from marsupials and monotremes in many rather subtle details of anatomy and physiology but the most notable differences are the possession, in general, of a proportionately larger brain and the birth of fully formed young. This second characteristic is to be interpreted in contrast with the condition of newborn marsupials, which are in a decidedly incomplete condition, and does not imply that newborn placental mammals are capable of independent existence. Some, indeed, are able to run after their mothers within an hour or so of birth but others are born naked and with closed eyes and spend some time in a state of absolute dependence upon their mothers.

In comparison with the monotremes and the marsupials, which have probably been in Australia for not less than 50 million years, the eutherians are recent migrants. The Cat, Fox, Rabbit, Hare, Horse, Pig, Camel, Goat, deer, cattle and sheep have been on the continent for less than 200 years. The Dingo may have arrived about 5000 years ago, long after the first humans, who came to Australia not less than 40,000 and possibly as long as 50,000 years ago. True rats (members of the cosmopolitan genus *Rattus*) probably crossed Torres Strait less than a million years ago: other rodents (the "old endemics") arrived between five and ten million years ago. The first bats may have flown in some five million years earlier. Fur-seals, sea-lions and seals have probably been visiting Australian coasts for as long as they have existed in the southern hemisphere — possibly one or two million years ago. The same is probably true of the Dugong.

# AUSTRALIAN MAMMALS: WORDS AND PICTURES

The oldest known illustrations of Australian animals were painted on rock faces more than 10,000 years ago in what is now Kakadu National Park. These include four species of kangaroos, the Rock Ringtail Possum, a bandicoot, the Numbat, Long- and Short-beaked echidnas, the Thylacine and the Tasmanian Devil. The antiquity of these paintings is underlined by the fact that the Long-beaked Echidna appears to have become extinct in Australia more than 15,000 years ago and that, at the time of European settlement of Australia, the Thylacine and Tasmanian Devil had long been restricted to Tasmania.

Vague European references to Australian mammals can be traced back to 1629 when Pelsaert's ship, *Batavia*, was wrecked on the Houtman Abrolhos: he described "cats" which we now assume to have been Tammar Wallabies. Volckertzoon in 1656 and de Vlamingh in 1696 saw Quokkas on Rottnest Island and referred to them, respectively, as "cats" and "rats". De Vlamingh also saw a "yellow dog" or Dingo near Jurien Bay. Dampier saw a Dugong near King Sound and what was probably a Banded Hare-wallaby on the Kimberley coast. Unfortunately, none of these reports was supported by an illustration, however crude.

The oldest known European representation of a mammal indigenous to Australia is a simple outline sketch of a dead kangaroo made by Sydney Parkinson, draughtsman to Sir Joseph Banks, when Cook's *Endeavour* was beached on the north Queensland coast. This sketch was the basis of a more lifelike painting by George Stubbs, itself the model for an engraving in Hawesworth's account, *An Account of the Voyages undertaken by order of His Present Majesty for making Discoveries in the Southern Hemisphere* (1773). This was the first published illustration of an Australian mammal.

Cook and Banks had seen a Spotted-tailed Quoll and a Common Ringtail Possum but the former was not illustrated and an engraving of the latter did not appear until the publication of an official account of Cook's voyages in 1804. Considering the scientific and artistic talents of his crews and the wealth of botanical and zoological information accumulated on the voyages, the mammals of Australia received remarkably little attention.

No interest seems to have been shown in setting traps and, because most mammals are nocturnal, they escaped the guns of naturalists who seldom spent the night ashore.

Greater contact was inevitable when the penal colony was established in New South Wales in 1788. The first two years saw the discovery and at least the preliminary description of the Common Brushtail Possum, Long-nosed Potoroo, Greater Glider and Squirrel Glider, but the level of illustration of these species was variable. The unidentified illustrator of an anonymous work, *The Voyage of Governor Phillip to Botany Bay* (1789), provided a barely recognisable engraving of a Common Brushtail Possum and an extremely elongated kangaroo. In strong

contrast, Surgeon General John White made very good sketches from which Frederick Nodder, in England, made paintings of the Greater Glider and Long-nosed Potoroo which later appeared as engravings in White's *Journal of a Voyage to New South Wales* (1790).

Nodder was associated for a time with the naturalist-publisher George Shaw (who had written the zoological part of White's narrative) in the production of a part-work, "the Naturalist's Miscellany", the first issue of which included an illustration of the Eastern Grey Kangaroo under the scientific name by which it is still known, *Macropus giganteus*. Even though Shaw thought that kangaroos were gigantic hopping rodents, he has the distinction of being the first person to have given a generic name to an indigenous Australian mammal. (In 1780 Storr had given the name *Phalanger* to a cuscus, but it was from Melanesia.)

Further discoveries of Australian mammals up to the end of the century were few but notable. In 1794, Shaw published the first part of his *Zoology of New Holland*, which included an illustration (probably based on a sketch by the convict artist, Thomas Watling) of the Feathertail Glider. In his *Account of the English Colony in New South Wales*, Judge-Advocate David Collins published very primitive drawings of the Common Wombat ("from a living subject") and a Platypus ("on the spot"), both the work of Governor John Hunter. A future governor of New South Wales was also involved in illustration at this time: in 1792, while in command of H. M. S. *Providence*, William Bligh made an excellent drawing of a Short-beaked Echidna which he found at Adventure Bay, Tasmania. This, together with his detailed notes, formed the basis of a learned paper published 10 years later by the anatomist Everard Home.

At the end of the seventeenth century, knowledge of Australian mammals remained slight and disorganised. The peculiarities of the Platypus and the Echidna were marvelled at but little sense could be made of them. Marsupials were regarded as variants on the South American opossums or as strange hybrids between familiar creatures of the Old World: kangaroos were seen as rodents akin to jerboas. On the other hand, birds, fishes and insects were simply accepted into the body of zoological knowledge and fairly accurately portrayed but because artists and

## GREATER GLIDER
*Petauroides volans*

*Journal of a voyage to New South Wales, with sixty-five plates of nondescript animals, birds, lizards, serpents, curious cones of trees and other natural productions.* John White, Surgeon General to the Settlement, London, 1790, pl. 61, Hepoona Roo.

*"Between the fore and hind legs, on each side, is placed a doubling of the skin of the side, which, when the legs are extended laterally, is as it were pulled out, forming a broad lateral wing or fin . . . In this respect it is very similar to the flying squirrel of America . . . The hind foot has also five toes but differs considerably from the fore foot; one of the toes may be called a thumb, having a broad nail, something like that of the Monkey or Opossum; what answers to the fore and middle toes are united in one common covering and appears like one toe; this is rather similar to the kangaroo."*

In an excellent description, here severely abridged, White draws attention to the similarity between the gliding possums and squirrels but does not, like many of his contemporaries, assume that this implies a close relationship. His description of the hindfoot makes a point that few writers recognise, even today: namely, that a thumblike first toe is found only in marsupials and primates. He also mentions the peculiar syndactyl condition of the second and third toes of this possum and the kangaroo, but fails to relate this to what Buffon, in 1765, had regarded as a peculiar characteristic of what he called "phalangers" and are now known as cuscuses.

draughtsmen had still to get the "feel" of marsupials, these were depicted with artificial stiffness.

Mammals suffered also from a relative lack of popularity. While individual kangaroos, platypuses and wombats were themselves of great interest as zoological novelties, they did not arouse the same curiosity or urge to collect as did birds, beetles or seashells. Thousands of amateur naturalists might enthuse about a new species or race of bird but only a small number of more or less professional zoologists were interested in variations on the theme of possums or bandicoots, and still less with the bats and rodents which, together, make up more than half the Australian mammal species. On the other hand, there was a strong tradition of official botanising, for it was almost an article of faith of the Colonial Office that every new land would provide new plants of agricultural potential. Sadly, Australia produced only the Macadamia Nut, which was not exploited until the twentieth century.

The lack of systematic interest in mammals is reflected in the scientific personnel, if any, of British and colonial exploratory voyages of the nineteenth century. Matthew Flinders was accompanied on the voyages of the *Investigator* by the botanist, Robert Brown, and a botanical draughtsman, Ferdinand Bauer. In addition to plants, they collected many birds but found no new mammals. P. P. King, who completed the exploratory voyages begun by Flinders, had the services of Alan Cunningham, a very competent botanist, but the voyages yielded only six mammal specimens, all of which were already well known. One might have expected that Thomas Henry Huxley, on H. M. S. *Rattlesnake* and Charles Darwin on H. M. S. *Beagle* would have grasped the opportunity to search for new marsupials during their respective visits to Australia but Huxley showed no interest and Darwin, or one of his assistants, managed no more than to trap a Bush Rat near Albany, Western Australia, just before the *Beagle* departed the continent.

Most terrestrial explorers sent out by colonial governments were similarly bereft of mammalogical assistance. In 1817 and 1818, Oxley was accompanied by Alan Cunningham but Sturt, on his several expeditions between 1828 and 1846, and Mitchell, between 1831 and 1836, were their own naturalists. Mitchell and Sturt were good draughtsmen and made excellent pencil sketches of birds but Mitchell's illustrations of the Pig-footed Bandicoot and Mitchell's Hopping-mouse, both discovered by him (although described by William Ogilby) are very wooden. It was not until 1856, under the leadership of William Blandowski, that a land expedition, primarily for natural history purposes, was organised to explore any part of inland Australia. Gerard Krefft, an all-round naturalist who was a member of the expedition, brought back some interesting observations on the mammals of inland Victoria but no illustrations arose from the exercise.

The French had a different approach. In the late eighteenth and early nineteenth centuries, a number of exploratory voyages centred on Australia, most notably those of d'Entrecasteaux (1792–93), Baudin (1801–03), Freycinet (1818), and Dumont d'Urville (1826–27). Of these, Baudin's expedition — originally with three botanists and five zoologists out of an initial complement of 16 scientists and skilled draughtsmen — was the most significant in terms of mammalogy. Many of the expert staff left Baudin's two ships at Mauritius, refusing to proceed any further, and the success of the expedition, in terms of zoology, was due to two men, François Péron, an indefatigable zoologist, and Charles Lesueur, an artist who worked closely with him. Péron brought more than 100,000 zoological specimens back to the Paris Museum but, dying in 1810, he described only two new species of Australian mammals, the Banded Hare-wallaby and the Australian Fur-seal. Lesueur made thousands of sketches on paper and paintings on vellum, some of which are yet to be published. The real value of the work of these two men lay in the documented specimens which they added to the collection of the Paris Museum, and which were later described by such zoologists as de Blainville, Desmarest, Lacépède and Geoffroy Saint-Hilaire, mainly in the encyclopaedias that flourished in post-Napoleonic France. Lesueur's paintings cannot be said to have been totally representative but they give indications of having been drawn from living or recently dead specimens. Illustrations in the French encyclopaedias tend to lack this quality, being made largely from museum skins.

It was not necessary to be an explorer in order to contribute to Australian natural history or the illustration thereof. John Lewin arrived in Sydney as an immigrant in 1800, accompanied two minor and unsuccessful expeditions and thereafter remained resident in Sydney, from which base he produced the first book on Australian insects and the first book on Australian birds (the latter being the first illustrated book to be produced in Australia). His contribution to mammalogy was negligible but it is of interest that, at the request of Governor King, he made a painting of the first living Koala to be brought into Sydney. A sketch made from the painting was sent by King to Sir Joseph Banks and copies of this copy, successively less accurate, turned up in European handbooks of zoology for the next 50 years. Nothing was known of the fate of the original painting until it was offered for sale in 1982 by a distant descendant of the Governor; it is now in the Mitchell Library, Sydney. The first published illustration of the Koala appeared in Perry's *Arcana*, published in 1811, but this bore no relation to Lewin's portrait, being obviously reconstructed from a skin.

Australian mammalogy could perhaps be dated from 1808 when G. P. Harris, Deputy Surveyor of Van Diemen's Land (Tasmania) not only illustrated the Tasmanian Devil and Thylacine for the first time, but published a scientific description of the two species in the *Transactions of the Linnean Society of London*. His drawings were by no means artistic nor particularly accurate but they convey a reasonable impression of these very unusual animals. Harris regarded both species as members of the genus *Didelphis*, that of the Virginian Opossum, and it was not until several decades later that they were placed, respectively, in the genera *Sarcophilus* and *Thylacinus*.

Another of the very few mammals to be described by a resident of Australia was the Brown Antechinus. Captain J. Stuart, Assistant Colonial Surgeon, sketched a specimen and made notes on its anatomy, passing these to W. S. Macleay, a gentleman of means in Sydney. Macleay fleshed out the notes and published a description and the illustration on the *Annals and Magazine of Natural History* in 1842. In his initial description, Macleay referred to the animal as a member of the order Insectivora—and thus related to the shrews and hedgehogs—but, chancing to look at the skull (an action that might have been taken earlier), he recognised that it must be that of a carnivorous marsupial. A correction was published in the next issue of the *Annals*.

Publications based on Péron's collections and material subsequently acquired by the Paris Museum dominated the systematic literature of Australian mammals until the 1830s. Even the very useful *Animal Kingdom* of E. Griffith, C. H. Smith and E. Pidgeon was based on a translation of the work of Baron Cuvier. A more idiosyncratic work, the 14-volume *Allgemeine Naturgeschichte* by L. Oken, a transcendentalist professor of natural history at the University of Zurich, illustrated all the marsupials known at the time of writing (1833–42) but in a stylised manner.

A higher standard of mammal illustration was established by Richardson and Gray in their report of the voyage of the *Erebus* and *Terror* (1844), but this included only a few Australian mammals. Of equal quality were the illustrations in G. R. Waterhouse's *A Natural History of the Mammalia*, the first volume of which (dealing with marsupials) was published in 1846. Unfortunately, the only species illustrated were those described for the first time in the book.

A turning point in the study of Australian mammals and birds was the visit, between September 1838 and April 1840, of the naturalist-publisher John Gould. At that time he was already famous for his large and beautifully illustrated books on birds of various parts of the world, mostly produced without leaving England. He had begun a volume on the birds of Australia but found it unsatisfactory and decided to look at them first-hand. Almost as an afterthought, he also studied such mammals as he could find in his 20 months of travel in Tasmania, South Australia, Victoria and New South Wales. His own observations were recorded in the form of quick but fluent pencil sketches with copious annotations indicating colour and texture and these were developed into paintings by assistant artists, including his wife, Elizabeth, Edward Lear and, for the majority of his mammal studies, H. C. Richter. Clearly, there was no possibility of covering all the mammals and birds in the course of his visit, but he had the invaluable assistance of a brilliant and assiduous collector, John Gilbert. Between 1838 and the middle of 1845 when (accompanying Leichhardt on an expedition through northern Queensland to Port Essington) he was killed in an affray with Aborigines, Gilbert spent more than six years travelling through Australia, collecting specimens for Gould and making detailed notes of the behaviour of the species that he trapped or shot.

Two years after his return to London, Gould published a large *Monograph of the Macropodidae*, including every known species of kangaroo, wallaby and rat-kangaroo and excellent accounts of their natural history, mostly the result of his and Gilbert's direct observations. This material was later absorbed into his two-volume *The Mammals of Australia*, published in 13 parts between 1845 and 1863. There had been nothing remotely approaching this standard previously and, in terms of accuracy, originality and scope, nothing like it could ever be produced again. In addition to his beautiful and expensive publications, Gould also published descriptions of new species in scientific journals (though these were seldom graced with his illustrations) and he is the author of descriptions of 38 currently recognised species of Australian mammals: no other worker has exceeded this number, although it is approached by two great mammalogists of the British Museum, J. E. Gray (31 species) and M. R. O. Thomas (36 species). And, Gould, it should be noted, regarded himself as an ornithologist!

Thomas was responsible, in 1888, for a magnificent work of scholarship, the *Catalogue of the Marsupialia and Monotremata in the Collections of the British Museum (Natural History)*. Where Gould had dealt primarily with appearance and behaviour, Thomas addressed himself to the anatomy and systematics of the Platypus, Echidna and marsupials. He included some fine colour plates, but only of the few species that were described for the first time in this work.

No other major works dealing with Australian mammals were published in the nineteenth century but these animals were included, of course, in many general treatises of general zoology, published in French, German and English. Of the English works, mention might be made of Wood's *The Illustrated Natural History* (1864), which contains a number of reasonable black and white engravings of Australian marsupials.

Between 1923 and 1925, F. W. Jones, professor of anatomy at the University of Adelaide, produced two paperback volumes, *The Mammals of South Australia* which, for the first time, attempted a synthesis of the natural history and anatomy of the mammals of that State; it has been a great disappointment to Australian mammalogists that his canvas was so limited, for it is a remarkably stimulating text. Jones was not an artist but he was a competent draughtsman who knew exactly what he wished to portray when he put pen to paper and this, too, adds greatly to the value of his work.

The next milestone in Australian mammalogy was Troughton's *Furred Animals of Australia*, of which this book is, in some respects, a continuation. Remarks about it will be found in the Foreword.

Two major works of the second half of the twentieth century must also be mentioned. One is D. W. L. Ride's *A Guide to the Native Mammals of Australia*, which provides a fine introduction to the subject but has few and rather poor black and white illustrations. The second is *The Australian Museum Complete Book of Australian Mammals*, a survey of the general biology of all the species that were recognised by the end of 1982. The joint work of 110 specialist authors and about the same number of photographers, it is currently the best general reference.

## FEATHERTAIL GLIDER
*Acrobates pygamaeus*

*Zoology and Botany of New Holland and the Isles Adjacent.* G. Shaw and J. E. Smith (figures by J. Sowerby), London, 1793, pl. 2, *Didelphis pygmaea*, Pygmy Opossum.

*"The figures are taken from coloured drawings made on the spot and communicated to Mr. Wilson [T. Wilson, F.L.S., to whom book is dedicated] by John White, Esq. Surgeon General to the Colony . . ."*

*"Among the most curious quadrupeds yet discovered in the Antarctic regions, may be numbered the animal represented on the present plate; which . . . forms, as it were, a kind of connecting link between . . . the Opossum and Squirrel."*

In the search for systematic zoological placement of the Australian marsupials, few early commentators could avoid regarding the herbivorous species as somehow related to the rodents.

*Didelphis pygmaea*

## EASTERN GREY KANGAROO
*Macropus giganteus*

*Museum Leverianum containing Select Species from the museum of the late Sir Ashton Lever, Kt with descriptions in Latin and English. G. Shaw M.D., F.R.S. (No. 6), London, 1796, opp. p. 35, (pl. 69?), Macropus giganteus.*

*". . . if external form or habit alone were to be regarded, we might consider the Kangaroo as a gigantic kind of Jerboa, since it has the same length of hind-legs, the same brevity of fore-legs and the same springing motions and shape: yet the teeth are almost as different from those of the Jerboa as those of the Opossum. In fact, we need not have the slightest hesitation in forming for the Kangaroo a distinct species."*

Shaw's conclusion that a kangaroo was no less different from a jerboa than it was from an opossum led him to the conclusion that the Eastern Grey Kangaroo was a distinct species. This was an advance on the position that kangaroos were giant jerboas but it fell short of recognising that opossums and kangaroos are representatives of the group that we now call marsupials.

## TASMANIAN DEVIL
*Sarcophilus harrisii and*
## THYLACINE
*Thylacinus cynocephalus*

*Description of two new species of*
Didelphis *from Van Diemen's Land.* By
G. P. Harris, Esq. Communicated by
the Right Honourable Sir Joseph
Banks, Bart . . . Trans. Linn. Soc.,
1808, p. 174, *Didelphis cynocephala,
Didelphis ursina.*

*Didelphis ursina*
*"These animals were very common on our
first settling at Hobart Town and were
particularly destructive to poultry etc. They,
however, furnished the convicts with a fresh
meal, and the taste was said to be not
unlike veal."*

*Didelphis cynocephala*
*"Only two specimens (both males) have yet
been taken. It inhabits among caverns and
rocks in the deep and impenetrable glens in
the highest mountain parts of Van
Diemen's Land . . . It is vulgarly called the
Zebra Opossum, Zebra Wolf, etc."*

Recognition that animals such as the
Thylacine and Tasmanian Devil were
marsupials was a great step forward in
mammalogy. However, since the only
previously recognised marsupials were
the American opossums of the genus
*Didelphis,* the new Australian species
were assigned to this genus.

## KOALA
### *Phascolarctos cinereus*

*Arcana; or the museum of natural history,*
Vol. 1. G. Perry, London, 1811,
opp. p. 53, Koala.

*"Among the most numerous and curious
tribes of animals which the hitherto almost
undiscovered regions of New Holland have
opened to our view, the creature which we
are now about to describe stands singularly
pre-eminent. Whether we consider the
uncouth and remarkable form of its body,
which is particularly awkward and
unweildy [sic], or its strange physiognomy
and manner of living, we are at a loss to
imagine for what particular scale of
usefulness or happiness such an animal
could by the great Author of Nature
possibly be destined."*

This is an interesting echo of the
Judeo-Christian view, set down in
Genesis, that all creatures were made
to serve humans. The concept was
elaborated between the sixteenth and
nineteenth centuries by natural
theologians to such an extent that, in
principle, every species could be cited
as contributing to humans by being
useful, entertaining, instructional or
edifying. It is difficult to see why the
Koala scored so low on every count.

## BANDED HARE-WALLABY
*Lagostrophus fasciatus*

*Voyage de découvertes aux Terres Australes . . . sur les corvettes* le Géographe, le Naturaliste *et la goëlette* le Casuarina *pendant les années 1800, 1801, 1802, 1803 & 1804.* Rédigé par François Péron et continué par Louis de Freycinet. Atlas, 1816, pl. 4, Kanguruh à Bandes.

Lesueur's illustration of the Banded Hare-wallaby, which falls far short of his usual high standard, was copied and recopied for a century with increasing inaccuracy, each copy increasing the impression that the species normally occurred as Siamese twins. The original painting, on vellum, survived Allied bombing in World War II and remains in the Le Havre Museum.

## EASTERN QUOLL
*Dasyurus viverrinus*

*Voyage autour du Monde entrepis par ordre du roi . . . exécuté sur les corvettes de S. M.* l'Uranie la Physicienne *pendant les années 1817, 1818, 1819, 1820.* L. de Freycinet, Paris, 1824, pl. 4, Dasyure de Maugé.

*"We were able to keep one of these on the corvette* Uranie *for five months. This elegant little animal was confident and did not seek to bite when disturbed. Avoiding bright light and seeking darkness, it was very satisfied with the narrow kennel that we had made for it . . . It was not savage; on the contrary it made an attachment to whoever fed and stroked it."*

This account, here abridged, includes one of the earliest descriptions of the behaviour of an Australian marsupial.

*LONG-NOSED POTOROO*
*Potorous tridactylus and*
*WOMBAT*
*Vombatus ursinus*

E. Geoffroy Saint-Hilaire in G. Cuvier (ed.) *Dictionnaire des Sciences Naturelles (1816–1829)*. Paris, Planches, 2nd part, pl. 52, Potoroo and Wombat.

*"M. Desmarest has established that this genus of rat-kangaroo links the possums with the true kangaroos. Potoroos have the general appearance of kangaroos but their dentition is very similar to that of possums."*

Recognition that the dentition of the rat-kangaroo is, in some respects, intermediate between that of possums and the typical kangaroo was of considerable zoological significance. So far as Geoffroy was concerned, this helped to classify the animals; after Darwin, it would be seen to have evolutionary significance. We now recognise that kangaroos evolved from possum-like ancestors. Which of the modern possums is most closely related to the kangaroo remains an open question.

*"The wombat is found in the mountains around Port Jackson, also King Island in the middle of Bass Strait and the Furneaux Islands. The sealers on King Island eat its flesh, which they find to be very good."*

It is interesting that the first wombats to become known to the British colony in New South Wales were eaten by shipwrecked sailors. The wombat continued as a component of colonial diet until at least the middle of the nineteenth century.

## SPRINGHARE
*Pedetes capensis* and
## EASTERN GREY KANGAROO
*Macropus giganteus*

*Oeuvres complètes de Buffon suivies de ses continuateurs,*—Vol. III, Mammifères. Brussels, 1829, pl. 274, Gerboise du Cap, Kanguruh.

*"The kangaroo or gigantic jerboa of New Holland is not the same animal as the great jerboa or jumping hare of the Cape of Good Hope; and Messrs. Forster, who have been inclined to make this comparison, consider, as we do, that they are different species of the genus of jerboas."*

The possibility that kangaroos could be other than large, jumping rodents took some time to be accepted. The Springhare is a large hopping rodent from southern Africa.

Th. Lejeune éditeur.                    Lith. de Burggraaff, a Brux.

## LONG-NOSED BANDICOOT
### Perameles nasuta

*Illustration of zoology, being representations of new, rare, or remarkable subjects of the animal kingdom.* J. Wilson, Edinburgh–London, 1831, pl. 10, *Perameles nasuta.*

"*The order [Marsupalia] of which I shall not at present attempt to give any definition, contains all those animals which are provided with an abdominal pouch . . . Let each of the marsupial genera be classed according to the position pointed out by a careful study of its natural and influential characters: and if, for example, the structure of its teeth indicate a carnivorous disposition in one genus, an insectivorous one in another, or a herbivorous one in a third, then let each be referred to its appropriate station . . . as a member of the* Carnivora, *the* Insectivora, *or in closer connection with the more harmless* Glires."

This comment indicates the difficulty with which some European zoologists accepted the fact that the Australian marsupials had evolved into *ecological equivalents* of the better-known eutherian mammals.

## BUSH RAT
### Rattus fuscipes

*The Zoology of the voyage of H. M. S.* Beagle *under the command of Captain Fitzroy, R.N. during the years 1832 to 1836.* Edited and superintended by Charles Darwin, Esq. M.A., F.R.S., Sec GS, Part II Mammalia. Described by George R. Waterhouse with a notice of their habits by Charles Darwin, Esq., M.A., F.R.S., et. London, 1839, p. 66, pl. 25, *Mus fuscipes.*

"*Mammalia not belonging to the order* Marsupiala *are rare in the continent. Besides the dog, we are acquainted with none excepting a few species of Rodents, and all these belong to the family* Muridae *. . . 'This animal was caught in a trap baited with cheese, amongst the bushes at King George's Sound.'—D.*"

This is Charles Darwin's only claim to Australian mammalogical fame—a common rodent caught in a trap just before H. M. S. *Beagle* departed from Australia. The scientific description was made by George Waterhouse, Darwin's contribution being reproduced above in its entirety.

## STRIPED POSSUM
*Dactylopsila trivirgata*

*List of species of mammalia sent from the Aru Islands by Mr A. R. Wallace to the British Museum.* J. E. Cray, Proc. Zool. Soc., London, 1858, *26*, p. 106, pl. 43.

*"The forefeet elongate, toes very slender, compressed, very unequal in length, quite free; the outer and third or middle toe nearly equal, the second or ring-finger much the longest, the fourth and fifth short . . ."*

This detailed scientific description mentions, but does not comment upon, the enormously elongated third digit of the hand, a feature unique among the marsupials and otherwise present only on the Aye-aye of Madagascar, a primitive primate. It may be noted, in passing, that this publication appeared in the same year that Wallace, still in the East Indies, produced his short account of the theory of evolution by natural selection, leading to a joint publication with Charles Darwin.

## THYLACINE
*Thylacinus cynocephalus*

*Zoological Sketches by Joseph Wolf made for the Zoological Society of London from animals in their vivarium in the Regent's Park.* Edited with notes by Philip Lutley Sclater M.A., F.L.S. etc., London, 1861, pl. 31, Thylacine.

*"The Zoological Society are indebted to the exertions of Mr. Ronald Gunn and Dr James Grant, of Lancaster, for the first pair of Thylacines ... they arrived in perfect safety and the female survives to the present time [c. 1860]. The Thylacine originally preyed on the Kangaroos and Bandicoots, but since the introduction of sheep into the colony, it has become more addicted to attack the sheepfolds. Perpetual war is therefore waged against it by the Tasmanian shepherds, whose determined persecution must eventually lead to its extinction."*

## SOUTHERN HAIRY-NOSED WOMBAT
*Lasiorhinus latifrons*

*Zoological Sketches by Joseph Wolf made for the Zoological Society of London from animals in their vivarium in the Regent's Park.* Edited with notes by Philip Lutley Sclater M.A., F.L.S. etc., second series, 1867, pl. 27, Hairy-nosed Wombat, *Phascolomys latifrons.*

*"In the spring of 1862, the Zoological Society of London received from the Acclimatisation Society of Melbourne two Wombats of this new species. These had been brought to Melbourne from South Australia ... The muzzle clothed with dense coarse hair ... led me to suggest the name* lasiorhinus.*"*

All hairy-nosed wombats are now placed in the genus *Lasiorhinus*. A second species, long thought to be extinct, is now known to survive in a small area of Queensland and there is suggestive evidence of a remnant population in New South Wales.

## RED KANGAROO
*Macropus rufus*

*Dictionnaire universel d'Histoire Naturelle (ed. M. C. D'Orbigny) I. Geoffroy Saint-Hilaire, 1861, pl. 19, Kangurus laniger.*

*"Kangaroos have reproduced several times in our zoos: it would seem desirable to try, as is being attempted in England, to acclimatise and breed them in Europe to provide a new source of wealth. Unfortunately our Parisian climate seems unfavourable: living specimens received by the museum have survived only for several months."*

Red-necked Wallabies were eventually acclimatised in the Black Forest of Germany, where they remained feral until World War II.

## PLATYPUS
*Ornithorhynchus anatinus*

*Dictionnaire universel d'Histoire Naturelle (ed. M. C. D'Orbigny) I. Geoffroy Saint-Hilaire, 1861, pl. 20, Kangurus laniger.*

*"... the anonymous author of an article published in 1827 in the* Anthologie de Florence *says that in the nests of these animals are sometimes two white eggs ... and that the females hatch these like birds. But this is far from proven and it now seems to be demonstrated that they are really viviparous ..."*

It was so difficult for European zoologists to accept the possibility of egg-laying mammals that direct affirmations of this fact were passed off as "unproven".

## NUMBAT
### Myrmecobius fasciatus

The Mammals of Australia, Vol. 1.
J. Gould, London, 1863, pl. 14,
Myrmecobius fasciatus, Numbat.

"Sterile sandy districts thinly studded with
moderately sized trees appear to be
congenial to its habits and mode of life. As
the form of its teeth would indicate, insects
constitute a great part of its food; but I
believe it also feeds upon honey and a
species of manna which exudes from the
leaves of the Eucalpyti. Wherever the
Myrmecobius takes up its abode, these
ants are found to be very abundant, and in
all probability, for I have no evidence that
such is the case, it is upon this insect or its
larvae that it mainly subsists."

Although a long tongue and degenerate
teeth are often associated with a diet of
nectar, these are also common
adaptations in animals which feed upon
small colonial insects. We now know
that the Numbat feeds exclusively upon
termites. Ants that are preying upon
the termites disturbed by a Numbat
may be ingested incidentally.

## KULTARR
### Antechinomys laniger

On Antechinomys and its allies.
E. R. Alson, Proc. Zool. Soc.,
London, 1880, p. 454, pl. 45.

"From the structure of the limbs and the
characters of the soles of the feet, it is
evident that it is strictly terrestrial and
digitigrade; while the powerful muscles of
the loins indicates that, when going at
speed, it probably moves by a succession of
leaps."

From its resemblance to a jerboa, the
Kultarr might well be thought to
progress by leaps. It in fact moves by
bounds, kicking off with the hindlegs
and landing on the forelegs.

# EGG-LAYING MAMMALS

*SUBCLASS PROTOTHERIA*
*(proh'-toh-thee'-ree-ah)*

DERIVATION   Gk, *protos*, first; *therion*, animal, mammal.

The characteristics of the living prototherians are those of the order Monotremata.

# ORDER MONOTREMATA

*(mon'-oh-trem-ah'-tah)*

DERIVATION.   Gk, *monos*, single; *trema*, orifice.

There can be no doubt that monotremes are mammals. They are warm-blooded, have a covering of hair and suckle their young on milk. Yet they are peculiar because, like reptiles, they hatch their young from soft-shelled eggs. The Platypus usually lays two eggs in a nest at the end of a burrow and curls its body around these to incubate them. A female echidna, on the other hand, develops a temporary pouch on its abdomen and the egg is hatched here. Nobody has yet seen how the egg is placed in the pouch but it seems probable that the body is curled in such a way that the egg is transferred directly into it. As in reptiles, birds and lower vertebrates, monotremes pass their urine, faeces and eggs to the exterior through the same external orifice, the cloaca. The scientific name of the group draws attention to this condition.

# MONOTREMES

PLATE 1

1  PLATYPUS *Ornithorhynchus anatinus* (see page 6)

2  SHORT-BEAKED ECHIDNA (Tasmanian subspecies) *Tachyglossus aculeatus aculeatus* (see page 7)

3  SHORT-BEAKED ECHIDNA (south-eastern subspecies) *Tachyglossus aculeatus setosus* (see page 7)

*1*

*2*

*3*

FAMILY
# Ornithorhynchidae
*(or'-nith-oh-rink'-id-ee)*

DERIVATION.   sci., *Ornithorhynchus* platypus; *-idae*, familial suffix.

This family contains only one species, the Platypus, a monotreme that is beautifully adapted to an aquatic life and for sifting small animals such as crustaceans and molluscs from the sediment at the bottom of a river or lake.

# Platypus
*Ornithorhynchus anatinus*
*(orn'-ith-oh-rink'-us an'-ah-teen'-us)*

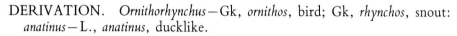

PLATE.   1:1

DERIVATION.   *Ornithorhynchus*—Gk, *ornithos*, bird; Gk, *rhynchos*, snout: *anatinus*—L., *anatinus*, ducklike.

LENGTH.   440–550 mm.

HABITAT.   Vicinity of riverbanks and lakes in well-watered coastal sclerophyll forests.

NOTES.   Sleeps most of the day in a nest in burrow in the bank of the waterbody. Solitary. Feeds at evening and night (also by day during winter in cooler latitudes) on a wide variety of bottom-living invertebrates, sifted from mud and water by flexible, ducklike snout. Webbed feet, nostrils at tip of snout, absence of external ears, and water-repellent fur make it the most aquatically adapted of all Australian mammals apart from the seals.

Mating begins in August in the warmer part of the range, progressively later to October in the southern part. Female lays two eggs, incubated for about two weeks, young suckled for four to five months.

STATUS.   Common.

FAMILY
# Tachyglossidae
*(tak'-ee-glos'-id-ee)*

DERIVATION.   sci., *Tachyglossus*, echidna; *-idae*, familial suffix.

This family contains two species: the Short-beaked Echidna which inhabits most of Australia and the lowlands of New Guinea; and the Long-beaked Echidna, a much larger and less spiny animal that is confined to the highlands of New Guinea. The Short-beaked Echidna feeds mostly upon ants, but its larger relative uses its long tongue to forage in rainforest litter mainly for worms.

# Short-beaked Echidna
*Tachyglossus aculeatus*
*(tak'-ee-glos'-us ak-yue'-lay-ah'-tus)*

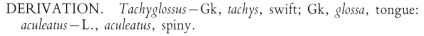

PLATE.   1:2 and 3

DERIVATION.   *Tachyglossus* — Gk, *tachys*, swift; Gk, *glossa*, tongue: *aculeatus* — L., *aculeatus*, spiny.

LENGTH.   330–450 mm.

HABITAT.   Wet sclerophyll forest to deserts.

NOTES.   Inhabits almost all of Australia and lowlands of New Guinea. Sleeps most of day under shelter of fallen timber or in rocky crevice. Feeds around evening and dawn (often by day under cold conditions) on termites, excavated from nest with powerful forefeet and collected on long, sticky tongue. Solitary. Excellent passive defence provided by spiny coat, and ability to roll into ball and to dig itself into ground rapidly while maintaining a horizontal posture.
   Mating occurs in July and August. Single egg transferred (laid into?) temporary pouch on belly of mother. Egg hatches in about 10 days, young suckled for at least three months.

STATUS.   Four Australian subspecies: *T. a. aculeatus*, wetter regions of eastern mainland; *T. a. acanthion*, north-western mainland and arid areas; *T. a. multiaculeatus*, Kangaroo Island; and *T. a setosus*, Tasmania. All common.

# MARSUPIALS

*SUBCLASS METATHERIA OR MARSUPIALIA*
*(mar-syue'-pee-ah'-lee-ah)*

DERIVATION.   L., *marsupium*, pouch, bag.

Although the name of these animals indicates that they are pouched, as in the familiar kangaroos, some female marsupials lack this structure; in others, the pouch is represented by a mere flap of skin, partially surrounding the teats. In general, the pouch is well developed in the larger species and absent in the very small ones. A much more characteristic feature of marsupials is that their newborn young are born in a foetal condition; naked, blind and with embryonic hindlimbs. The forelimbs are precociously developed and armed with sharp, curved claws but the hindlimbs are represented only by fan-shaped buds, with shallow creases indicating where the toes will eventually form. Newborn marsupials are also relatively much smaller than those of the more familiar (placental) mammals: in marsupials about the size of a mouse, newborn individuals are no larger than a grain of rice.

As soon as it is born, a newborn marsupial crawls, by its forelegs, from the cloacal orifice of its mother towards the teats. Having located one, it clamps its mouth firmly around it and settles down to a second period of growth and development. In this stage of attachment to the maternal teats, the young are appropriately referred to as "pouch-embryos". Until recently, this style of reproduction was regarded as markedly inferior to that of placental mammals but we now recognise that—since it obviously works—the marsupial way is simply *different*.

The same appears to be the case with most other differences between marsupials and placental mammals, such as a slightly lower body temperature and metabolic rate. In at least one feature, however, marsupials appear to be inferior to placental mammals. With few exceptions, they have relatively smaller brains and—although there has been insufficient research to establish the difference—it appears that their behaviour is less flexible. To put it simply and brutally, it appears that a marsupial is not as "bright" as a placental mammal of similar size. In ways of life, such as hunting, where flexible behaviour, learning and prediction are at a premium, we may expect a placental mammal to displace a marsupial and this seems to have happened, for example, when the Dingo came into competition with the Thylacine. On the other hand, where survival depends largely upon physiological fitness for a particular way of life, the placental mammal has no inbuilt advantage: without human assistance, sheep could not displace kangaroos.

There is considerable uncertainty about the interrelationships of the marsupials and hence of their appropriate classification. The view taken here is the conservative one that they fall into two orders, the Polyprotodonta and Diprotodonta, based on their dentition.

# Order Polyprotodonta

*(pol'-ee-proh-toh-don'-tah)*

DERIVATION.   Gk, *polys*, many; *protos*, first; *odous,* tooth

The marsupials that are classified in this group have three or four pairs of narrow, pointed upper incisors and three lower pairs of similar shape. In this respect they differ fundamentally from the Diprotodonta (see p. 67). Additionally, polyprotodont marsupials usually have well-developed upper and lower canines, two or three pairs of upper and lower premolars, and four pairs of upper and lower molars with sharp, shearing cusps. Such a dentition, which is well suited to a carnivorous, insectivorous or omnivorous diet, probably represents an ancient and relatively unspecialised mammalian condition which preceded the evolutionary separation of the marsupial and eutherian mammals. Thus, the fact that we find it in the carnivorous and omnivorous Australian mammals and in the omnivorous opossums of the Americas is not very strong evidence that these groups are closely related. However, there is other anatomical and biochemical evidence of such a relationship, indicating that the diprotodonts stand apart. At our present stage of understanding, it is therefore reasonable to regard the polyprotodonts as all those marsupials which are not diprotodonts.

The Australian polyprotodonts can be divided into three suborders: the essentially carnivorous Dasyuromorphia; the Notoryctemorphia, with a single species, the Marsupial Mole; and the omnivorous Peramelomorphia, or bandicoots. Each of these suborders comprises only a single superfamily. They are raised to subordinal status in order to express the degree of difference between the groups.

# VARIOUS DASYUROID MARSUPIALS

*1*

2

3

4

5

6

# VARIOUS DASYURID MARSUPIALS

PLATE 3

*1*

# ANTECHINUSES

PLATE 4

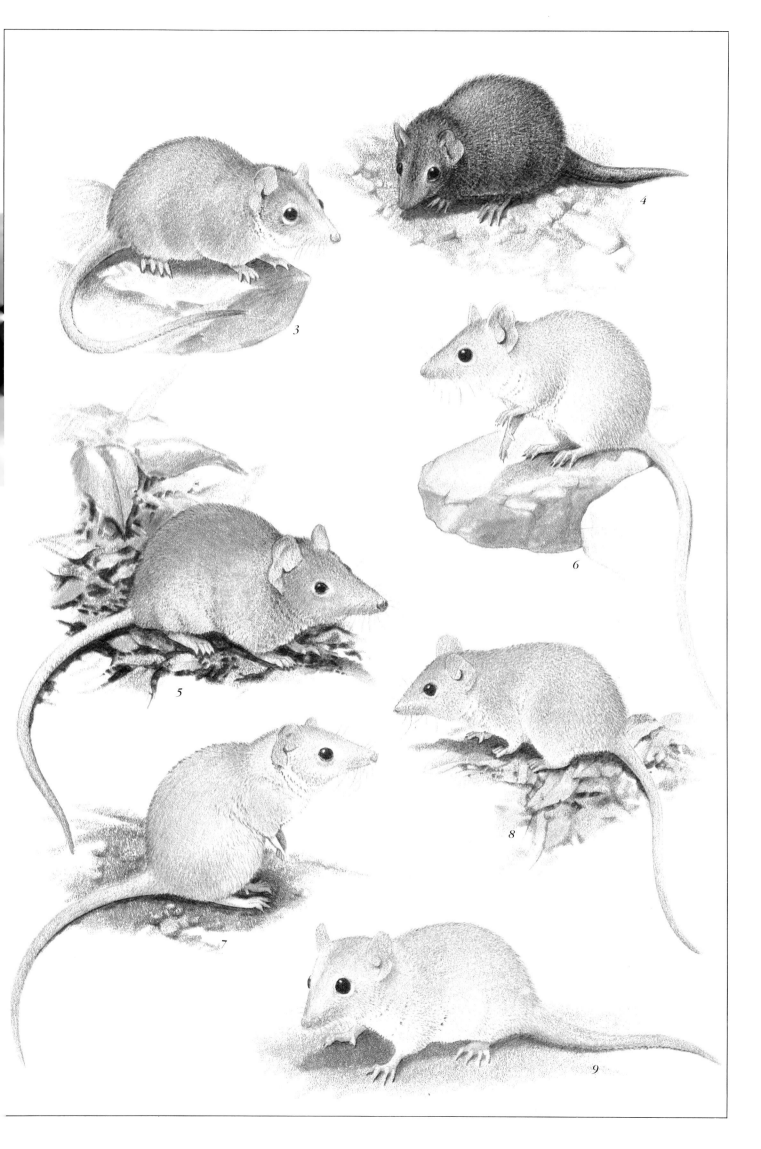

# PLANIGALES AND NINGAUIS

PLATE 5

# DUNNARTS AND KULTARR

# Dunnarts

PLATE 7

1  STRIPE-FACED DUNNART (western form) *Sminthopsis macroura* (see page 49)

2  STRIPE-FACED DUNNART (eastern form) *Sminthopsis macroura* (see page 49)

3  LONG-TAILED DUNNART *Sminthopsis longicaudata* (see page 50)

4  RED-CHEEKED DUNNART *Sminthopsis virginiae* (see page 49)

5  HAIRY-FOOTED DUNNART *Sminthopsis hirtipes* (see page 50)

6  OOLDEA DUNNART *Sminthopsis ooldea* (see page 48)

# DUNNARTS

PLATE 8

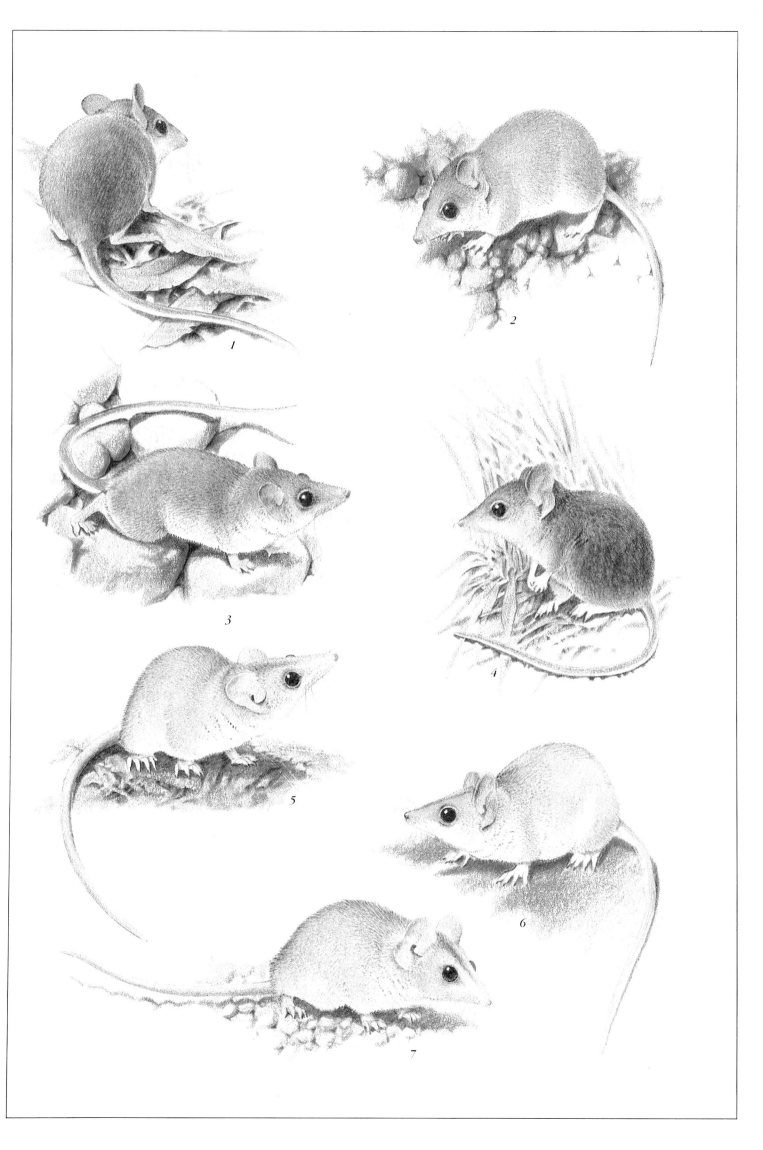

# SPECIALISED DASYUROIDS

PLATE 9

# BANDICOOTS AND BILBIES

4

5

6

7

8

9

10

11

12

SUBORDER **Dasyuromorphia**
*(daz'-ee-yue-roh-mor'-fee-ah)*

DERIVATION.   sci., *Dasyurus*, quoll; Gk, *morphos*, form.

The Dasyuromorphia includes all the typically predatory Australian polyprotodonts, such as the quolls, antechinuses and dunnarts. It also includes the termite-eating Numbat and the recently extinct Thylacine. The Dasyuromorphia comprises a single superfamily, the Dasyuroidea.

SUPERFAMILY **Dasyuroidea**
*(daz'-ee-yue-roy'-day-ah)*

DERIVATION.   sci., *Dasyurus*, quoll; *-oidea*, superfamilial suffix.

Dasyuroids are the typical predatory marsupials of Australia. They do not differ very much in shape but range in size from that of a dog (the recently extinct Thylacine) to much smaller than a mouse (planigales). Typically, a dasyuroid has an elongate, pointed snout and a long, continuous row of teeth comprising pointed incisors, strong canines and serrated, blade-like premolars and molars. (The single exception is the Numbat, in which the teeth—which are not used in feeding—are reduced to a row of similar pegs.) The forelegs and hindlegs are of approximately the same length and the first toe of the hindfoot (if present) is at a right angle to the other four. The tail is usually long and flexible, but not prehensile, and may be covered with long or short hair or have a terminal brush. The name of the group is not diagnostic: it is derived from that of the first of its members to be described, *Dasyurus* (now *Dasyurops*) *maculatus*—which happens to have a very hairy tail.

The living dasyuroids are classified into three families: the Dasyuridae, including all but one of the species; the Thylacinidae; and the Myrmecobiidae, comprising only the Numbat.

FAMILY
# Dasyuridae
*(daz'-ee-yue'-rid-ee)*

DERIVATION.   sci., *Dasyurus*, quoll; *-idae*, familial suffix.

The major characteristics of the family are also those of superfamily Dasyuroidea, mentioned above. Following the extinction of the Thylacine, the largest dasyuroid is now the Tasmanian Devil (up to nine kilograms) which, uniquely in the group, is more a scavenger than a predator. Next in size are the quolls (one to seven kilograms), which are generalised predators in relatively wet forested areas. The phascogales, which are arboreal predators in forests and woodlands, weigh up to 200 grams. Antechinuses, and related forms, which are mostly hunters on the forest floor, vary in range from about 25 grams to about 100 grams. Dunnarts (20–50 grams) have habitats ranging from wet forests to the arid interior. The Kultarr, a close relative of the dunnarts but differing from these and all other dasyurids in having very long hindlegs, is a small desert animal (about 25 grams). Little is known of the biology of ningauis, the first of which was described in 1975: they inhabit dry country and range from about seven grams to about 15 grams. Smallest of the marsupials—and among the smallest known mammals—are the planigales (four to twelve grams); their habitats range from wet forests to deserts.

# Kowari

*Dasyuroides byrnei*
*(daz'-ee-yue-roy'-dayz ber'-nee)*

PLATE.   2:2

DERIVATION.   *Dasyuroides*—sci., *Dasyurus*, quoll; Gk, *-oides*, resembling: *byrnei*—after P. M. Byrne, of Charlotte Waters, Qld, who collected the first specimens.

LENGTH.   250–320 mm.

HABITAT.   Stony ("gibber") desert of central Australia.

NOTES.   Sleeps by day in a burrow but may spend periods basking in sun. At night preys upon large insects, rodents and other small ground-dwelling vertebrates. Does not need to drink. Sexually mature at about nine months but probably does not breed until second year. Breeding continuous except from February to April. Female has six teats in a vestigial pouch and carries up to six young for about eight weeks; thereafter young suckled in a nest to the age of about 16 weeks.

STATUS.   Range has contracted during the twentieth century. Not endangered but possibly vulnerable.

# Eastern Quoll

*Dasyurus viverrinus*
*(daz'-ee-yue'-rus viv'-er-een'-us)*

PLATE.  2:3

DERIVATION.  *dasyurus*—Gk, *dasys*, hairy; *ouros*, tail: *viverrinus*—L., *viverra*, a ferret; referring to the general appearance and behaviour.

LENGTH.  520–730 mm.

HABITAT.  Wet to dry eucalypt forest, extending to savannah and heathland.

NOTES.  Much smaller than the Spotted-tailed Quoll (about one-fifth of weight). Sleeps by day in a nest in a natural crevice, hollow log or short burrow. At night hunts on the ground for large insects and small vertebrates, supplemented by carrion and grasses.
  Both sexes sexually mature at about 11 months, mating in May and June. Female has six to eight teats and five to eight young are carried in the shallow pouch for about 10 weeks and suckled in a nest to age of about 20 weeks.

STATUS.  Widespread on south-eastern mainland within historical times but now apparently surviving only in Tasmania, where it is common.

# Western Quoll

*Dasyurus geoffroii*
*(zhe-froy'-ee)*

PLATE.  2:4

DERIVATION.  *geoffroii*—after Etienne Geoffroy Saint-Hilaire (1772–1844), French zoologist who made notable contributions to Australian mammalogy.

LENGTH.  540–640 mm.

HABITAT.  Arid scrubland, sand plain and desert south of the Tropic of Capricorn (*D. g. geoffroii*); cooler subarid savannah to wet eucalypt forest (*D. g. fortis*).

NOTES.  Sleeps by day in a nest in a shallow excavation or natural crevice. At night preys upon small vertebrates, large insects and carrion when available. Despite non-prehensile tail and the absence of a first toe on hindfoot, is an agile climber, but lives mainly on the ground.
  Both sexes sexually mature at about one year. Mating in May and June. Female has six teats and up to six young are suckled in the pouch for about 12 weeks, and in nest to age of 15–16 weeks.

STATUS.  The once widespread desert subspecies, *D. g. geoffroii*, is apparently extinct in inland Australia but persists in New Guinea. *D. g. fortis* is sparsely distributed in south-western Western Australia.

# Spotted-tailed Quoll

*Dasyurops maculatus*
*(daz'-ee-yue'-rops mak'-yue-lah'-tus)*

PLATE.   2:5

DERIVATION.   *Dasyurops*—sci., *Dasyurus*, quoll; Gk, *opsis*, appearance:
   *maculatus*—L., *maculatus*, spotted.

LENGTH.   750–1310 mm.

HABITAT.   Cool temperate to tropical wet sclerophyll forest and rainforest.

NOTES.   Sleeps most of day in nest in hollow log or rock crevice. Feeds at
   night (sometimes by day) on a variety of prey ranging from small
   mammals and birds to reptiles and insects. Excellent climber but tail not
   prehensile; catches most prey on ground.
      Sexually mature at about one year. Mating from April to July. Female
   has six teats and usually rears five young, independent at about 18 weeks.

STATUS.   Common to sparse over extensive range.

# Northern Quoll

*Satanellus hallucatus*
*(say'-tan-ell'-us hal'-ue-kaht'-us)*

PLATE.   2:1

DERIVATION.   *Satanellus*—*Satan*, devil; L., *-ellus*, diminutive suffix:
   *hallucatus*—L., *hallux*, inner digit of foot, "big toe".

LENGTH.   250–620 mm.

HABITAT.   Tropical to subtropical open forest, savannah, scrubland,
   favouring rocky country.

NOTES.   Smallest of the quolls. Sleeps by day in nest in hollow log or
   natural crevice. At night preys upon rodents, other small vertebrates and
   large insects, and eats succulent fruits.
      Sexually mature at about one year; mating in June and July. Female
   has six to eight teats in vestigial pouch and usually carries six young for
   about 10 weeks; these are suckled in a den to age of about 20 weeks.

STATUS.   Unlike the other quolls, has not suffered reduction in range since
   European settlement. Common.

# Tasmanian Devil

*Sarcophilus harrisii*
*(sar-kof'-il-us  ha'-ris-ee-ee)*

PLATE.  2:6

DERIVATION.  *Sarcophilus*—Gk, *sarx*, flesh; Gk, *philos*, loving: *harrisii*—after G. P. R. Harris, who described the species in 1808.

LENGTH.  910 mm.

HABITAT.  Wet and dry sclerophyll forest, woodland, scrubland.

NOTES.  Largest and least predatory of the living dasyurids. Sleeps by day in hollow log or natural crevice. At night, scavenges for carcasses but also eats beetle larvae and may attack weak or immobilised animals such as lambs and penned poultry.

    Females become sexually mature in the second year of life, mating in March or April. They have four teats in a complete, backwardly directed pouch and carry up to four young which detach from teats at the age of about 15 weeks and are suckled in a den to the age of about 30 weeks.

STATUS.  No more than 3000 years ago, was widespread over Australia. May have persisted on the Australian mainland until 600 years ago but now restricted to Tasmania. Common.

# Mulgara

*Dasycercus cristicauda*
*(daz'-ee-ser'-kus  kris'-tee-kaw'-dah)*

PLATE.  3:6

DERIVATION.  *Dasycercus*—Gk, *dasys*, hairy; Gk, *kerkos*, tail: *cristicauda*—L., *crista*, crest; L., *cauda*, tail.

LENGTH.  200–345 mm.

HABITAT.  Sandy inland deserts.

NOTES.  Sleeps by day in a complex burrow, often with several pop-holes; may emerge for periods to bask in sun. At night preys upon large arthropods and small vertebrates. Does not need to drink.

    Sexually mature at age of 10–11 months; mating mainly in March and April but may extend to July in response to variable rainfall. Female has four to eight teats in vestigial pouch; five to seven young are carried for about seven weeks and suckled in a nest to age of about 14 weeks.

STATUS.  Distribution may have diminished greatly in recent decades, but common in the Northern Territory.

# Brush-tailed Phascogale

*Phascogale tapoatafa*
*(fas'-koh-gah'-lay ta'-poh-ah-tah'-fah)*

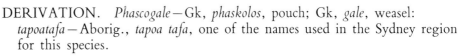

PLATE. 3:5

DERIVATION. *Phascogale*—Gk, *phaskolos*, pouch; Gk, *gale*, weasel: *tapoatafa*—Aborig., *tapoa tafa*, one of the names used in the Sydney region for this species.

LENGTH. 350–450 mm.

HABITAT. Open, well-watered sclerophyll forest, often on ridges with sparse ground cover.

NOTES. Spends the day in a tree-hole; at night hunts in trees for insects, other arthropods and small vertebrates, but tail not prehensile. Also forages on the ground, and may attack penned poultry.

Sexually mature at the age of about 11 months; mating around June. The female has eight teats but no pouch. Young remain attached to the teats for about six weeks and thereafter are suckled until about 20 weeks old. Males die shortly after mating.

STATUS. Two subspecies: *P. t. tapoatafa* in south-eastern and south-western coastal Australia; *P. t. pirata* in northern coastal Australia. Southern subspecies has suffered a reduction in distribution but both remain common in limited parts of range.

# Red-tailed Phascogale

*Phascogale calura*
*(kal-yue'-rah)*

PLATE. 3:1

DERIVATION. *calura*—Gk, *kalos*, beautiful; Gk, *oura*, tail.

LENGTH. 240–270 mm.

HABITAT. Dry, stunted eucalypt forest with relatively continuous canopy and abundant tree-holes and hollow trees.

NOTES. Similar to Brush-tailed Phascogale but much smaller and arid-adapted. Sleeps by day in tree-hole. An agile climber but finds most of its food—small insects, birds and rodents—on the ground.

Sexually mature at about one year; mating from May to June. Female has eight teats but no pouch; carries six to eight young, which are weaned at age of about 20 weeks. Males probably die shortly after mating.

STATUS. Distribution severely reduced since European settlement; now restricted to relatively small area in south-western Australia. Locally common but vulnerable.

# Brown Antechinus

*Antechinus stuartii*
*(an'-te-kie'-nus styue'-ar-tee-ee)*

PLATE. 3:2

DERIVATION. *Antechinus*—Gk, *anti-*, against or equivalent to; Gk, *echinos*, hedgehog: *stuartii*—after J. Stuart, army surgeon who made a preliminary description of a specimen found near Sydney in 1837.

LENGTH. 150–250 mm.

HABITAT. Wet eucalypt forest with dense ground cover.

NOTES. Sleeps by day in a nest in a natural crevice. At night burrows through leaf litter in search of insects, spiders and other small arthropods and vertebrates. In the drier parts of its range, where ground cover and leaf litter are sparse, it may seek much of its food in trees.

    Sexually mature at about 11 months; mating in August or September. Females have from six to 10 teats but lack a definite pouch. All teats usually occupied; young attached for about five weeks, thereafter suckled in a nest to age of about 17 weeks. All males die soon after mating. Females may survive to breed in a second or even a third year.

STATUS. Two subspecies: *A. s. stuartii* from south-eastern Australia; and *A. s. adustus* from Queensland. Both abundant.

# Dusky Antechinus

*Antechinus swainsonii*
*(swayn'-sun-ee-ee)*

PLATE. 3:3

DERIVATION. *swainsonii*—after W. Swainson, from whose private collection the type specimen of this species was obtained.

LENGTH. 190–330 mm.

HABITAT. Wet eucalypt forest with a dense understorey; alpine heath.

NOTES. Sleeps by day in nest in natural crevice on the ground. At night digs among leaf litter and friable soil for insects, other arthropods, and small reptiles, supplemented by fruits such as blackberries. Juvenile animals occasionally climb trees.

    Sexually mature at about eleven months; mating in June or July. Female has 10 teats in a shallow pouch and carries six to eight young for seven to eight weeks. Thereafter young suckled in a subterranean leaf-lined nest to the age of about 14 weeks. Males die within three weeks of mating.

STATUS. Two subspecies: *A. s. swainsonii* in Tasmania and *A. s. mimetes* on the mainland. Both abundant.

# Swamp Antechinus

*Antechinus minimus*
*(min'-im-us)*

PLATE.  3:4

DERIVATION.  *minimus* — L., *minimus*, smallest.

LENGTH.  200–270 mm.

HABITAT.  Wet heathland, tussock grassland and sedges.

NOTES.  Sleeps by day in a well-made nest of grass and leaves. In early part of the night forages among dense vegetation, digging in leaf litter and soil for a variety of insects and spiders.
   Sexually mature at the age of about 11 months; mating from June to August; earlier in the southern part of the range than in the northern part. Females from Tasmania have six teats; those from the mainland have eight. Commonly all teats are occupied by pouch young. Males die soon after mating but females may breed in a second or third year.

STATUS.  Two subspecies: *A. m. minimus* from Tasmania and Bass Strait islands; and *A. m. maritimus* from southern Victoria and South Australia. Both rare.

# Cinnamon Antechinus

*Antechinus leo*
*(lay'-oh or lee'-oh)*

PLATE.  4:8

DERIVATION.  *leo* — L., *leo*, lion, in reference to "lion-like" colour and to Leo Creek, in the McIlwraith Range, Qld, where many specimens were trapped.

LENGTH.  205–295 mm.

HABITAT.  Tropical vine-forest.

NOTES.  Probably sleeps by day in nest in tree-hole. An agile climber which probably forages at night for insects high in the rainforest as well as on the ground. Little is known of its biology. Female has 10 teats. Probable that mating occurs in October and that all males die shortly afterwards.

STATUS.  Common in limited range.

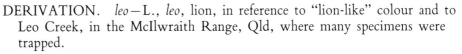

## Atherton Antechinus

*Antechinus godmani*
*(god'-man-ee)*

PLATE.  4:5

DERIVATION.  *godmani*—after F. D. Godman, whose widow endowed an exploration fund which financed the expedition on which the first specimen was found.

LENGTH.  225–305 mm.

HABITAT.  Very wet montane tropical rainforest (mist forest).

NOTES.  By far the largest member of the genus (males up to 120 grams). Sleeps by day in nest in natural crevice. At night forages among deep litter and decomposing timber on forest floor.

  Sexually mature at the age of about 11 months; mating in July. Female has six teats in a rudimentary pouch and may carry up to six young for about five weeks. Subsequently these are suckled in a nest but duration of dependency not known. Males die soon after mating.

STATUS.  Not described until 1923; since then, found at only five localities within its small range. Rare.

## Fawn Antechinus

*Antechinus bellus*
*(bel'-us)*

PLATE.  4:7

DERIVATION.  *bellus*—L., *bellus*, beautiful.

LENGTH.  225–275 mm.

HABITAT.  Tropical open eucalypt forest to woodland with abundant tree-holes and hollow trees.

NOTES.  Resembles the Yellow-footed Antechinus but adapted to tropical monsoon conditions. Sleeps by day in nest in tree hollow or fallen hollow log. Preys at night upon insects taken on the ground or on the trunks of trees.

  Sexually mature at about 11 months; mating in August and September. Female has 10 teats and carries up to 10 young. Details of developmental biology not known. Males die shortly after mating.

STATUS.  Common over most of range.

# Yellow-footed Antechinus

*Antechinus flavipes*
*(flah'-vi-pez)*

PLATE. 4:3

DERIVATION. *flavipes* — L., *flavus*, yellow; L., *pes*, foot.

LENGTH. 160–320 mm.

HABITAT. From tropical rainforest through wet and dry eucalypt forest to mulga woodland.

NOTES. Sleeps by day in rough nest in natural crevice on ground. At night, hunts on the ground for rodents, small birds and insects; also eats flowers and nectar.
　　Sexually mature about one year; mating in about August (in the northern part of the range) or September (in the southern part). The female has 12 teats in a poorly developed pouch and carries eight to 12 young for about five weeks, after which they are suckled in the nest to the age of 19 or 20 weeks. All males die shortly after mating.

STATUS. Three subspecies: *A. f. flavipes* in south-eastern Australia; *A. f. rubeculus* in central coastal Queensland; and *A. f. leucogaster* in south-western Australia. All abundant.

# Ningbing Antechinus

*Antechinus* sp.

PLATE. 4:9

DERIVATION. Common name refers to Ningbing Station, Kimberleys, WA, where first specimen was discovered.

LENGTH. 170–190 mm.

HABITAT. Tropical woodland on dissected sandstone country.

NOTES. Species has been known for many years but has not yet been officially described.
　　Little known of biology. Apparently breeds annually and males probably survive to breed in their second year.

STATUS. Locally common.

# Little Red Antechinus

*Dasykaluta rosamondae*
*(daz'-ee-kah-lue'-tah roz'-ah-mon'-dee)*

PLATE.   4:4

DERIVATION.   *Dasykaluta* — Gk, *dasys*, hairy (but in reference to the family Dasyuridae); *kaluta*, Nyamal Aboriginal name: *rosamondae* — refers to red-haired Rosamond, mistress of Henry II.

LENGTH.   150–180 mm.

HABITAT.   Arid spinifex tussock country.

NOTES.   Sleeps by day in shelter of spinifex tussock. Preys at night on insects and lizards.
   Sexually mature at about 11 months; mating in September. Female has eight teats and may carry up to eight young which become independent at an age of about 16 weeks. All males die shortly after mating.

STATUS.   Common in parts of range.

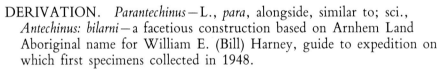

# Sandstone Antechinus

*Parantechinus bilarni*
*(pa'-ran-te-kie'-nus bil'-ar-nee)*

PLATE.   4:6

DERIVATION.   *Parantechinus* — L., *para*, alongside, similar to; sci., *Antechinus: bilarni* — a facetious construction based on Arnhem Land Aboriginal name for William E. (Bill) Harney, guide to expedition on which first specimens collected in 1948.

LENGTH.   140–215 mm.

HABITAT.   Well-vegetated tropical quartz sandstone country.

NOTES.   Sleeps by day in rock crevice. An agile climber, but forages on the ground for insects. In the dry season, animals may move from rocky country to the more humid shelter of vine thickets.
   Sexually mature at about 11 months; mating from June to August. Female has six teats but no pouch; seldom carries more than four or five young, which are suckled for 16–20 weeks. Males do not die shortly after mating. Some males breed in their second year and some females produce a third litter.

STATUS.   Common.

# Dibbler

*Parantechinus apicalis*
*(ap'-ik-ah'-lis)*

PLATE.   4:1

DERIVATION.   *apicalis* — L., *apex*, a point, referring to shape of tail.

LENGTH.   240–260 mm.

HABITAT.   Banksia heathland.

NOTES.   Sleeps by day in nest of twigs and grass. Burrows through leaf
litter at night to forage for terrestrial insects; also climbs banksia trees to
sip nectar and possibly to eat insects attracted to the flowers.
   Sexually mature at the age of 10–11 months; mating around April.
Female has eight teats in a very shallow pouch and may carry up to eight
young, suckled for approximately 16 weeks. No evidence that males die
after mating.

STATUS.   Immense reduction in range since European settlement; now
known only vicinity of Albany, WA, and an offshore island. Rare,
endangered.

# Fat-tailed Antechinus

*Pseudantechinus macdonnellensis*
*(sued'-an-te-kie'-nus mak-don'-el-en'-sis)*

PLATE.   4:2

DERIVATION.   *Pseudantechinus* — Gk, *pseudes*, false; sci., *Antechinus:*
*macdonnellensis* — from Macdonnell Range, NT.

LENGTH.   170–185 mm.

HABITAT.   Rocky arid or desert country.

NOTES.   Sleeps by day in nest in rock crevice or termite mound, but may
bask for periods in sun. Preys at night on a variety of small insects and
other arthropods. Well-nourished individuals store fat in base of tail.
   Sexually mature at age of 10 or 11 months. Mating usually in June
and July or August and September but females breed only once a year. Female has six teats in a moderately developed pouch and carries up to six
young. Both sexes survive to breed in a second year.

STATUS.   Common over much of range.

# Common Planigale

*Planigale maculata*
*(pla'-nee-gah'-lay mak'-yue-lah'-tah)*

PLATE. 5:1

DERIVATION. *Planigale*—L., *planus*, flat; Gk, *gale*, weasel: *maculata*—L., *macula*, spot.

LENGTH. 130–195 mm.

HABITAT. Hot to warm rainforest, wet sclerophyll forest, woodland, grassland and marsh, usually with wettish soil.

NOTES. Largest of the planigales (10–12 grams). Head not notably flattened. Sleeps by day in nest under a rock, log, or similar natural crevice. At night, forages for insects and small vertebrates up to or even slightly exceeding its own size.

   Females possibly sexually mature at eight months; breeding occurs from October to January in southern part of range, but in the Northern Territory occurs throughout the year with peaks in autumn and spring. Female has eight to twelve teats in a well-developed pouch; usually carries eight young.

STATUS. Two subspecies: *P. m. maculata*, mainland and *P. m. sinualis*, Groote Eylandt. Both common.

# Long-tailed Planigale

*Planigale ingrami*
*(in'-gram-ee)*

PLATE. 5:2

DERIVATION. *ingrami*—after Sir William Ingram, sponsor of William Stalker, who collected the type specimen.

LENGTH. 110–125 mm.

HABITAT. Seasonally flooded tropical grassland.

NOTES. Smallest of the planigales (average head and body length less than 60 millimetres, weight four to five grams). By day sleeps in natural crevices, particularly in sun-dried muddy soil, sometimes emerging to bask in sun. At night preys upon insects, including grasshoppers as large as or even larger than itself. Age of sexual maturity not known. Mating occurs throughout the year but mainly from December to April. Female has eight to 12 teats in a well-developed pouch and carries four to 12 young for six weeks; thereafter young suckled in a nest to age of about 12 weeks. Females can breed more than once a year.

STATUS. Three subspecies: *P. i. ingrami* from the Gulf country; *P. i. subtilissima* from the Kimberley region, WA; and *P. i. brunnea* from central northern Queensland. Rare over most of range.

# Narrow-nosed Planigale

*Planigale tenuirostris*
*(ten'-yue-ee-ros'-tris)*

PLATE.  5:7

DERIVATION.  *tenuirostris* — L., *tenuis*, slender; L., *rostrum*, snout.

LENGTH.  100–140 mm.

HABITAT.  River and lake flood plains with dense grass; well-vegetated creek channels.

NOTES.  Sleeps in a short burrow by day but may emerge to sunbathe. At night hunts small and large insects. In cold weather, may hunt during the daylight hours or reduce energy requirement by becoming torpid.
  Breeding from August to February. Female has a temporary pouch surrounding 10 or 12 teats but average litter is six. Details of development not known. Females can breed more than once a year.

STATUS.  Sparse.

# Paucident Planigale

*Planigale gilesi*
*(jile'-zee)*

PLATE.  5:5

DERIVATION.  *gilesi* — after inland explorer Ernest Giles who, as Peter Aitken, describer of the species, remarked, was also "an accomplished survivor in deserts".

LENGTH.  115–150 mm.

HABITAT.  Arid to semi-arid river flats, creek channels and floodouts with cover of shrubs, grasses or sedges. Clay soils which develop cracks when dry appear to be essential.

NOTES.  Whereas other planigales have three premolar teeth, this species has only two. Sleeps by day in a crevice in dried clay soil but may emerge to bask in sun. At night hunts among litter at the base of grasses for large and small insects. On cold days may hunt for several hours during daylight. May also respond to cold conditions by becoming torpid for hours at a time.
  Breeds from July to January, with a peak in September. Female has a well-developed pouch with 12 teats but the average litter is six. Young detach from the teats at age of five to six weeks and are thereafter suckled in a nest until age of 11 weeks. Female may rear two litters in one year.

STATUS.  Sparse.

# Pilbara Ningaui

*Ningaui timealeyi*
*(nin-gow'-ee tim-ee'-lee-ee)*

PLATE.   5:3

DERIVATION.   *Ningaui*—Aborig., *ningaui*, mythical small nocturnal flesh-eating being with large feet: *timealeyi*—after zoologist E. H. M. ("Tim") Ealey.

LENGTH.   105–140 mm.

HABITAT.   Semi-arid shrubland and hummock grassland.

NOTES.   Tiny independent juveniles may weigh as little as two grams. Largest adult less than 10 grams. Sleeps during day in shelter of spinifex hummock and hunts by night on the ground and over the hummocks or shrubs for centipedes, cockroaches and grasshoppers, some larger than itself.

Age of sexual maturity is not known; may be as low as six to eight months. Female has four to six nipples on a slight depression in the belly: no pouch. Up to six young carried on the six teats, probably for about six weeks. Probably weaned and independent when about 13 weeks old.

STATUS.   Common.

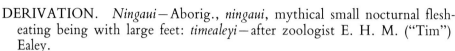

# Wongai Ningaui

*Ningaui ridei*
*(ry'-dee)*

PLATE.   5:4

DERIVATION.   *ridei*—after W. D. L. Ride, distinguished Australian mammalogist.

LENGTH.   115–145 mm.

HABITAT.   Arid to semi-arid hummock grassland.

NOTES.   Sleeps during the day in the shelter of spinifex hummock. At night hunts insects, including those of its own size. Probably does not need to drink.

Age of sexually maturity not known. Mating from September to January. Female has six or seven teats in a rudimentary pouch and may carry up to seven young which probably detach themselves from the teats when about six weeks old and become independent at about thirteen weeks. Two litters may be reared in a year.

STATUS.   Common.

# Southern Ningaui

*Ningaui yvonneae*
*(ee-von'-ee)*

PLATE.  5:6

DERIVATION.  *yvonneae* — after Yvonne C. Kitchener, wife of the describer.

LENGTH.  *c.* 120 mm.

HABITAT.  Arid temperate sand plain and dunes with mallee and spinifex cover.

NOTES.  Southernmost of the known ningauis. Habits little known. Nocturnally active, probably as a predator upon invertebrates and vertebrates its own size or smaller.
    Female has seven teats; probably breeds in spring.

STATUS.  Common to sparse.


# Kultarr

*Antechinomys laniger*
*(an'-te-kie'-noh-mis lan'-i-jer)*

PLATE.  6:3

DERIVATION.  *Antechinomys* — sci., *Antechinus*; Gk, *mys*, mouse: *laniger* — L., *lana* wool; L., *gero*, I carry or wear.

LENGTH.  180–250 mm.

HABITAT.  Arid to semi-arid grassland and scrubland, stony desert.

NOTES.  The head and body of a Kultarr resemble those of a dunnart but the hindlegs are long and slender like those of a hopping-mouse. Does not hop but bounds, pushing off with hindlegs and landing on forelegs. Sleeps by day under a rock or log, beneath a clump of vegetation or in a soil-crack. Preys at night on insects and other arthropods.
    Females sexually mature at eight months; mating from July to November (perhaps February). Female has six or eight teats in rudimentary pouch. Usually four young carried until age of about 30 days; suckled in nest to age of about 90 days. Females may breed more than once a year.

STATUS.  Two subspecies: *A. l. laniger* from eastern Australia and *A. l. spenceri* from central and western Australia. Both rare, particularly the eastern form.

# Common Dunnart

*Sminthopsis murina*
*(smin-thop'-sis myue-ree'-nah)*

PLATE. 6:1

DERIVATION. *Sminthopsis* — Gk, *sminthos*, mouse; Gk, *opsis*, appearance: *murina* — L., *murinus*, pertaining to a mouse.

LENGTH. 140–180 mm.

HABITAT. Open forest, woodland, heathland.

NOTES. Sleeps during the day in a nest of grass and leaves constructed in a natural crevice. At night forages for spiders, beetles, roaches and caterpillars.

    Age of sexual maturity not known but may be as little as six months; mating from July to December. Female has 10 teats completely enclosed in a pouch which develops after mating and regresses after the young are weaned. Four to 10 young carried on the teats for about five weeks, and thereafter suckled in a nest to age of nine to ten weeks. Females typically produce two litters each year.

STATUS. Common.

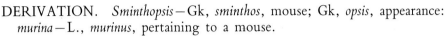

# Sandhill Dunnart

*Sminthopsis psammophila*
*(sam-o'-fil-ah)*

PLATE. 6:4

DERIVATION. *psammophila* — Gk, *psammos*, sand; Gk, *philos*, loving, fond of.

LENGTH. 205–245 mm.

HABITAT. Desert sand ridges partially covered with spinifex and with open scrub or woodland between the ridges.

NOTES. Very little known of biology. Active for at least part of the day as well as at night. In captivity, has been observed to eat spiders and a variety of insects. One of the largest dunnarts, comparable in size to Red-cheeked Dunnart.

STATUS. Known from one specimen captured in 1984 and five in 1969. Rare, possibly scattered populations.

# Fat-tailed Dunnart

*Sminthopsis crassicaudata*
*(kras'-ee-kaw-dah'-tah)*

PLATE. 6:2

DERIVATION. *crassicaudata* — L., *crassus*, fat; L., *cauda*, tail.

LENGTH. 100–160 mm.

HABITAT. Arid to moderately wet woodland, shrubland, and tussock grassland on clay, sand and stony desert.

NOTES. Sleeps by day in a nest of grass in a variety of natural crevices, including deep cracks in dried muddy soil. In colder part of the year, several individuals may huddle together in the same nest to conserve body heat; alternatively may become torpid. Forages at night, often in areas bare of vegetation, for insects and other arthropods. Well-nourished individuals store fat in base of tail. Does not need to drink.

Females sexually mature at the age of five or six months but not demonstrated to breed in the first year of life. Mating extends from July to February. Females have eight to 10 teats in well-developed pouch and usual litter is six to eight young. Young detach at the age of four to five weeks and are suckled in a nest to age of nine to 10 weeks. Females normally rear two litters each year.

STATUS. Common over much of range.

# White-tailed Dunnart

*Sminthopsis granulipes*
*(gran-yue'-li-pez)*

PLATE. 6:5

DERIVATION. *granulipes* — L., *granum*, grain, granule; L., *pes*, foot.

LENGTH. 125–155 mm.

HABITAT. Low mallee shrubland, mostly on sand.

NOTES. Although this species has been trapped fairly regularly since the early 1960s, its biology is very little known. Eats a wide variety of insects and their larvae, spiders and centipedes. Probable that mating occurs in May and June.

STATUS. Common.

# White-footed Dunnart

*Sminthopsis leucopus*
*(lue'-koh-poos)*

PLATE.  6:6

DERIVATION.  *leucopus* — Gk, *leukos*, white; Gk, *pous*, foot.

LENGTH.  140–200 mm.

HABITAT.  Cool closed or open forest and woodland with dense ground cover; coastal scrub, heathland, sedgeland and tussock grassland.

NOTES.  Sleeps by day in a roughly constructed nest in hollow logs, woodpile or tree-hole. At night hunts on the ground for insects, small reptiles and possibly small mammals.
   Little is known of breeding biology. Mating probably from July to September. Females have 10 teats (mainland) or eight (Tasmania) and usually rear eight to 10 young.

STATUS.  Two subspecies: *S. l. leucopus* in Tasmania; *S. l. ferruginifrons*, southern Victoria. Both common.

# Ooldea Dunnart

*Sminthopsis ooldea*
*(ule-day'-ah)*

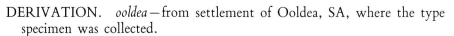

PLATE.  7:6

DERIVATION.  *ooldea* — from settlement of Ooldea, SA, where the type specimen was collected.

LENGTH.  125–180 mm.

HABITAT.  Arid woodland, shrubland, tussock grassland on sandy or stony soil.

NOTES.  Little is known of biology but in the laboratory it is nocturnal and readily kills and eats such large insects as locusts and moths.
   Females sexually mature at 10 months; mating from August to December, possibly with a peak in October. Females have eight teats, enclosed in a temporary pouch, and usually carry about seven young. Young detach from teats when four to five weeks old and are suckled in a nest to the age of about 10 weeks. Females not known to breed more than once a year.

STATUS.  Common.

# Red-cheeked Dunnart

*Sminthopsis virginiae*
*(ver-jin'-ee-ee)*

PLATE.   7:4

DERIVATION.   *virginiae* — significance unknown.

LENGTH.   170–260 mm.

HABITAT.   Tropical woodland, including swampy savannah.

NOTES.   The only dunnart to be found in both Australia and New Guinea. Little known of biology. Animals studied in captivity were nocturnal and ate insects and small vertebrates. Females from Australia have eight nipples; those from New Guinea have six. Mating appears to extend from October to March. Probable that two litters can be reared in one year.

STATUS.   Two Australian subspecies: *S. v. virginiae*, north-eastern Queensland; and *S. v. nitela*, Northern Territory and Kimberleys. Both common in parts of range.

# Stripe-faced Dunnart

*Sminthopsis macroura*
*(mak'-roh-yue'-rah)*

PLATE.   7:1 and 2

DERIVATION.   *macroura* — Gk, *makros*, large; Gk, *oura*, tail.

LENGTH.   150–210 mm.

HABITAT.   Arid to semi-arid woodland, shrubland and tussock grassland.

NOTES.   Sleeps during the day under cover or in soil cracks and may enter a state of torpor. At night forages for insects and other arthropods. Well-nourished individuals store fat in base of tail.

   Females sexually mature at about five months and may rear two litters in the breeding season, which extends from July to February. Female has eight teats and usually rears about six young, which detach from teats at about six weeks of age and are suckled in nest to age of about 10 weeks.

STATUS.   Three subspecies: *S. m. macroura*, central eastern Australia; *S. m. froggatti*, central Australia; and *S. m. monticola* in the Blue Mountains. All sparse in their ranges.

# Hairy-footed Dunnart

*Sminthopsis hirtipes*
*(her'-ti-pez)*

PLATE. 7:5

DERIVATION. *hirtipes*—L., *hirtus*, hairy; L., *pes*, foot.

LENGTH. 150–180 mm.

HABITAT. Arid to semi-arid woodland, shrubland and hummock grassland, usually on sand.

NOTES. A very unusual feature, reflected in the scientific and common names of this species, is its hairy soles and palms. These bristles, which also extend as short fringes around the feet, are apparently an adaptation for locomotion on soft sand.

    Almost nothing is known of biology but likely that mating occurs in winter.

STATUS. Common in parts of extensive range.

# Long-tailed Dunnart

*Sminthopsis longicaudata*
*(lon'-jee-kaw-dah'-tah)*

PLATE. 7:3

DERIVATION. *longicaudata*—L., *longus*, long; L., *cauda*, tail.

LENGTH. 280–310 mm.

HABITAT. Stony lateritic breakaways and screes with open woodland and hummock grassland.

NOTES. Has a long slender tail twice the length of head and body, used as a balancer when the animal runs and jumps among the rocks. Little is known of the biology of this species; appears to eat spiders, centipedes and insects ranging in size from ants and flies to beetles and grasshoppers. Probably breeds from October to February.

STATUS. Rare.

# Lesser Hairy-footed Dunnart

*Sminthopsis youngsoni*
*(yung'-sun-ee)*

PLATE.  8:6

DERIVATION.  *youngsoni* — after W. K. Youngson of the Western
  Australian Museum.

LENGTH.  130–140 mm.

HABITAT.  Arid tropical sand plain and dunes with tussock and hummock
  grasses.

NOTES.  Very similar in appearance to Hairy-footed Dunnart but slightly
  smaller. First described in 1982, little known of biology.
    Mating occurs at least in August and September, apparently not from
  April to June. No information for other months.

STATUS.  Common.

# Julia Creek Dunnart

*Sminthopsis douglasi*
*(dug'-las-ee)*

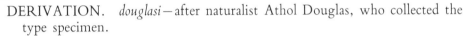

PLATE.  8:7

DERIVATION.  *douglasi* — after naturalist Athol Douglas, who collected the
  type specimen.

LENGTH.  *c.* 200 mm.

HABITAT.  Not known with certainty but probably subtropical woodland
  with dense grass cover.

NOTES.  Only four specimens of this species are known, none of which
  was studied in captivity. The only female to be collected had six young
  on seven teats.

STATUS.  Rare, possibly extinct.

# Carpentarian Dunnart

*Sminthopsis butleri*
*(but'-ler-ee)*

PLATE.  8:5

DERIVATION.  *butleri* — after naturalist Harry Butler, who collected the type specimen.

LENGTH.  180 mm.

HABITAT.  Tropical eucalypt forest with thick grass understorey.

NOTES.  Not described until 1965; and almost nothing is known of biology. Captive animals behave like other dunnarts, being nocturnal predators on insects. Data from two trapped animals indicate that mating occurs in spring.

STATUS.  Assumed to be common in the Kimberley part of the range; status unknown in Cape York.

# Little Long-tailed Dunnart

*Sminthopsis dolichura*
*(dol'-i-kue-rah)*

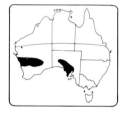

PLATE.  8:3

DERIVATION.  *dolichura* — Gk, *dolichos*, long; Gk, *oura*, tail.

LENGTH.  160–180 mm.

HABITAT.  Semi-arid temperate mallee.

NOTES.  Described in 1984. No information on biology.

STATUS.  At least locally common.

# Aitken's Dunnart

*Sminthopsis aitkeni*
*(ayt'-ken-ee)*

PLATE.  8:4

DERIVATION.  *aitkeni* — after P. Aitken, Australian zoologist.

LENGTH.  170–200 mm.

HABITAT.  Mallee.

NOTES.  Known only from Kangaroo Island, South Australia. Described in 1984. No details of biology.

STATUS.  Sparse or rare.

# Grey-bellied Dunnart

*Sminthopsis griseoventer*
*(griz'-ay-oh-vent'-er)*

PLATE.   8:2

DERIVATION.   *griseoventer* — L., *griseus*, grey; L., *venter*, belly.

LENGTH.   140–180 mm.

HABITAT.   Warm to cool temperate, well-watered to semi-arid eucalypt woodland, mallee, banksia scrub and heath.

NOTES.   Described in 1984. No details of biology.

STATUS.   Common.

# Gilbert's Dunnart

*Sminthopsis gilberti*
*(gil'-ber-tee)*

PLATE.   8:1

DERIVATION.   *gilberti* — after J. Gilbert, collector for J. Gould.

LENGTH.   150–180 mm.

HABITAT.   Heathland, mallee and eucalypt woodlands.

NOTES.   Described in 1984. No information on biology.

STATUS.   Common.

FAMILY
# Thylacinidae
*(thie'-lah-see'-nid-ee)*

DERIVATION.  sci., *Thylacinus*, Thylacine; *-idae*, familial suffix.
The characteristics of the family are those of the species.

# Thylacine

*Thylacinus cynocephalus*
*(thie'-lah-see'-nus  sie'-noh-sef'-al-us)*

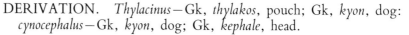

PLATE.  9:3

DERIVATION.  *Thylacinus* — Gk, *thylakos*, pouch; Gk, *kyon*, dog:
   *cynocephalus* — Gk, *kyon*, dog; Gk, *kephale*, head.

LENGTH.  150–200 cm.

HABITAT.  Open forest and woodland, with or without adjacent
   grassland.

NOTES.  Head and forequarters bear strong resemblance to those of wolf.
   Despite its great scientific significance, was subject to very little study
   prior to its presumed extinction in the 1930s. Slept by day, probably
   under shelter, and hunted other marsupials by night, singly, in pairs or
   with dependent young. Could not run fast but jogged after its prey until
   the latter was fatigued. Probably also preyed upon slow-moving wallabies
   not long out of the pouch. Following European settlement, attacked lambs
   and weak or immobilised sheep.
      Breeding extended throughout the year but with a peak of births in
   winter and spring. Females had four teats in a backwardly directed pouch.
   Up to four young (usually two or three) were reared.

STATUS.  Extinct.

FAMILY
# Myrmecobiidae
*(mer'-mek-oh-bee'-id-ee)*

DERIVATION.   sci., *Myrmecobius*, Numbat; *-idae*, familial suffix.

The Numbat, sole member of this family, is unique among the marsupials in its adaptations for feeding upon colonial insects. On the other hand, its feeding adaptations are remarkably similar to those adopted by quite unrelated animals that are also specialised for this diet. Like the echidnas, the Aardvark, the anteaters of South America and the pangolins of Asia, it has degenerate teeth and a very long, sticky tongue which is flicked rapidly in and out of a long snout to collect insects which are individually small but which occur locally in large numbers. It differs from the other ant-eaters in the lack of powerful digging claws on the forelimbs. It differs from all other marsupials in being thoroughly diurnal.

Perhaps the most surprising aspect of the Numbat is its rather small size (less than 500 grams) and relative weakness. The Short-beaked Echidna may reach a weight of seven kilograms; the Giant Anteater of South America, and the Aardvark, are very much larger. It is also characteristic of all the anteaters except the Numbat that they have extremely powerful forelimbs and hands that are armed with stout claws, whereas the forelimbs of the Numbat are not noticeably overdeveloped nor are the claws particularly strong. It cannot breach termite mounds made of cemented soil and is limited to rooting around fallen timber and opening the runways, just below the surface of the soil, in which termites travel between the nest and the feeding sites. It is difficult to understand why the processes of evolution have not produced large numbats capable of exploiting the enormous populations of Australian termites that live in large nests above the ground.

# Numbat
*Myrmecobius fasciatus*
*(mer'-mek-oh-bee'-us fas'-ee-ah'-tus)*

PLATE.   9:2

DERIVATION.   *Myrmecobius*—Gk, *myrmex*, ant; Gk, *bios*, life, way of life: *fasciatus*—L., *fasciatus*, banded.

LENGTH.   360–490 mm.

HABITAT.   Reasonably watered eucalypt woodland and, in the past, arid to semi-arid savannah.

NOTES.   Sleeps at night in hollow log. Active by day. Feeds exclusively upon termites, collected on its very long and mobile sticky tongue. Seldom able to breach a free-standing termitarium ("ant-nest") but often exposes the tunnels, just below the soil surface, by which foraging termites enter and leave the termitarium. Is able to breach the nests made in or on fallen logs.

Sexual maturity probably reached at about 11 months. Female has four teats but no pouch. Mating extends from December to February and up to four young may be reared, becoming independent at the age of about 28 weeks.

STATUS.   Rare, endangered.

SUBORDER **Notoryctemorphia**
*(noh'-toh'-rik-te-mor'-fee-ah)*

> DERIVATION. sci., *Notoryctes*, Marsupial Mole; Gk, *morphos*, form
> The characteristics of the suborder are those of the genus.

SUPERFAMILY **Notoryctoidea**
*(noh'-toh-rik-toy'-day-ah)*

> DERIVATION. sci., *Notoryctes*, Marsupial Mole; *-oidea*, superfamilial suffix.
> The characteristics of the superfamily are those of the genus.

FAMILY
# Notoryctidae
*(noh'-toh-rik'-tid-ee)*

DERIVATION.   sci., *Notoryctes*, Marsupial Mole; *-idae*, familial suffix.

This animal is so different from the dasyuroids that it must be placed in a separate superfamily and suborder, Notoryctemorphia, indicating that the Marsupial Mole is no less different from the dasyuroids than are the bandicoots. Unfortunately, it is such an elusive animal that little research has been carried out and much of its biology remains a mystery.

Interestingly, its anatomical adaptations to a life below the desert sand are so similar to those of the (placental) Golden Mole of Africa, that it is difficult, at first glance, to tell the two apart. In both, the eyes lie below the skin and are without function; the nostrils are protected by a horny shield at the end of the snout; there are no external ears and the tail is reduced to a short stub. The hand is reduced essentially to two fingers, the claws of which form a spade-like structure. The body is covered with long, silky fur.

# Marsupial Mole
*Notoryctes typhlops*
*(noh'-toh-rik'-tayz tif'-lops)*

PLATE.   9:1

DERIVATION.   *Notoryctes*—Gk, *notos*, south; Gk, *oryktes*, digger: *typhlops*—Gk, *typhlos*, blind.

LENGTH.   140–190 mm.

HABITAT.   Sandy desert.

NOTES.   Undoubtedly the most specialised of all the marsupials. Blind. Lacks external ears. Feet converted into blade-like shovelling organs. Spends most of its life below the surface of the desert, forcing its way through the sand with its horny-shielded head. Its food, mainly insect larvae, is captured below the surface and the oxygen it consumes must presumably come from the spaces between sand grains. Does not need to drink.

Nothing known of its reproduction other than that the female has two teats in a pouch that opens to the rear and that the male does not have a scrotum.

STATUS.   Probably common but rarely encountered.

SUBORDER # Peramelomorphia
*(pe'-rah-mel-oh-mor'-fee-ah)*

DERIVATION. sci., *Perameles*, long-nosed bandicoot; Gk, *morphos*, form. The characteristics of the suborder are those of the family.

SUPERFAMILY # Perameloidea
*(pe'-rah-mel-oy'-day-ah)*

DERIVATION. sci., *Perameles*, long-nosed bandicoot; *-oidea*, superfamilial suffix.

The perameloids include the bandicoots, spiny bandicoots and bilbies. For a long time the group was classified into two families: one including all the bandicoots, the other containing the two known bilbies (one of which is almost certainly extinct). Recent research indicates that a more natural division is into a large family, Peramelidae, including the bandicoots and bilbies, and a smaller one, consisting only of the spiny bandicoots, an essentially New Guinean group.

In fact, the perameloids are all similar in basic structure and general behaviour. They have long, pointed snouts and a dentition that is fairly similar to that of a dasyuroid. The ears are of "normal" mammalian size and shape, except in the bilbies, where they are long and rabbit-like, probably serving as heat-exchangers in these desert animals. The fur is sleek but stiff in typical bandicoots, bristly in spiny bandicoots, long and silky in bilbies. The forelimbs are much shorter than the hindlimbs but are quite powerful and armed with stout digging claws on the second, third and fourth toes (the first and fifth toes are either reduced or absent).

The long hindlimbs are very muscular and used to propel the animal in a bounding gait. The hindfoot is long and extends into a long, powerful fourth toe which terminates in a strong claw. The fifth toe is much shorter than the fourth and the first toe is either reduced to a stub or absent. The second and third toes are slender and bound together in the same covering of skin, so that only their claws are separate. They form a two-toothed comb that is used to groom the fur.

The Pig-footed Bandicoot, which became extinct in the nineteenth century, had longer legs than other perameloids and appears to have supported itself on the tips of its toes. The forelimbs had only two functional toes (the second and third) and their claws appear to have acted as hooves.

FAMILY

# Peramelidae

*(pe'-rah-mel'-id-ee)*

DERIVATION.   sci., *Perameles*, long-nosed bandicoot; *-idae*, familial suffix.

This family includes the typical bandicoots, bilbies and the extinct Pig-footed Bandicoot. The typical bandicoots forage for insects, other invertebrates and the succulent parts of plants by digging conical pits with their forefeet. They sleep by day on or within a rough nest. Bilbies include small vertebrates in their diet and they differ markedly from typical bandicoots in making their nests at the end of long burrows. Bandicoots range in weight from about 200 grams to two kilograms. The only surviving species of bilby may weigh as much as 2.5 kilograms.

The peramelid embryo forms a placental connection with the uterus of its mother but gestation is remarkably brief. The record for the shortest known gestation period in mammals (12.5 days) is shared by the Long-nosed Bandicoot and Northern Brown Bandicoot.

# Long-nosed Bandicoot

*Perameles nasuta*
*(pe'-rah-mel'-ayz naz-yue'-tah)*

PLATE.   10:7

DERIVATION.   *Perameles* — Gk, *pera*, pouch; Gk, *meles*, badger: *nasuta* — L., *nasutus*, pertaining to the nose.

LENGTH.   450–700 mm.

HABITAT.   Tropical rainforest to cool temperate woodland.

NOTES.   Sleeps by day in rough nest of vegetation in shallow scrape in soil. Forages at night for subterranean insects, other invertebrates and succulent parts of plants by digging conical pits with forelegs. Solitary. Aggressively defends territory.

Females sexually mature at five months, males at about a year. Female has eight teats in backwardly directed pouch but usually rears two or three young which are suckled for about eight weeks and become independent at nine to ten weeks. Breeding proceeds throughout year but is reduced in winter.

STATUS.   Two subspecies: *P. n. nasuta*, south of about Townsville; and *P. n. pallescens*, north of Townsville. Both common to abundant.

# Eastern Barred Bandicoot

*Perameles gunni*
*(gun'-ee)*

PLATE.   10:6

DERIVATION.   *gunni*—after R. Gunn, who forwarded the first specimen to the British Museum.

LENGTH.   340–460 mm.

HABITAT.   Seasonally wet woodland and grassland.

NOTES.   Sleeps by day within a nest of grass and soil. At night forages for insect larvae and other burrowing arthropods, earthworms and berries. Individuals defend territories.

Females sexually mature at about three months. Mating extends throughout the year, with a peak from June to November. Female has eight teats in a backwardly directed pouch and usually rears two or three young, which become independent at the age of about 12 weeks. Several litters may be reared in a year.

STATUS.   Mainland population now limited to a small area around Hamilton, Vic. Common over much of Tasmania.

# Western Barred Bandicoot

*Perameles bougainville*
*(bue'-gan-veel)*

PLATE.   10:9 and 10

DERIVATION.   *bougainville*—after Baron Bougainville, French navigator and leader of scientific expeditions.

LENGTH.   275–420 mm.

HABITAT.   Semi-arid woodland to shrubland and dunes.

NOTES.   Little is known of natural history. Sleeps by day in a grass nest situated in a hollow dug in the soil. At night forages for burrowing insects and their larvae, seeds, and succulent roots.

Breeding extends from April to August. Female has eight teats in a backwardly directed pouch but usually rears two young.

STATUS.   Four subspecies: *P. b. bougainville*, Bernier and Dorre Islands, Shark Bay (abundant); *P. b. fasciata*, New South Wales, Victoria (extinct); *P. b. myosura*, south-western Western Australia (extinct); and *P. b. notina*, South Australia, south-eastern Western Australia (extinct).

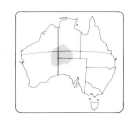

# Desert Bandicoot

*Perameles eremiana*
*(e'-rem-ee-ah'-nah)*

PLATE.  10:3

DERIVATION.  *eremiana*—L., *eremus*, desert.

LENGTH.  350 mm.

HABITAT.  Spinifex grassland on desert sand plain and ridges.

NOTES.  This species became extinct before any studies had been made on its natural history. Slept by day in a grass nest and presumably foraged at night for insects. Had long ears (acting as thermal "radiators") and feet fringed with stiff hairs.

 Females had eight teats in a backwardly directed pouch and are said to have reared two young in a litter.

STATUS.  No specimen collected for more than fifty years. Extinct.

# Southern Brown Bandicoot

*Isoodon obesulus*
*(ie-soh'-oh-don ob-es'-yue-lus)*

PLATE.  10:8

DERIVATION.  *Isoodon*—Gk, *isos*, equal; Gk, *odous*, tooth: *obesulus*—L., *obesus*, fat.

LENGTH.  390–500 mm.

HABITAT.  Woodland or scrubland with low ground cover.

NOTES.  Sleeps by day below the surface of a well-constructed nest of grass, twigs and earth, which is sometimes situated in a scrape in the ground but, in damp conditions, may be on a raised platform of soil. At night forages for insect larvae and worms dug from the soil with its forepaws. Individuals maintain territories which they defend fiercely.

 Sexually mature at three to four months. Mating from about May to about November. Females have eight teats in a backwardly directed pouch but seldom rear more than four young, which become independent at the age of about eight weeks. As many as three litters may be reared in one breeding season.

STATUS.  Four subspecies: *I. o. obesulus* on the south-eastern mainland; *I. o. affinis* in Tasmania; *I. o. peninsulae* on Cape York; and *I. o. fusciventer* in south-western Australia. Common in parts of range.

# Northern Brown Bandicoot

*Isoodon macrourus*
*(mak'-roh-yue'-rus)*

PLATE. 10:12

DERIVATION. *macrourus* — Gk, *makros*, large; Gk, *oura*, tail.

LENGTH. 390–690 mm.

HABITAT. Rather wet closed and open forest, woodland and scrubland, always with dense ground cover of shrubs or grass.

NOTES. Sleeps by day, usually within a pile of grasses and sticks. At night forages for insects and other arthropods, small fruits, seeds and tubers. Solitary, territorial and aggressive.
   Females sexually mature at three months. Mating throughout the year in warmer parts of the range but not in autumn in the south. Female has eight teats in a backwardly directed pouch and usually rears about four young, which become independent when about seven weeks old. Three litters may be reared in a year.

STATUS. Two subspecies: *I. m. macrourus* from the Northern Territory and the Kimberleys; and *I. m. torosus* in eastern Australia. Both common.

# Golden Bandicoot

*Isoodon auratus*
*(or-ah'-tus)*

PLATE. 10:2

DERIVATION. *auratus* — L., *auratus*, golden.

LENGTH. 270–420 mm.

HABITAT. From wet vine thickets to woodland and arid tussock grassland.

NOTES. Little known of natural history. Apparently behaves like other members of the genus *Isoodon*, sleeping in a nest of grass during the day and foraging for insects, other arthropods and succulent plant material at night.
   Breeding extends throughout the year. Female has eight teats in a backwardly directed pouch but seldom carries more than three young, of which only one or two survive to weaning.

STATUS. Two subspecies: *I. a. auratus* from the Kimberleys (severely reduced in range) and *I. a. barrowensis* from Barrow Island (abundant).

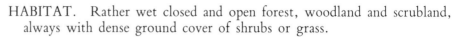

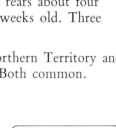

# Bilby

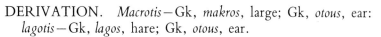

*Macrotis lagotis*
*(mak-roh'-tis lag-oh'-tis)*

PLATE.   10:5

DERIVATION.   *Macrotis* — Gk, *makros*, large; Gk, *otous*, ear:
*lagotis* — Gk, *lagos*, hare; Gk, *otous*, ear.

LENGTH.   500–840 mm.

HABITAT.   Arid to semi-arid woodland, shrubland, hummock grassland,
particularly regenerating areas.

NOTES.   Sleeps by day in a deep, well-constructed burrow, sometimes in
company with another individual or with recently weaned juveniles. At
night digs pits in the sand in search of burrowing insect larvae and
succulent plant material.
   Breeding extends throughout the year. Female has eight teats in a
backwardly directed pouch but seldom rears more than two young. Young
remain in the pouch for about 11 weeks and are weaned at about 13
weeks.

STATUS.   Two subspecies: *M. l. lagotis* from the southern Northern
Territory and parts of northern Western Australia; and *M. l. sagitta* from
south-western Queensland. Range now severely reduced. Sparse to rare.

# Lesser Bilby

*Macrotis leucura*
*(luke-yue'-rah)*

PLATE.   10:4

DERIVATION.   *leucura* — Gk, *leukos*, white; Gk, *oura*, tail.

LENGTH.   365–440 mm.

HABITAT.   Desert sandhills.

NOTES.   Similar to Bilby but about one-third its weight. Rested by day in
burrow, exit of which was closed while animal in residence. Fierce
nocturnal predator upon small mammals, possibly also ate seeds and fruits.
Female had eight teats in backwardly directed pouch; usually reared two
young.

STATUS.   Only six specimens known; not seen since 1931; presumed
extinct.

# Pig-footed Bandicoot

*Chaeropus ecaudatus*
*(kee'-roh-poos ay'-kaw-dah'-tus)*

PLATE.  10:11

DERIVATION.  *Chaeropus* — Gk, *choiros*, young pig; Gk, *pous*, foot:
   *ecaudatus* — L., *e-*, without; L., *cauda*, tail.

LENGTH.  330–410 mm.

HABITAT.  Semi-arid to arid woodland, shrubland and tussock grassland.

NOTES.  Common name refers to the two-toed forefoot, likened to a pig's
   "trotter". Species name arose from accidental absence of a tail from the
   first specimen to be described. Slept by day in a nest of grass and was
   active by night. Females had eight teats in a backwardly directed pouch
   and usually reared two young.

STATUS.  Extinct. Was locally common over much of southern and central
   inland Australia at the time of European settlement but disappeared by the
   end of the nineteenth century.

FAMILY
# Peroryctidae*
*(pe'-roh-rik'-tid-ee)*

DERIVATION.   sci., *Peroryctes*, a spiny bandicoot; *-idae*, familial suffix.

This family includes the spiny bandicoots, which are a New Guinean group, one species of which, the Rufous Spiny Bandicoot, also occurs in Cape York Peninsula. The hair of spiny bandicoots is bristly and much less sleek than in the typical bandicoots of the family Peramelidae. Little is known of the biology of these animals.

* This name, coined by C. P. Groves and T. F. Flannery was in press at the time of publication of this book. It is used with the permission of the authors and is not intended, here, to imply a formal definition of the family.

# Rufous Spiny Bandicoot
*Echymipera rufescens*
*(ek'-ee-mip'-er-ah rue-fes'-enz)*

PLATE.   10:1

DERIVATION.   *Echymipera* — Gk, *echinos*, hedgehog; Gk, *pera*, pouch: *rufescens* — L., *rufescens* reddish.

LENGTH.   375–500 mm.

HABITAT.   Tropical rainforest to woodland and adjoining heath.

NOTES.   The genus *Echymipera* is essentially New Guinean and this species is much more widely distributed in New Guinea than in Australia: the Cape York population is an outlier.
   Almost nothing is known of its natural history.

STATUS.   Common in New Guinea, locally common in Australian range.

# ORDER DIPROTODONTA

*(die-proh'-toh-don'-tah)*

DERIVATION.   sci., *Diprotodon*, large extinct example of this group; Gk,
   *dis*, twice; *protos*, first; *odous*, tooth.

The diprotodont marsupials have only one pair of well-developed incisors in
the lower jaw (a vestigial second pair may also be present). As in bandicoots,
the second and third toes of the hind foot are slender and joined together to
form a structure with two claws. Diprotodonts are primarily herbivorous but
some became secondarily insectivorous and a few are omnivorous, also eating
eggs, nestling birds and lizards.

   Modern diprotodonts fall into four groups, currently regarded as
superfamilies: the Vombatoidea, comprising the wombats and the koala; the
Phalangeroidea, including the cuscuses and the various possums; the
Tarsipedoidea, with only one species, the Honey-possum; and the
Macropodoidea, including the kangaroos and their relatives. Three of these
groups are easily definable but it is not clear whether all possums should be
grouped together, in other words whether they all share a common ancestor
that is not shared by any of the other diprotodonts.

# VARIOUS DIPROTODONT MARSUPIALS

PLATE 11

3

4

5

6

7

# BRUSH-TAILED POSSUMS

*1*

*2*

*3*

*4*

*5*

*6*

# RINGTAIL POSSUMS

## PLATE 13

1

2

3

4

5

6          7

# GLIDERS AND LEADBEATER'S POSSUM

# HONEY-POSSUM, FEATHERTAIL GLIDER, STRIPED POSSUM AND PYGMY-POSSUMS

PLATE 15

3

4

5

6

7

8

# MUSKY RAT-KANGAROO, DESERT RAT-KANGAROO, BETTONGS AND POTOROOS

PLATE 16

*1*

# HARE-WALLABIES

PLATE 17

# ROCK-WALLABIES, NAILTAIL WALLABIES AND NABARLEK

1

2

3

4

5

6

7

8

# ROCK-WALLABIES, TREE-KANGAROOS AND WARABI

PLATE 19

3

4

5

6

7

# PADEMELONS, WALLABIES AND QUOKKA

PLATE 20

*1*

# WALLABIES

PLATE 21

*1*

*2*

*3*

*4*

*5*

*6*

# KANGAROOS AND WALLAROOS

# WALLAROOS

PLATE 23

*1*

*2*

*3*

*4*

*5*

SUPERFAMILY # Vombatoidea
*(vom'-bat-oy'-day-ah)*

DERIVATION. sci., *Vombatus* (see below); *-oidea*, superfamilial suffix.

Wombats and the Koala share many basic anatomical features—such as the structure of the skull, teeth, vertebral column, stomach and pouch—but the two types of marsupial are adapted to such very different ways of life that the differences are much more obvious than the underlying similarities. We can deduce from the anatomy and blood chemistry of vombatoids that they are survivors of a rather early group of diprotodonts—or, in other words, that their common ancestor represents an early branch on the diprotodont evolutionary tree, long before possums or kangaroos had begun to come into existence. Thus, they have had a longer time than the other living diprotodonts to evolve away from what can be thought of as the "standard model".

Wombats are the most terrestrial of the diprotodonts, for they have underground dens. They are extremely efficient burrowers, with powerful limbs, a compact head and a short neck that can exert powerful leverage. They are grazing animals.

The Koala is a very efficient arboreal leaf-eater. Like the wombats, its tail is reduced to an insignificant stub but, in contrast to wombats, in which the limbs are compact, it has very long arms and legs and its hands and feet are the most efficient grasping organs to be found among the marsupials.

FAMILY
# Vombatidae
*(vom-bah'-tid-ee)*

DERIVATION.   sci., *Vombatus*, wombat; *-idae*, familial suffix.

Although various types of wombats existed in Pleistocene times—one as large as a cow—only three species survive at present. The genus *Vombatus*, which lives in forests and feeds on grasses at the forest edge, comprises a single species which is abundant over much of south-eastern Australia. The genus *Lasiorhinus* had a wide distribution in more arid woodland but its range has declined severely since European settlement. One species now exists in reasonable numbers and security on the eastern edge of the Nullarbor Plain. The other, with a total population no more than a few hundred, has a precarious existence in a small area of Queensland. There are some indications that another remnant population may still survive near Deniliquin, NSW, but its existence has not been confirmed.

# Common Wombat
*Vombatus ursinus*
*(vom-bah'-tus er-see'-nus)*

PLATE.   11:6

DERIVATION.   *Vombatus*—Aborig., *wombat*, one of the names of the species in the Sydney region: *ursinus*—L., *ursus*, bear.

LENGTH.   900–1150 mm.

HABITAT.   Forested areas with adjacent grassy areas.

NOTES.   A large marsupial (about same weight as female Red Kangaroo). Usually sleeps by day in one of several long burrows but activity pattern may be reversed when and where winter is very cold. Grazes on native grasses and sedges, usually travelling several kilometres over home range, which may overlap with that of other individuals. Solitary and aggressive: cornered individuals may attack humans; inflicting severe bites.

  Sexually mature at two years. Mating throughout year with peak from September to November. Female has two teats in backwardly directed pouch but usually rears one young which remains in pouch for about six months and follows its mother until about 17 months old.

STATUS.   Three subspecies: *V. u. ursinus*, Flinders Island; *V. u. hirsutus*, south-eastern mainland; and *V. u. tasmaniensis*, Tasmania. Mainland range reduced since European settlement but species still common.

# Southern Hairy-nosed Wombat

*Lasiorhinus latifrons*
*(laz'-ee-oh-rine'-us lat-i-fronz)*

PLATE.   11:7

DERIVATION.   *Lasiorhinus* — Gk, *lasios*, hairy; Gk, *rhis*, nose: *latifrons* — L., *latus*, broad; L., *frons*, forehead.

LENGTH.   770–940 mm.

HABITAT.   Semi-arid woodland and shrubland on rather friable soil.

NOTES.   Slightly smaller than Common Wombat and distinguished by silky fur, hairy rhinarium, and adaptation to arid habitat. Sleeps by day in complex warren of burrows which accommodate up to ten animals. Grazes at night on tough native grasses (and agricultural pastures or crops). Does not need to drink; low metabolic rate is an adaptation to sparse and variable food supply.
   Sexually mature at three years. Mating mostly from August to November. Female has two teats in backwardly directed pouch but rears single young which remains in pouch for six to nine months and is weaned at about 12 months.

STATUS.   Range has contracted since European settlement but present populations, mostly on non-agricultural land, are secure and the species is common.

# Northern Hairy-nosed Wombat

*Lasiorhinus krefftii*
*(kref'-tee-ee)*

PLATE.   11:2

DERIVATION.   *krefftii* — after Gerard Krefft, zoologist who found fossil skull from which species was named.

LENGTH.   *c.* 1000 mm.

HABITAT.   Semi-arid woodland and grassland on sandy soil.

NOTES.   Similar in appearance to Southern Hairy-nosed Wombat but somewhat larger. Sleeps by day in burrows which may be solitary or grouped in warren. Emerges at night to graze on native grasses and herbs.
   Reproductive biology unknown.

STATUS.   Early in European settlement, populations existed in southern New South Wales and southern Queensland but these disappeared at turn of century. In 1937 very small remnant population discovered at Epping Forest, Queensland. Rare, endangered.

FAMILY
# Phascolarctidae
*(fas'-koh-lark'-tid-ee)*

DERIVATION.   sci., *Phascolarctos*, Koala; *-idae*, familial suffix.

This family has only one living member, the well-known Koala, the general characteristics of which are mentioned in the account of the species. Like wombats, the Koala is virtually tail-less and has powerful rodent-like incisors. Its fingers end in strong, curved claws, with which it can climb smooth-barked trees of large diameter but, when moving along branches, it employs an unusual grip, opposing the first two digits of the hand against the other three (in much the same way as a parrot opposes two of its toes against the other two). This "split-hand" or "two-thumbed" grip is also employed by cuscuses and ringtail possums but reaches its greatest development in the Koala.

The hind foot is also very well adapted to gripping. The first toe is larger and more strongly muscled than in other marsupials and works against the other four as a powerful pincer. As in other diprotodonts, the second and third fingers are combined to form a two-clawed comb.

The Koala feeds almost exclusively upon the leaves of eucalypt trees, a diet which has a very high content of fibre and a rather low content of available carbohydrate or protein. Nutrient is released from this food by fermentation in an extremely large caecum, proportionately the longest of any mammal.

Although it is beautifully adapted to life in the trees, the Koala can gallop quite fast on the ground and is a good swimmer.

# Koala

*Phascolarctos cinereus*
*(fas'-koh-lark'-tos sin'-er-ay'-us)*

PLATE.   11:3

DERIVATION.   *Phascolarctos* — Gk, *phaskolos*, pouch; Gk, *arktos*, bear: *cinereus* — L., *cinereus*, ash-coloured.

LENGTH.   750–820 mm.

HABITAT.   Wet and dry eucalypt forests and woodland.

NOTES.   Feeds almost exclusively on leaves of eucalypts; local populations restricted to a few eucalypt species. Excellent climber and jumper; can gallop on ground; swims efficiently. No nest or den is constructed or used; sleeps in fork of tree during most of day; feeds at night. Essentially solitary but mature males monopolise several females in vicinity.

Both sexes mature at two years; males may not mate until three to four years old. Mating from October to February. Female has two teats but usually rears a single young which remains in pouch for five to six months and thereafter accompanies mother, often on her back, to age of 12 months.

STATUS.   Range reduced since European settlement, mainly due to clearing of forests. Common in parts of range; some populations unhealthily dense.

SUPERFAMILY # Phalangeroidea
*(fal'-an-je-roy'-day-ah)*

DERIVATION.   sci., *Phalanger*, cuscus; *-oidea*, superfamilial suffix.

The first member of this group to be described by a European was a cuscus, probably from Sulawesi (Celebes) and in 1765, four years before Cook landed at Botany Bay, the great French zoologist, Buffon, had drawn attention to the fusion of the second and third toes of its hindfoot. This led to the name *Phalanger*, from the French *phalange*, a bone of the finger or toe. However, when Sir Joseph Banks found a prehensile-tailed arboreal marsupial (*Pseudocheirus peregrinus*) at Botany Bay, he regarded it as a close relative of the American opossums and this misapprehension passed into common language. The Australian "opossums" are diprotodonts and vastly different from the true opossums of the Americas, which are polyprotodonts (see p. 11).

Nineteenth-century zoologists attempted to establish "phalanger" as a common name for the arboreal diprotodonts but ordinary Australians persisted in calling them opossums. In an endeavour to make some compromise between common usage and zoological reality, we now refer to the arboreal diprotodonts of Australia as "possums", restricting "opossum" to the American polyprotodonts. It is confusing, the more so because there are grounds for doubting whether the possums themselves constitute a natural group of species representing a single branch of the marsupial tree. This is certainly the case with the Honey-possum, which we now recognise to be so different as to require a superfamily of its own.

Within the Phalangeroidea we currently recognise five families: Phalangeridae (cuscuses and brushtail possums); Pseudocheiridae (ringtail possums and Greater Glider); Petauridae (other furry-tailed gliders); Burramyidae (pygmy-possums); and Acrobatidae (feathertails).

FAMILY
# Phalangeridae
*(fal'-an-je'-ri-dee)*

DERIVATION.   sci., *Phalanger*, cuscus; *-idae*, familial suffix.

This group includes the cuscuses (*Phalanger*), the Scaly-tailed Possum (*Wyulda*), and the brushtail possums (*Trichosurus*).

Cuscuses are basically a New Guinean group of arboreal diprotodonts characterised by a slow, deliberate method of climbing, aided by a long, prehensile tail. Like the Koala, a cuscus can oppose the first two fingers of its hand against the other three when gripping a branch but the hand itself is proportionately much smaller than that of a Koala. Many cuscuses have very short snouts and the combination of a flat face, large forwardly-directed eyes and a prehensile tail led early explorers to regard them as monkeys. No cuscuses are peculiar to Australia but two New Guinea species are represented in the rainforests of Cape York Peninsula. Cuscuses vary in size from about two to five kilograms.

The Scaly-tailed Possum (*Wyulda*) has a strongly prehensile tail similar to that of a cuscus. It weighs about 1.5 kilograms.

Brush-tailed possums (*Trichosurus*) have a long, hairy tail which is only weakly prehensile. Unlike cuscuses and the Scaly-tailed Possum, brushtails are fast, agile climbers which often leap from one branch to another. They range in weight from about 1.5 to 4.5 kilograms.

# Spotted Cuscus

*Phalanger maculatus*
*(fal'-an-jer mak'-yue-lah'-tus)*

PLATE.   11:5

DERIVATION.   *Phalanger* — Fr., *phalange*, joint of finger: *maculatus* — L., *macula*, spot.

LENGTH.   660–875 mm.

HABITAT.   Tropical rainforest.

NOTES.   Remarkably short snout, large forward-directed eyes, short ears; up to 3.5 kilograms. Sleeps most of the day, crouched on a branch. At night and sometimes for periods in day, climbs very deliberately in canopy, with aid of "two-thumbed" hands and long, very prehensile tail; seldom descends to ground. Feeds on fruits and leaves supplemented by large insects, eggs and nestling birds. Solitary. Male scent-marks territory and defends it aggressively.

Reproductive biology little known. Females have four teats in well-developed pouch but normally rear only one young, which is carried on mother's back after leaving the pouch.

STATUS.   An abundant New Guinean species with four subspecies. Australian population, an outlier of the subspecies *P. m. nudicaudatus*, is sparse to rare.

# Grey Cuscus

*Phalanger orientalis*
*(o'-ree-en-tah'-lis)*

PLATE. 11:1

DERIVATION.   *orientalis* — L., *orientalis*, eastern.

LENGTH.   350–400 mm.

HABITAT.   Tropical rainforest.

NOTES.   Smaller than Spotted Cuscus (up to 2.5 kilograms), with longer snout, and more visible ears. Sleeps by day in tree-hole. At night, climbs deliberately through canopy, aided by strongly prehensile tail. Eats fruits, leaves and buds. Solitary.

　　Reproductive biology little known. Females have four teats in well-developed pouch and usually rear two young.

STATUS.   Species distributed from Ceram and Timor through New Guinea to Solomons. At least eight subspecies, of which Australian population is an outlier of *P. o. peninsulae*. Sparse to rare in Australia.

# Scaly-tailed Possum

*Wyulda squamicaudata*
*(wie-ool'-dah skwah'-mee-kaw-dah'-tah)*

PLATE. 11:4

DERIVATION.   *Wyulda* — Aborig., *wyulda*, a name of the Common Brushtail Possum, mistakenly applied to this species by the describer, J. Alexander: *squamicaudata* — L., *squama*, scale; L., *cauda*, tail.

LENGTH.   700 mm.

HABITAT.   Vine thickets, open woodland in rugged country.

NOTES.   Distal four-fifths of tail covered with conical scales. Sleeps in a rock crevice by day. At night climbs trees with aid of very prehensile tail, to feed on flowers, probably also fruits, leaves, nuts.

　　Reproductive biology little known. May not be sexually mature until second year. Mating probably from February to July. Indications are that single young leaves pouch at age of about 25 weeks and may not be weaned until about 35 weeks.

STATUS.   First described in 1919 but only three specimens taken between then and 1965, when resident populations recognised. Common in parts of range, rare elsewhere.

# Common Brushtail Possum

*Trichosurus vulpecula*
*(trik'-oh-syue'-rus vool-pek'-yue-lah)*

PLATE. 12:4, 5 and 6

DERIVATION. *Trichosurus* — Gk, *trix*, hair; Gk, *oura*, tail: *vulpecula* — L.,
  *vulpes*, fox; L., *-ecula*, diminutive suffix.

LENGTH. 600–950 mm.

HABITAT. Wet and dry sclerophyll forest and woodland.

NOTES. Sleeps by day in tree-hole or similar cavity (including ceilings of
  houses). At night climbs in trees, with some aid from a prehensile tail, to
  feed on eucalypt leaves, fruits and blossoms. May also forage on the
  ground. Males scent-mark territories and defend these against other males.
    Females sexually mature at 12 months, males at 24 months. Mating
  occurs throughout the year but with peaks in March to April and
  September to October. Females have two teats in a well-developed pouch
  and rear one young which leaves the pouch at 17–22 weeks and is suckled
  in the nest or riding on its mother's back to the age of about 26 weeks.
  Females can breed twice a year.

STATUS. Three subspecies recognised: *T. v. vulpecula* from the central and
  south-western mainland; *T. v. johnstoni* from the eastern and south-eastern
  mainland and *T. v. fuliginosus* from Tasmania. All common.

# Northern Brushtail Possum

*Trichosurus arnhemensis*
*(arn'-em-en'-sis)*

PLATE.   12:3

DERIVATION.   *arnhemensis* — from Arnhem Land.

LENGTH.   620–755 mm.

HABITAT.   Dry sclerophyll forest and woodland.

NOTES.   Sleeps by day in a tree hole or ground cavity; males singly; females sometimes sharing. At night climbs through trees and forages on the ground (more than the Common Brushtail) in search of leaves and fruits.

    Sexually mature at about 12 months. Breeding throughout year. Single young weaned at age of about 26 weeks. Two young may be reared in a year.

STATUS.   Common over much of range.

# Mountain Brushtail Possum

*Trichosurus caninus*
*(kah-nee'-nus)*

PLATE.   12:1 and 2

DERIVATION.   *caninus* — L., *caninus*, doglike.

LENGTH.   740–920 mm.

HABITAT.   Wet and (wettish) dry sclerophyll forests.

NOTES.   Sleeps by day in a tree-hole. At night climbs through trees, aided by moderately prehensile tail, and on forest floor. Eats leaves, fruits, fungi. Solitary; marks and defends territory.

    Sexually mature at two years but usually does not breed successfully until third year. Female has two teats but rears single young which leaves pouch at 22–26 weeks and is suckled to age of 30–40 weeks. Young adults may remain close to the mother until two to three years old.

STATUS.   Common over much of range.

FAMILY
# Pseudocheiridae
*(sue'-doh-kie'-rid-ee)*

DERIVATION.   sci., *Pseudocheirus*, ringtail possum; *-idae*, familial suffix.

This group includes the typical arboreal ringtail possums, the terrestrial Rock Ringtail, the Greater Glider, the Lemuroid Ringtail and the peculiar striped possums. No pseudocheirids have become adapted to arid conditions and most live in wet forests or rainforests: there are a number of species in New Guinea and nearby islands.

Ringtail possums are arboreal and characterised by a long, well-furred tail which is bare on the underside for part of its length from the tip: the tail is strongly prehensile and used in climbing. The Rock Ringtail is exceptional in sheltering among rocks by day and climbing trees to eat at night: its tail is short, but prehensile.

The Greater Glider is superficially similar to a typical glider of the family Petauridae but many features of its anatomy and blood chemistry testify to its close relationship with the ringtails. It has an extremely long tail and its gliding membrane extends only to the elbows (not to the wrist as in typical gliders). It feeds entirely upon eucalypt leaves.

The leaf-eating Lemuroid Ringtail has a flattened face and looks very different from typical ringtails. Recent research indicates that it is closely related to the Greater Glider.

# Common Ringtail Possum

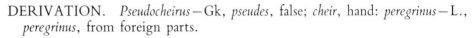

*Pseudocheirus peregrinus*
*(syue-doh-kie-rus pe'-re-green'-us)*

PLATE.   13:1, 2 and 6

DERIVATION.   *Pseudocheirus*—Gk, *pseudes*, false; *cheir*, hand: *peregrinus*—L., *peregrinus*, from foreign parts.

LENGTH.   600–700 mm.

HABITAT.   Rainforest to wet and dry sclerophyll with thick shrub understorey.

NOTES.   Sleeps by day in a globular nest constructed in a tree-hole or among dense foliage (animals in the tropical part of the range may utilise a tree-hole without a nest). Unusually sociable for a marsupial; a number of individuals may build adjacent nests. At night climbs through the forest canopy, aided by a very prehensile tail, feeding mainly upon eucalypt leaves, also fruits and flowers. Soft and hard faeces produced alternately; soft faeces eaten and subjected to further digestion.

Sexually mature at 12 months; mating extends from March to November. Female has four teats in forwardly directed pouch; usually rears two young. Young detach from teats at six weeks, leave pouch at about 18 weeks; independent at about 26 weeks. Two litters may be reared in one year.

STATUS.   Five subspecies: *P. p. peregrinus*, Cape York to about Maryborough, then inland from Dividing Range to South Australia and Kangaroo Island; *P. p. pulcher*, Maryborough southward to about Sydney on eastern side of Dividing Range; *P. p. cooki*, seaward side of Dividing Range in southern New South Wales and Victoria; *P. p. viverrinus*, Tasmania; and *P. p. occidentalis*, south-western Western Australia. All common.

# Herbert River Ringtail Possum

*Pseudocheirus herbertensis*
*(her'-bert-en'-sis)*

PLATE.   13:4

DERIVATION.   *herbertensis* — from Herbert River region, north Queensland.

LENGTH.   625–770 mm.

HABITAT.   Tropical rainforest at high altitude.

NOTES.   Sleeps during the day in a nest made in a tree-hole or in dense vegetation. Moves deliberately through the canopy at night, with aid of very prehensile tail, eating leaves plus some fruits and flowers. Solitary.
   Sexually mature at about 12 months; mating extends from March to November, with a peak of births from May to July. Females born with four teats, two disappearing before maturity; pouch well-developed. Young detach from teats at nine to ten weeks; leave pouch at 16–17 weeks; carried on mother's back or left in nest until about 22 weeks old.

STATUS.   Two subspecies: *P. h. herbertensis* in southern part of range (black and white); and *P. h. cinereus* in northern part of range (fawn and white). Both sparse, verging on rare.

# Green Ringtail Possum

*Pseudocheirus archeri*
*(ar'-cher-ee)*

PLATE.   13:3

DERIVATION.   *archeri* — after the Archer family, host to Carl Lumholtz, who collected specimens described by Robert Collett of the Oslo Museum.

LENGTH.   650–710 mm.

HABITAT.   Wet tropical rainforest.

NOTES.   Spends the day crouched compactly on a branch or in a fork. At night, moves through the canopy, often at speed but seldom leaping, in search of a wide variety of leaves. Tail very prehensile. Solitary.
   Sexually mature at about 12 months. Female has two teats in well-developed pouch. Mating probably extends from July to October.

STATUS.   Sparse over limited range, probably vulnerable.

# Rock Ringtail Possum

*Pseudocheirus dahli*
*(dah'-lee)*

PLATE.   13:7

DERIVATION.   *dahli*—after K. Dahl, Norwegian zoologist, who collected first specimens.

LENGTH.   530–600 mm.

HABITAT.   Rocky outcrops in tropical woodland.

NOTES.   Sleeps during the day in clefts between boulders or rock fissures; not known to make a nest. At night feeds on leaves, flowers and fruits of shrubs and trees; retreats to rocks when disturbed. By far the least arboreal of all the ringtails.

Reproductive biology unknown. Female has two teats in well-developed pouch but usually rears one young; probably born in the wet season.

STATUS.   Common in appropriate habitat.

# Lemuroid Ringtail Possum

*Hemibelideus lemuroides*
*(hem'-ee-bel-id'-ay-us lee'-mer-oy-dayz)*

PLATE.   13:5

DERIVATION.   *Hemibelideus*—Gk, *hemi-*, half; sci., *Belideus*, earlier name for *Petaurus*, marsupial gliders: *Lemuroides*—sci., *Lemur*, lemur; Gk, *-oides*, resembling.

LENGTH.   650–730 mm.

HABITAT.   Tropical rainforest at high altitude.

NOTES.   Sleeps by day in a tree-hole. At night, climbs through forest canopy, eating a wide variety of leaves. A much less deliberate climber than Green and Herbert River Ringtails, it characteristically makes long leaps between branches. Less solitary than these species; several animals may share a den or feed in the same tree.

Little known of reproduction. Female has two teats in well-developed pouch and normally rears one young.

STATUS.   Sparsely distributed over limited range. Vulnerable.

# Greater Glider

*Petauroides volans*
*(pet'-aw-roy'-dayz voh'-lanz)*

PLATE.   14:2 and 3

DERIVATION.   *Petauroides* — sci., *Petaurus*; Gk, *-oides*, resembling: *volans* — L., *volans*, flying.

LENGTH.   800–1050 mm.

HABITAT.   Wet to dry sclerophyll forest to woodland.

NOTES.   Largest of gliders, up to 1.7 kilograms. Sleeps by day in a tree-hollow. Forages at night for leaves of limited number of eucalypt species. An efficient climber with a long, rather weakly prehensile tail, it also glides from tree to tree, using square patagium extending from elbows to ankles. Solitary, territorial. Various colour phases ranging from chocolate to cream may occur in same population.

Females sexually mature at 18 months; males at 12 months; mating from March to May. Females have two teats in well-developed pouch but usually rear one young, which leaves pouch at 12–16 weeks and is suckled in nest or rides on mother's back until aged about 35 weeks.

STATUS.   Still common in appropriate habitat but dependent upon old trees for nesting holes and therefore vulnerable to clear-felling forestry practice.

FAMILY
# Petauridae
*(pet-or'-id-ee)*

DERIVATION.  sci., *Petaurus*, glider; *-idae*, familial suffix.

All but two of the Australian members of this family are gliding marsupials, equipped with a roughly rectangular membrane stretching from the sides of the body to the wrist and the ankle which acts as an aerofoil. One exception is the rare Leadbeater's Possum, which is extraordinarily similar in appearance to the Sugar Glider (commonest of the petaurids) but lacks a patagium. Leadbeater's Possum seems not to be a relic of a pre-gliding stage in petaurid evolution but a "glider" which has lost its patagium, probably as a consequence of living in Mountain Ash forests which provide such dense and continuous canopy that climbing provides a better means of getting about. (A similar loss of gliding ability is demonstrated by a New Guinean species closely related to the Feathertail Glider of Australia.)

It seems that petaurids are fairly closely related to pseudocheirids (one species of which is a glider), but they differ markedly in diet. Petaurids do not eat leaves or fruits, but feed mainly upon insects, the gum of acacias, the exudates of certain sap-sucking insects, and upon the sap of eucalypts. Gliders score the bark of smooth-skinned eucalypts with their sharp incisors and feed on the sap that seeps from these wounds.

It may be noted that the ability to glide has evolved independently in three marsupial groups: the Pseudocheiridae, Petauridae and (as will be mentioned later) the Acrobatidae.

Four striped possums (three restricted to New Guinea) are aberrant members of the family. Unlike the others, they are insectivorous and have several unusual adaptations to this way of life. The lower incisors are long and sharp and the upper ones chisel-like: they are used to bite or gouge away bark and wood to expose burrowing insect larvae. These are then picked up with the very long tongue or extracted with the greatly elongated fourth finger. These adaptations are similar to those of the Aye-aye, a rare prosimian from Malagasy (Madagascar).

# Squirrel Glider
*Petaurus norfolcensis*
*(pet'-aw-rus nor'-foh-ken'-sis)*

PLATE.  14:1

DERIVATION.  *Petaurus*—Gk, *petaurista*, tightrope walker: *norfolcensis*— (mistakenly) from Norfolk Island.

LENGTH.  400–530 mm.

HABITAT.  Dry sclerophyll forest to woodland.

NOTES.  Closely related to Sugar Glider but larger (about 250 grams) and, although distributions overlap, prefers drier habitat. Agile climber with weakly prehensile tail and patagium from wrists to ankles. Feeds on sap, gum, pollen, nectar and insects.

Sexually mature at about 12 months; mating from May to December. Female has two teats in well-developed pouch and rears one or two young which are weaned by the age of about 17 weeks.

STATUS.  Two subspecies: *P. n. norfolcensis*, most of range; and *P. n. gracilis*, north of Cardwell, Qld. Both sparse.

# Yellow-bellied Glider

*Petaurus australis*
*(os-trah'-lis)*

PLATE. 14:6

DERIVATION. *australis*—L., *australis*, southern.

LENGTH. 690–780 mm.

HABITAT. Wet and dry sclerophyll forest.

NOTES. Sleeps by day, often with other members of a social group, in a leaf-lined tree-hole. An agile climber with a weakly prehensile tail; also glides from tree to tree, using a square patagium extending from wrists to ankles. Feeds on sap obtained by biting pieces out of tree trunks; also eats pollen, nectar and insects. Social groups may have nests and defend common territory.

   Sexually mature at about 12 months; mating extends from July to April. Female has two teats in a well-developed pouch, partially divided into two compartments. Normally rears one young which leaves pouch at about 14 weeks and is weaned at about 23 weeks.

STATUS. Two subspecies: *P. a. australis* from central coastal Queensland to South Australia; and *P. a. reginae*, from north Queensland. Southern species common in parts of range; northern race becoming rare. Both dependent upon old trees for nesting.

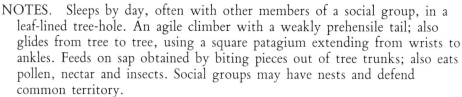

# Sugar Glider

*Petaurus breviceps*
*(bre'-vi-seps)*

PLATE. 14:4

DERIVATION. *breviceps*—L., *brevis*, short; L., *ceps*, head.

LENGTH. 325–420 mm.

HABITAT. Wet and dry sclerophyll forest and woodland; preference for open forest with abundant acacia.

NOTES. Smallest of the petaurids (about 130 grams). Sleeps by day together with other members of family in leaf-lined nest in tree-hollow. Agile climber with weakly prehensile tail; glides, using patagium extending from fifth finger to ankle. May become torpid in cold weather. Feeds on sap exuded from incisions bitten into tree trunks, and acacia gum and insects.

   Sexually mature at about 12 months; mating from June to November. Female has four teats in a well-developed pouch; rears one or two young which leave pouch at ten weeks and are weaned at about 14–15 weeks. Juveniles may remain with mother's group until 30–40 weeks old.

STATUS. Seven subspecies, four of these in New Guinea. *P. b. breviceps* in south-eastern mainland and Tasmania; *P. b. longicaudatus* in north-eastern mainland; and *P. b. ariel* in northern and north-western mainland. All common.

# Leadbeater's Possum

*Gymnobelideus leadbeateri*
*(jim'-noh-bel-id'-ay-us led'-beet-er-ee)*

PLATE.   14:5

DERIVATION.   *Gymnobelideus*—Gk, *gymnos*, naked; sci., *Belideus*, earlier name for *Petaurus*. *Leadbeateri*—after J. Leadbeater, taxidermist in National Museum of Victoria.

LENGTH.   295–350 mm.

HABITAT.   Mountain Ash forest.

NOTES.   Scientific name, loosely translated as 'naked glider', refers to resemblance to Sugar Glider except for absence of patagium. Sleeps by day as social group in leaf-lined nest in hole or hollow trunk of *old* Mountain Ash tree. An agile climber with a non-prehensile tail. Feeds on tree exudates including acacia gum and on insects and their exudates.

   Sexually mature at about 18 months but males may not mate until second year. Mating from March to May and October to December. Females have four teats in a well-developed pouch and rear one or two young which leave the pouch at about 12 weeks and are weaned at the age of about 17 weeks.

STATUS.   Described in 1867, species assumed to be extinct in early twentieth century. Rediscovered in 1961; now known in limited area of Mountain Ash forest in Victoria. Rare and vulnerable.

# Striped Possum

*Dactylopsila trivirgata*
*(dak'-til-op'-sil-ah trie'-ver-gah'-tah)*

PLATE.   15:5

DERIVATION.   *Dactylopsila*—Gk, *daktylos*, finger; Gk, *psilos*, naked: *trivirgata*—L., *tres*, three; L., *virgatus*, striped.

LENGTH.   570–610 mm.

HABITAT.   Tropical rainforest and adjacent woodland.

NOTES.   Scientific name refers to very long fourth finger on rather hairless hand. Sleeps by day in leaf-lined nest in tree-hole. At night, climbs and runs and leaps through forest canopy. Tail non-prehensile. Feeds mostly on wood-boring insect larvae obtained by biting into cavity made by insect and extracting it with the long tongue or elongate finger.

   Reproductive biology little known. Mating perhaps from February to August. Female has two teats in a well-developed pouch and rears one or two young.

STATUS.   There are four species of striped possums, three restricted to New Guinea. The Australian population of this species is an outlier. Common in New Guinea; sparse or rare in Australia.

FAMILY
# Burramyidae
*(bu'-rah-mie'-id-ee)*

DERIVATION.   sci., *Burramys*, Mountain Pygmy-possum; *-idae*, familial suffix.

The pygmy-possums are small marsupials (7–40 grams), most of which live in rather wet forests although one species extends into arid woodland. Another, the Mountain Pygmy-possum, is restricted to an alpine habitat. All except the Mountain Pygmy-possum are arboreal and have long and (except for the Mountain Pygmy-possum) strongly prehensile tails. Diet varies with the species, ranging from insects and seeds to nectar.

Associated with their small size and vulnerability to predators, pygmy-possums produce more young than other diprotodont marsupials. While phalangerids seldom rear more than one young at a time and pseudocheirids and petaurids raise one or two, burramyids typically rear a litter of four (and up to six in one species). Also related to their small size is a difficulty in maintaining a high body temperature when food is scarce or when the external temperature is low. To cope with such conditions, a pygmy-possum may become torpid for a few hours or days, entering a deep sleep and permitting its body temperature to drop to within a few degrees of its surroundings, thus conserving its energy resources. Torpor resembles hibernation but is a much more temporary state: no Australian marsupial is known to hibernate.

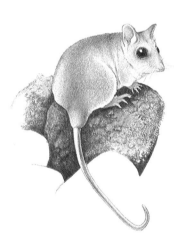

# Mountain Pygmy-possum
*Burramys parvus*
*(bu'-rah-mis par'-vus)*

PLATE.   15:2

DERIVATION.   *Burramys* — Aborig., *burra-burra*, stony place; Gk, *mys*, mouse: *parvus* — L., *parvus*, small.

LENGTH.   240–270 mm.

HABITAT.   Dense shrubs, with or without cover of Snow Gums, in alpine and subalpine regions.

NOTES.   Sleeps most of day in nest in vegetation or in crevice. Feeds at night (or during day in cold conditions) on seeds, fruits and insects. In winter, moves about in runways under snow-covered vegetation. May enter ski lodges for food and shelter. During warmer months, stores seeds and fruits to be eaten later. Gregarious. May become torpid for several days during periods of extreme cold or shortage of food. Largest of the pygmy-possums.

Sexually mature at two years. Mating in October and November. Female has four teats, usually rears four young, independent at about 14 weeks, but may remain with mother until nearly 12 months old.

STATUS.   Generally rare, but common in very restricted parts of range.

# Eastern Pygmy-possum

*Cercartetus nanus*
*(ser'-kar-tay'-tus nah'-nus)*

PLATE.   15:7

DERIVATION.   *Cercartetus* — Gk, *kerkos*, tail: *nanus* — L., *nanus*, dwarf.

LENGTH.   145–215 mm.

HABITAT.   Temperate rainforest to woodland and heath.

NOTES.   One of the larger pygmy-possums (up to 40 grams). Sleeps by day in woven nest in tree-hole, or crevice, becoming torpid in cold weather. At night climbs among foliage with agility, aided by prehensile tail about as long as head and body. Feeds on nectar and pollen gathered with a brush-tipped tongue; also eats fruits and insects. When well fed, stores fat in base of tail. Solitary, but juveniles may sleep with mother.

   Sexually mature in first year. Mates from July to March on mainland; in Tasmania from August to November. Female has four to five teats in well-developed pouch and usually rears four young, which detach from teats at six weeks of age and are weaned by eight weeks. Two litters may be reared in a breeding season.

STATUS.   Common.

# Western Pygmy-possum

*Cercartetus concinnus*
*(kon-sin'-us)*

PLATE.   15:3

DERIVATION.   *concinnus* — L., *concinnus*, elegant.

LENGTH.   140–200 mm.

HABITAT.   Dry sclerophyll forest and woodland with dense understorey, heathland.

NOTES.   Smaller than Eastern Pygmy-possum (up to 20 grams). Sleeps by day in a nest of leaves in a tree hollow or crevice; often torpid. At night climbs through low foliage, aided by very prehensile tail, or forages on the ground. Eats insects, nectar, fruits. Solitary.

   Sexually mature in first year. Mates throughout the year. Female has six teats and may rear up to six young, which leave pouch at three to four weeks and are suckled in nest to age of about 10 weeks. Several litters may be born in a year.

STATUS.   Common.

# Little Pygmy-possum

*Cercartetus lepidus*
*(lep'-id-us)*

PLATE.   15:1

DERIVATION.   *lepidus* — L., *lepis*, scale.

LENGTH.   110–140 mm.

HABITAT.   Wet and dry sclerophyll to woodland.

NOTES.   Smallest of the pygmy-possums (up to nine grams). Sleeps by day in a nest of bark fibre in a crevice, usually in a tree but sometimes in soil or in artifacts; usually torpid in cold weather. At night climbs among low foliage or forages on ground for insects and other small animals. Tail very prehensile and may store fat in thickened base. Solitary.

    Sexually mature in first year. Mating from August to January. Females have four teats in moderately developed pouch and usually rear four young. Young are independent at about 13 weeks. Several litters may be reared in a breeding season.

STATUS.   Sparsely distributed but not rare.

# Long-tailed Pygmy-possum

*Cercartetus caudatus*
*(kaw-dah'-tus)*

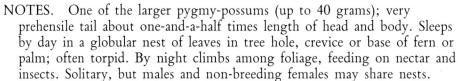

PLATE.   15:4

DERIVATION.   *caudatus* — L., cauda, tail.

LENGTH.   230–260 mm.

HABITAT.   Tropical rainforest and fringes.

NOTES.   One of the larger pygmy-possums (up to 40 grams); very prehensile tail about one-and-a-half times length of head and body. Sleeps by day in a globular nest of leaves in tree hole, crevice or base of fern or palm; often torpid. By night climbs among foliage, feeding on nectar and insects. Solitary, but males and non-breeding females may share nests.

    Sexually mature in first year. Mating from August to February with peaks in September–October and January–February. Female has four teats in well-developed pouch and usually rears two to three young, which leave pouch at about six weeks and are weaned at eight weeks. Usually two litters are reared in a year.

STATUS.   Two subspecies: *C. c. caudatus* in New Guinea and *C. c. macrurus* in Australia. Both are common.

FAMILY
# Acrobatidae
*(ak'-roh-bah'-tid-ee)*

DERIVATION.   sci., *Acrobates*, Feathertail Glider; *-idae*, familial suffix.

This family is probably allied to the Burramyidae and has been regarded as part of that group. There is only one Australian species, the delightful Feathertail Glider, by far the smallest of the gliding marsupials (total length averaging about 140 millimetres; weight about 12 grams). Its common name aptly describes the tail, which bears a fringe of stiff hairs on each side, forming a structure very like a feather. The patagium extends from the elbow to the knee.

A related but much larger New Guinean genus, *Distoechurus*, has no patagium but possesses a similar tail. On the reasonable assumption that the tail evolved as an adaptation to gliding, we must assume that the New Guinean feathertail is descended from a gliding ancestor.

The family is distinguished from the other phalangeroids by the feather-like tail.

# Feathertail Glider

*Acrobates pygmaeus*
*(ak'-roh-bah'-tayz pig-mee'-us)*

PLATE.   15:8

DERIVATION.   *Acrobates* — Gk, *akrobates*, acrobat: *pygmaeus* — L., *pygmaeus*, pygmy.

LENGTH.   135–160 mm.

HABITAT.   Wet and dry sclerophyll forest to woodland.

NOTES.   Very small (up to 14 grams), similar in appearance to pygmy-possum but with patagium from elbows to knees and feather-like tail. Sleeps by day in globular nest of leaves in tree-hole or crevice, usually with several other individuals; becomes torpid in cold weather. At night climbs and glides through foliage, feeding upon nectar, plant and insect exudates, and small insects.

Females sexually mature at eight months; males at twelve. Breeding throughout year in northern part of range; from June to December in the south. Female has four teats in well-developed pouch; usually rears two or three young which are weaned at the age of about 14 weeks.

STATUS.   Common.

SUPERFAMILY **Tarsipedoidea**
*(tar'-si-ped-oy'-day-ah)*

DERIVATION.   sci., *Tarsipes*, Honey-possum; *-oidea*, superfamilial suffix. Characteristics of the superfamily are those of the family.

FAMILY
# Tarsipedidae
*(tar'-si-ped'-id-ee)*

DERIVATION.   sci., *Tarsipes*, Honey-possum; *-idae*, familial suffix.

The single species of Honey-possum is placed in a superfamily of its own in recognition of considerable differences between it and those diprotodonts which are included in the Phalangeroidea. These differences, based on such characteristics as blood proteins and the ultrastructure of sperms are not easily described but we can note here that the teeth of the Honey-possum have degenerated to a row of similar pegs and that the tongue is a very long, brush-tipped structure. Both of these features are related to its exclusive diet of nectar and pollen.

   The Honey-possum is a very small animal (total length averages about 150 millimetres; weight about 10 grams). Like the pygmy-possums it becomes torpid in cold conditions or when food is scarce. Also like these animals, it normally rears several (two or three) young.

# Honey-possum

*Tarsipes rostratus*
*(tar'-si-pez ros-trah'-tus)*

PLATE.   15:6

DERIVATION.   *Tarsipes* — sci., *Tarsius*, a small prosimian; L., *pes*, foot: *rostratus* — L., *rostrum*, snout.

LENGTH.   85–200 mm.

HABITAT.   Shrubland and heathland with myrtaceous and proteaceous shrubs and trees.

NOTES.   Small (males up to 12 grams, females up to 22 grams), with long and very prehensile tail. Sleeps by day in crevices or tree-holes, sometimes with other individuals; often torpid. At night climbs with agility through foliage, collecting nectar from flowers with its very long, brush-tipped tongue.

   Females sexually mature at eight months. Breeding throughout year, but least in summer. Female has four teats in well-developed pouch and normally rears two or three young, which leave pouch at about eight weeks of age and are suckled in the nest to the age of ten to twelve weeks. Two litters may be reared in a year. As in many macropods, lactating female may carry quiescent embryos in its uterus.

STATUS.   Common in appropriate habitats within its range.

SUPERFAMILY **Macropodoidea**
*(mak'-roh-pod-oy'-day-ah)*

DERIVATION.   sci., *Macropus*, kangaroo; *-oidea*, superfamilial suffix.

Members of this group are characterised by powerfully developed hindlimbs with relatively long feet and an elongated fourth toe. In normal zoological terminology, members of this superfamily would be called macropodoids but, in general usage, the term has been shortened to macropods. The superfamily divides naturally into two subfamilies: the Potoroidae, including the potoroos, bettongs and Musky Rat-kangaroo; and the Macropodidae, comprising the familiar kangaroos and wallabies, rock-wallabies, tree-kangaroos and several other less familiar subgroups. In very broad terms, the potoroids may be regarded as the more "primitive" macropods and the macropodids as the more "advanced".

Most macropods employ their hindlegs to hop at high speed, both legs moving together. Even when moving slowly, they do not move their hindlegs independently; they progress by supporting the body on a tripod formed by the forelegs and the tail and swinging both hindlegs forward. To this general rule there are several exceptions. The tiny Musky Rat-kangaroo does not hop, but employs all four limbs in a bounding gait and some other potoroids place the forelegs on the ground when changing direction at high speed. When tree-kangaroos are on the ground, they hop in a typical macropod manner but, when moving along the branch of a tree, they walk like typical quadrupeds, moving the hindlimbs alternately. It is interesting that terrestrial kangaroos move their hindlimbs alternately when swimming.

In comparison with the hindlimbs, the forelimbs of many macropods appear to be puny. However, they are very powerful in adult male kangaroos and wallabies; in all tree-kangaroos; and in bettongs, which use the forelimbs for digging.

The tail of a macropod is much less flexible than that of any possum. In typical kangaroos, it is a rather stiff structure that can be moved up and down as a balancer when hopping, or slightly bent to support the weight of the body during slow locomotion. In potoroids, however, the tail retains a slight degree of prehensility and is used to carry nesting material. Potoroids are the only macropods to make nests; at most, macropodids make a shallow scrape in which to rest.

All female macropods have a well-developed pouch enclosing four teats but it is rare for more than one young to be born at a time (except in the Musky Rat-kangaroo, which normally gives birth to twins). Nevertheless, many female macropods may suckle two young at the same time. This arises from a phenomenon known as embryonic diapause or delayed implantation.

Very shortly after her first young is born, a typical female macropod mates again. The embryo from this mating ceases development at a very early stage (when no more than a tiny bag of undifferentiated cells), and does not become implanted in the wall of the uterus until a few weeks before the young from the previous mating leaves her pouch. The second embryo now resumes development and is born three to five weeks later (followed shortly by a third mating). The female is now suckling a young animal following her at heel, plus a pouch embryo (each receiving milk of a different composition from its teat) and holding a quiescent embryo in reserve in one of her uteruses. The stimulus to retain this embryo in a quiescent state is the suckling of a young animal in the pouch: if this should die or be lost from the pouch, the quiescent embryo resumes development.

Being diprotodonts, macropods are basically herbivorous, but some potoroids also eat insects. The macropodids are almost exclusively herbivorous but the more primitive species tend to be browsers. Typical kangaroos and wallabies are grazers and digest grass eaten by a process of fermentation in the stomach comparable with that employed by cattle.

FAMILY

# Potoroidae
*(pot'-oh-roh'-id-ee)*

DERIVATION.   sci., *Potorous*, Potoroo; *-idae*, familial suffix.

The anatomy of macropods makes it clear that they evolved from arboreal, possum-like ancestors. Members of the Potoroidae retain more possum-like characters than the kangaroos and other species that comprise the family Macropodidae and this is the basic difference between the two families. In potoroids, the upper and lower incisors bite against each other; the upper canine teeth are well developed; the molars are low-crowned; and there is only a short gap between the cutting and the grinding teeth. The hindlimb and foot are proportionately shorter than in macropodids and the tail is prehensile. Unlike macropodids, potoroids build nests and the tail is used to carry nesting material. Potoroids do not eat grass, feeding mainly on a wide range of more easily digested bulbs, tubers, fungi and invertebrates: the stomach is a simple sac.

One potoroid is sharply distinguished from the remainder by characters that are even more reminiscent of the possum condition. The Musky Rat-kangaroo retains a first toe, set at a right angle to the axis of the foot (as in arboreal marsupials): this digit has been lost in all other macropods. The hindlimb has the same overall structure as in other macropods but the difference in length of the fore- and hindlimbs is no greater than in some possums. It is therefore not surprising that the Musky Rat-kangaroo does not hop but bounds, on all four feet, rather like a rabbit. Uniquely among the macropods, it usually gives birth to two young.

The remaining potoroids fall into two sub-groups: the potoroos and the bettongs. Potoroos have tapering snouts and are rather more delicately built than the short-snouted and rather broad-faced bettongs. Both have powerful forelimbs armed with strong digging claws. Potoroos tend to be forest-dwellers while bettongs range into more arid vegetation. Both are largely restricted to habitats with a dense ground cover of shrubs.

No marsupial group has suffered more from the effects of European settlement than the potoroids. Of eight species known to be in existence in the early nineteenth century, two are now extinct, three have declined from extensive distributions on the mainland to last-ditch survival on island refuges; and only three appear to be secure. A ninth species, discovered in 1979 in Victorian wet sclerophyll forest near the NSW border, is extremely rare.

# Musky Rat-kangaroo

*Hypsiprymnodon moschatus*
*(hip'-see-prim'-noh-don mos-kaht'-us)*

PLATE. 16:4

DERIVATION. *Hypsiprymnodon*—sci., *Hypsiprymnus*, past generic name for the potoroos; Gk, *odous*, tooth: *moschatus*—L., *moschatus*, musky.

LENGTH. 285–430 mm .

HABITAT. Tropical rainforest.

NOTES. Smallest (500 grams) of the macropods; only macropod retaining the first digit ("big toe") of the hindfoot. Sleeps at night in a nest of vegetation. Forages by day on the forest floor for fallen fruits and for insects and other invertebrates. Fast gait employs four limbs. Solitary.

    Sexually mature at about 13 months. Mating takes place from February to July. Female has four teats in a well-developed, forwardly directed pouch and normally rears two young, which leave the pouch when 21 weeks old and are suckled in the nest to the age of about 24 weeks.

STATUS. Distribution has been reduced by clearing of rainforest. Remains reasonably common in limited area.

# Long-nosed Potoroo

*Potorous tridactylus*
*(pot'-oh-roh'-us trie-dak'-til-us)*

PLATE. 16:2 and 3

DERIVATION. *Potorous*—Aborig., *potto roo*, name of species in Sydney region: *tridactylus*—Gk, *tri-*, triple; Gk, *daktylos*, digit.

LENGTH. 580–650 mm.

HABITAT. Wet sclerophyll forest and cool rainforest with thick ground cover; heathland; mostly on sandy soil.

NOTES. Scientific name, given in 1792, refers to typical macropod foot, which appears to have only three toes: short, fused second and third digits; long fourth digit; and short fifth digit. Sleeps by day in a nest of vegetation. At night digs in the soil with its forelegs for succulent roots, fungi, and insect larvae. Solitary.

    Sexually mature in first year. Mates throughout year, with peaks in January–February and August–September. Female has four teats but rears only one young at a time. This leaves the pouch at the age of about 17 weeks and is suckled at foot to the age of about 21 weeks. Two young may be reared in one year.

STATUS. Two subspecies: *P. t. tridactylus* on south-eastern mainland; and *P. t. apicalis* in Tasmania. Distribution of both has declined since European settlement but still common in parts of range.

# Broad-faced Potoroo

*Potorous platyops*
*(plat'-ee-ops)*

PLATE.   16:5

DERIVATION.   *platyops*—Gk, *platys*, flat; Gk, *opsis*, appearance.

LENGTH.   *c.* 420 mm.

HABITAT.   Woodland and grassland.

NOTES.   This is the smallest of the potoroos, only a little larger than the Musky Rat-kangaroo. As the name implies, its face had a "fat-cheeked" appearance. Nothing is known of its natural history.

STATUS.   Only six specimens are known, taken between 1839 and the early 1870s. Extinct.

# Long-footed Potoroo

*Potorous longipes*
*(lon'-ji-pez)*

PLATE.   16:1

DERIVATION.   *longipes*—L., *longus*, long; L., *pes*, foot.

LENGTH.   695–740 mm.

HABITAT.   Dry sclerophyll forest with dense understorey of shrubs and grasses.

NOTES.   Similar to Long-nosed Potoroo but about twice the weight; hindfeet proportionately longer. Sleeps by day in a nest; forages at night, digging into the soil with its forepaws. Solitary.
   Sexually mature at 18–24 months. Breeds throughout year. Four teats but only one young reared at a time; leaves pouch at age of 18 weeks, suckled at foot to age of about 21 weeks.

STATUS.   First described in 1980 from small number of specimens, it appeared to be limited to an area of about 80,000 hectares in north-eastern Victoria and to be very rare. Since the discovery of its bones in fox scats in south-eastern New South Wales in late 1986, the possibility arises that it has a more extensive, but discontinuous, distribution.

# Brush-tailed Bettong

*Bettongia penicillata*
*(bet-ong'-gee-ah pen'-is-il-ah'-tah)*

PLATE.  16:8

DERIVATION.  *Bettongia* — Aborig., *bettong*, small wallaby: *penicillata* — L., *penicillus*, brush.

LENGTH.  590–740 mm.

HABITAT.  Dry sclerophyll forest to woodland with low shrubs or tussocks.

NOTES.  Sleeps by day in well-constructed nest of vegetation. Forages on the ground at night for succulent roots, fungi, seeds and insects. Solitary, territorial.
   Sexually mature at about 21 weeks of age; breeding continuous; embryonic diapause. Female has four teats but usually bears only one young, which vacates pouch at about 13 weeks and is suckled at heel to age of about 15 weeks.

STATUS.  Extreme contraction of range since European settlement. Now restricted to small areas in south-western mainland (*B. p. ogilbyi*) and in Queensland (*B. p. tropica*). Rare, possibly endangered. *B. p. penicillata* is extinct.

# Tasmanian Bettong

*Bettongia gaimardi*
*(gay-mar'-dee)*

PLATE.  16:9 and 11

DERIVATION.  *gaimardi* — after J. P. Gaimard, French naturalist.

LENGTH.  600–680 mm.

HABITAT.  Dry sclerophyll forest with grassy understorey; grassland.

NOTES.  Sleeps by day in well-constructed nest of grass and bark. Forages at night for fungi, succulent roots and seeds. Solitary, territorial.
   Sexually mature at about one year; breeding continuous; embryonic diapause. Female has four teats in a well-developed pouch which is occupied by one young at a time. It quits the pouch at the age of about 15 weeks and suckles at foot until about 22 weeks old.

STATUS.  Two subspecies: *B. g. gaimardi*, once extending over much of south-eastern Australia, is extinct; *B. g. cuniculus* remains common in Tasmania.

# Burrowing Bettong

*Bettongia lesueur*
*(le-swer')*

PLATE.   16:7

DERIVATION.   *lesueur*—after C. A. Lesueur, French naturalist.

LENGTH.   495–700 mm.

HABITAT.   Arid to semi-arid woodland, shrubland and grassland.

NOTES.   Sleeps by day in a nest at the end of a burrow, sometimes forming part of extensive warren system. At night digs with its forelegs for succulent roots and bulbs, fungi and termites; also seeds, fruits and leaves. Sociable.
   Sexually mature at five months; breeding continuous; embryonic diapause. Female has four teats but carries only one young in pouch; young quits pouch when about 16 weeks old.

STATUS.   Once distributed over about half of continent. Now restricted to four islands off the north-western coast of Western Australia.

# Rufous Bettong

*Aepyprymnus rufescens*
*(ee'-pee-prim'-nus ru-fes'-enz)*

PLATE.   16:10

DERIVATION.   *Aepyprymnus*—Gk, *aipys*, high; Gk, *prymnon*, rump: *rufescens*—L., *rufescens*, reddish.

LENGTH.   710–780 mm.

HABITAT.   Wet and dry sclerophyll forests with thick understorey.

NOTES.   Largest of the bettongs. Sleeps by day in a well-constructed nest of grass. At night, forages for grasses and succulent roots. Solitary, males aggressive.
   Sexually mature at about 12 months; continuous breeding; embryonic diapause. Female has four teats but carries only one young in pouch. Young quits pouch at age of about 16 weeks and is suckled at foot to age of about 23 weeks.

STATUS.   Only bettong not to have suffered disastrous reduction in range following European settlement. Common.

# Desert Rat-kangaroo

*Caloprymnus campestris*
*(kal'-oh-prim'-nus kam-pes'-tris)*

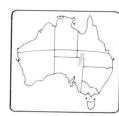

PLATE. 16:6

DERIVATION. *Caloprymnus*—Gk, *kalos*, beautiful; Gk, *prymnon*, rump: *campestris*—L., *campester*, open country.

LENGTH. 550–615 mm.

HABITAT. Arid stony desert.

NOTES. Slept by day in a well-constructed nest of grass and twigs. Foraged at night, but diet unknown. Reproductive biology unknown.

STATUS. Known from only a few specimens. Extinct.

FAMILY
# Macropodidae
*(mak'-roh-poh'-did-ee)*

DERIVATION.   sci., *Macropus*, kangaroo; *-idae*, familial suffix.

Whether reckoned in terms of number of species, variety of habitat or sheer biomass, the Macropodidae must be regarded as the most successful family of the herbivorous marsupials. Indeed, among the herbivorous mammals of the world, it ranks not far behind the deer, cattle and antelopes.

It is among the macropodids that the technique of bipedal locomotion reaches its greatest grace and efficiency—so efficient, in fact, that a fast-moving kangaroo expends less energy than a galloping animal of equivalent size. Among the rock-wallabies we find this style of locomotion even further developed for ricochetting progress in three dimensions with agility and speed that surpasses the performance of a chamois or mountain goat. Yet, despite the manifest success of hopping, one group of macropodids has reversed this evolutionary trend and returned to life in the trees.

Tree-kangaroos provide a textbook example of the generalisation, known as Dollo's Law, that a structure that has been lost in the course of evolution cannot be regained. Tree-kangaroos would benefit greatly from a prehensile tail but must make do with the rather stiff balancing organ inherited from their hopping ancestors. An opposable first toe would be invaluable for gripping branches, but that organ was lost very early in the evolution of kangaroos. A long foot is very inappropriate for climbing among branches: in the tree-kangaroos it has been secondarily shortened, broadened and provided with a granular sole but it remains a very makeshift device for arboreal life. Strengthening and lengthening the forelimbs was a relatively easy evolutionary step and, luckily, the hopping ancestors of the tree-kangaroos retained hands that could grasp, albeit far less effectively than those of the primarily arboreal cuscuses that occupy much the same rainforest habitat. The clumsiness of tree-kangaroos poses the question: how did they come to be? The answer seems to be that Australian and New Guinean rainforests provide an enormous amount of potential food in the form of leaves and that the tree-kangaroos are macropods that have found a way of exploiting this resource. Being virtually without competitors or enemies, they do not need to be very efficient.

Despite their generally similar appearance, the other macropodids have a range of adaptations. The hare-wallabies, pademelons, the Swamp Wallaby and the Quokka are predominantly browsing animals and, like the potoroids, tend to have fairly large canine teeth and rather low-crowned molars. In general, their feet are somewhat shorter than those of the typical wallabies and kangaroos.

Kangaroos, typical wallabies, rock-wallabies and nailtail wallabies are grazers. Grass is plentiful but it is a tough, abrasive food and those animals that eat it require a range of special adaptations. In the kangaroos and their grazing relatives the upper incisors are placed in a transverse row and behind this is a toughened area of the palate which functions as a "chopping block" for the lower incisors. There is a long gap between the cutting teeth and the grinding teeth, leaving room for the mobile tongue to arrange bundles of chopped grass and pass these to the broad molars, crowned with multiple ridges, that function as rasps, reducing the grass to a paste. The permanent molars erupt in very slow succession and, in the course of their existence, move forward in the jaw. A young adult may have only two molars in each tooth-row. As these wear down, they move forward and the third erupts. In its prime, a kangaroo may have four molars in each tooth-row but these are gradually shed, beginning with the foremost. The grinding teeth of an old animal may be reduced to the third and fourth molars, now with very low ridges: quite apart from any other factors related to age, such an animal has difficulty in processing enough food to feed itself. A fascinating exception to this general rule is the Nabarlek, a small rock-wallaby which feeds on extremely abrasive grasses and ferns. It continues to produce new molars at the rear of the tooth-rows throughout its life, shedding the worn ones from the front.

Even when grass has been reduced to a paste, it is of little food value since most of its carbohydrate is in the form of cellulose (the substance of which paper is made). No vertebrate animal is able to produce the enzymes that break cellulose down into its constituent sugars, but many micro-organisms have this ability. Thus, if enough space is provided in the gut for such micro-organisms to work on finely divided grass, this will eventually be reduced to material (including the bodies of the micro-organisms and their by-products) that can be digested and absorbed. In some marsupials, notably the Koala, Greater Glider and brushtail and ringtail possums, such microbial fermentation is carried out in a side-branch of the gut, the caecum. In kangaroos and wallabies fermentation takes place in a multi-chambered stomach—an arrangement similar to that which has evolved, quite independently, in cattle and sheep.

Understandably, the grazing macropods live where grass is available. They may retire to forests to sleep during the day but they feed in woodland or grassland and some species can live in all but the most barren central deserts. Unusually among the native mammals of Australia, kangaroos have benefited from the activities of European settlers, who vastly increased the area of grassland and made permanent water much more widely available.

# Eastern Hare-wallaby

*Lagorchestes leporides*
*(lag'-or-kes'-tayz lep'-or-ee'-dayz)*

PLATE.  17:3

DERIVATION.  *Lagorchestes*—Gk, *lagos*, hare; Gk, *orkhestes*, dancer: *leporides*—L., *lepus*, hare; L., *-ides*, akin to.

LENGTH.  770 mm.

HABITAT.  Tussock grassland.

NOTES.  Slept by day in a burrow, usually under a tussock. Active by night but diet unknown: probably tough grasses. A prodigious leaper when disturbed.

Reproductive biology unknown.

STATUS.  Apparently common in its range until the 1850s. Last specimen collected in 1890. Extinct.

# Spectacled Hare-wallaby

*Lagorchestes conspicillatus*
*(kon-spis'-il-aht-us)*

PLATE.   17:2

DERIVATION.   *conspicillatus* — N.L., *conspicillus*, spectacles.

LENGTH.   770–960 mm.

HABITAT.   Tropical sclerophyll forest to woodland, shrubland and tussock grassland.

NOTES.   Sleeps by day under shelter, particularly of tussock. Feeds at night on tough native grasses and shrubs; does not drink. Solitary, territorial.
   Sexually mature at about twelve months; breeding throughout year; embryonic diapause. Single young leaves pouch at about 21 weeks of age.

STATUS.   At least two subspecies: *L. c. conspicillatus*, common on Barrow Island; and *L. c. leichhardti*, common in Queensland, scattered elsewhere.

# Rufous Hare-wallaby

*Lagorchestes hirsutus*
*(hers-yue'-tus)*

PLATE.   17:4

DERIVATION.   *hirsutus* — L., *hirsutus*, hairy.

LENGTH.   570–640 mm.

HABITAT.   Semi-arid to arid spinifex grassland.

NOTES.   Sleeps by day in a deep excavation (sometimes a short burrow) in the shelter of a hummock or low shrub. At night grazes on tough native grasses or sedges and browses on shrubs and herbs.
   Reproduction biology little known.

STATUS.   Three subspecies. *L. h. hirsutus*, which once occupied most of the central and western deserts, now restricted to sparse population in part of Tanami Desert; *L. h. dorreae* in Dorre Island and *L. h. bernieri* on Bernier Island. Island populations unstable, varying from rare to locally common.

# Banded Hare-wallaby

*Lagostrophus fasciatus*
*(lag'-oh-stroh'-fus fas'-ee-aht'-us)*

PLATE.  17:1

DERIVATION.  *Lagostrophus* — Gk, *lagos*, hare; Gk, *strophe*, twist or turn: *fasciatus* — L., *fasciatus*, banded.

LENGTH.  750–850 mm.

HABITAT.  Semi-arid woodland and scrubland.

NOTES.  Sleeps by day in shelter of dense vegetation. At night grazes on native grasses and browses on shrubs. Solitary; males territorial and aggressive. Females slightly larger than males.

    Sexually mature at less than one year but usually does not breed until second year. Breeding throughout year except October and November; peak of births in January and February. Young remain in pouch to age of about 26 weeks. Females seldom rear more than one young in a year. Embryonic diapause.

STATUS.  Once relatively common in south-western Australia but mainland population (*L. f. albipilis*) now extinct. Survives on Bernier and Dorre Islands (*L. f. fasciatus*), where it is locally common. Vulnerable.

# Northern Nailtail Wallaby

*Onychogalea unguifera*
*(on'-ik-oh-gah-lay'-ah ung-wif'-er-ah)*

PLATE.  18:5

DERIVATION.  *Onychogalea* — Gk, *onyx*, nail, claw; Gk, *gale*, weasel: *unguifera* — L., *unguis*, nail, claw; L., *fero*, I bear.

LENGTH.  1140–1420 mm.

HABITAT.  Tropical woodland with grassy understorey to grassland.

NOTES.  Largest of the nailtail wallabies (males up to nine kilograms). Sleeps by day in shelter of low tree or shrub. Grazes at night. Solitary, but may form small feeding aggregations. Males notably larger than females.

STATUS.  Two reputed subspecies with no clear geographical demarcation: *O. u. unguifera*, north-western Australia; and *O. u. annulicauda*, north-eastern Australia. Both common in parts of range.

# Bridled Nailtail Wallaby

*Onychogalea fraenata*
*(free-nah'-tah)*

PLATE. 18:8

DERIVATION. *fraenata* — L., *fraenum*, bridle.

LENGTH. 890–1240 mm.

HABITAT. Dry sclerophyll forest to semi-arid woodland, both with grassy areas; shrubland.

NOTES. Sleeps by day in a saucer-shaped depression in shelter of low tree or shrub. Grazes at night on native grasses. Last surviving population shelters in brigalow scrub and feeds on grass in adjacent woodland. Solitary, but may form feeding aggregations. Males larger than females. Reproductive biology unknown.

STATUS. Range has declined severely since European settlement. Now exists only in restricted area near Dingo, Queensland. Rare, endangered.

# Crescent Nailtail Wallaby

*Onychogalea lunata*
*(lue-nah'-tah)*

PLATE. 18:7

DERIVATION. *lunata* — L., *lunatus*, of the moon, crescentic.

LENGTH. 424–838 mm.

HABITAT. Semi-arid to arid woodland and tussock grassland.

NOTES. Rested by day in shallow excavation below shrub or in hollow tree, sometimes basking in sun. Presumably grazed at night, but natural history unknown.

STATUS. Apparently abundant when described in 1841, but disappeared from south-western Australia by 1910. Said to be still surviving in central Australia as late as the 1950s. Probably extinct.

# Nabarlek

*Peradorcas concinna*
*(pe'-rah-dor'-kas kon-sin'-ah)*

PLATE. 18:2

DERIVATION. *Peradorcas*—Gk, *pera*, pouch; sci., *dorcas*, gazelle: *concinna*—L., *concinnus*, elegant.

LENGTH. 510–660 mm.

HABITAT. Rocky margins of tropical grasslands.

NOTES. A little larger (up to 1.4 kilograms) than Warabi. Sleeps by day in rock crevice. At night ventures some distance from rocks, foraging for native grasses and ferns; may be active by day during wet season. Only marsupial to produce continuous succession of new molars to replace those that are worn and drop out.

　　Sexually mature in second year. Breeding throughout year with peak of births in wet season. Young remain in pouch for about 26 weeks. Embryonic diapause.

STATUS. Three subspecies: *P. c. concinna*, north-western Northern Territory; *P. c. monastria*, Kimberleys; and *P. c. canescens*, eastern Arnhem Land. All rare.

# Black-footed Rock-wallaby

*Petrogale lateralis*
*(pet'-roh-gah'-lay lat'-er-ah'-lis)*

PLATE. 18:6

DERIVATION. *Petrogale*—Gk, *petra*, rock; Gk, *gale*, weasel: *lateralis*—L., *lateralis*, pertaining to the side.

LENGTH. 950–1160 mm.

HABITAT. Semi-arid to arid granite rock-piles with mallee or other scrub cover.

NOTES. Sleeps through most of the day in sheltered area among rocks. Emerges to feed, mainly on grasses, in the late afternoon or evening. In cool weather, animals may bask in sun. Feeding aggregations common. Males larger than females.

　　Sexually mature at one or two years; embryonic diapause.

STATUS. Five distinct populations: *P. l. lateralis*, semi-arid western–south-western Western Australia (rare); *P. l. purpureicollis*, western Queensland (common); Macdonnell Range race (common in parts of range); Western Kimberley race (rare); and *P. l. hackettii*, Recherche Archipelago.

# Yellow-footed Rock-wallaby

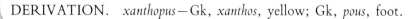

*Petrogale xanthopus*
*(zan'-thoh-poos)*

PLATE. 18:1

DERIVATION. *xanthopus*—Gk, *xanthos*, yellow; Gk, *pous*, foot.

LENGTH. 1050–1350 mm.

HABITAT. Arid rock-piles and outcrops with open woodland and acacia scrubland, sometimes associated with sources of water.

NOTES. Sleeps by day among vegetation between boulders or in rocky cleft. Emerges in evening to graze on native grasses, to browse on forbs and shrubs and to drink. Some indications that adults may be able to survive for long periods without drinking and interesting that juveniles seen to lap saliva from mother's lips. Feeding aggregations common. Males larger than females.

    Sexually mature at one to two years; breeding continuous; young quits pouch at age of about 29 weeks. Embryonic diapause.

STATUS. Two subspecies: *P. x. xanthopus*, South Australia and New South Wales (common in limited areas); and *P. x. celeris*, Queensland (rare).

# Short-eared Rock-wallaby

*Petrogale brachyotis*
*(brak'-ee-oh'-tis)*

PLATE. 18:4

DERIVATION. *brachyotis*—Gk, *brachys*, short; Gk, *otous*, ear.

LENGTH. 830–1070 mm.

HABITAT. Low rocky hills, cliffs and gorges in tropical savannah grassland.

NOTES. Sleeps by day in cool crevices in rock-pile. In late afternoon or evening, emerges to graze in surrounding grassland. Feeding aggregations common. Little known of general biology.

    Probably breeds continuously with peak in wet season; embryonic diapause.

STATUS. Three distinct populations: *P. b. brachyotis*, Kimberleys, Western Australia (abundant in eastern part of range); Victoria River race (abundant); Arnhem Land race (abundant).

# Brush-tailed Rock-wallaby

*Petrogale penicillata*
*(pen'-is-il-ah'-tah)*

PLATE. 18:3

DERIVATION. *penicillata* — L., *penicillus*, brush.

LENGTH. 1080–1150 mm.

HABITAT. Cliffs and rock slopes in wet and dry sclerophyll forest with grassy understorey or close to grassed areas.

NOTES. Sleeps by day in shelter of rocks but may emerge to bask in sun during cool weather. Feeds in evening and night on native grasses and a wide variety of other vegetation. Extremely agile on cliff faces.

STATUS. Two subspecies: *P. p. penicillata* in New South Wales and Victoria (common in New South Wales); and *P. p. herberti* in Queensland (common).

# Proserpine Rock-wallaby

*Petrogale persephone*
*(per-sef'-on-ay)*

PLATE. 19:6

DERIVATION. *persephone* — Persephone, Greek name for Roman goddess Proserpina; refers to Proserpine, Qld.

LENGTH. 1120–1320 mm.

HABITAT. Rocky outcrops in tropical rainforest surrounded by woodland with grassy understorey.

NOTES. Shelters by day in rock crevices and moves out to grassy areas to graze at night. Nothing more known of biology.
   Breeding probably continuous. Embryonic diapause.

STATUS. Described in 1982. Extremely small distribution. Rare and probably endangered by competition from *Petrogale inornata*.

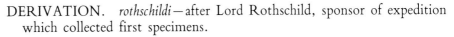

# Rothschild's Rock-wallaby

*Petrogale rothschildi*
*(roths'-chile-dee)*

PLATE.   19:5

DERIVATION.   *rothschildi*—after Lord Rothschild, sponsor of expedition which collected first specimens.

LENGTH.   900–1250 mm.

HABITAT.   Granite rock-piles and outcrops with partial grass and shrub cover.

NOTES.   Sleeps by day in deep clefts between rocks, where temperature is much lower than at the surface. At night, grazes on native grasses and browses on forbs and shrubs. Little known of biology.
   Probably sexually mature at one or two years.

STATUS.   Common over much of range.

# Unadorned Rock-wallaby

*Petrogale inornata*
*(in'-orn-ah'-tah)*

PLATE.   19:3

DERIVATION.   *inornata*—L., *inornatus*, unadorned, plain.

LENGTH.   845–1150 mm.

HABITAT.   Steep-sided rainforest to wet and dry sclerophyll forest and woodland, often without much outcropping rock.

NOTES.   Sleeps through most of the day in rock crevice. Feeds in late afternoon and night on native grasses. Some populations of this species inhabit the wettest areas in which rock-wallabies live and here they frequently climb sloping trees.
   Sexually mature at about eighteen months; breeding continuous but predominantly from March to July. Female has four teats in forwardly directed pouch but rears one young which quits pouch at 27–32 weeks. Embryonic diapause.

STATUS.   Five populations: *P. i. inornata, P. i. assimilis, P. i. puella,* Mount Claro race, and Mareeba race. All apparently common but status of *P. i. puella* uncertain.

# Godman's Rock-wallaby

*Petrogale godmani*
*(god'-man-ee)*

PLATE.  19:4

DERIVATION.  *godmani*—after F. D. Godman, sponsor of T. V. Sherrin, who found first specimen.

LENGTH.  935–1120 mm.

HABITAT.  Rainforest to dry sclerophyll forest with rocky slopes.

NOTES.  Sleeps by day in shelter of rocks. Feeds at night on grasses, forbs and shrubs. Feeding aggregations common. Males larger than females. Little known of biology.
   Probably sexually mature at one to two years; probably breeds throughout year.

STATUS.  Two distinct populations: *P. g. godmani*, Cooktown south to Mossman; Cape York race. Both abundant.

# Warabi

*Petrogale burbidgei*
*(ber'-bid-jee)*

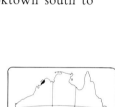

PLATE.  19:7

DERIVATION.  *burbidgei*—after A. Burbidge, Australian zoologist.

LENGTH.  570–650 mm.

HABITAT.  Rugged sandstone areas of open tropical woodland.

NOTES.  Sleeps most of day in rock crevice or cave. Feeds at night (also by day in the wet season) on grasses and ferns. Births at least from August to October.

STATUS.  Not described until 1978. Apparently common in limited range.

# Lumholtz's Tree-kangaroo

*Dendrolagus lumholtzi*
*(den'-droh-lah'-gus lum'-holt-zee)*

PLATE. 19:2

DERIVATION. *Dendrolagus*—Gk, *dendron*, tree; Gk, *lagos*, hare:
*lumholtzi*—after C. Lumholtz, Norwegian naturalist who collected
specimens from which species was named.

LENGTH. 1120–1330 mm.

HABITAT. Tropical rainforest.

NOTES. Sleeps by day, crouched on the branch of a tree. At night climbs
through the canopy, gripping with its large, strongly clawed forefeet and
balancing on its hindfeet (unusually short and broad for a kangaroo). Tail
non-prehensile. Feeds on leaves of trees, supplemented by fruits. Solitary.
Males much larger than females.
Breeding probably continuous but details not known.

STATUS. Range seriously reduced by logging of rainforest but still
reasonably common in limited areas.

# Bennett's Tree-kangaroo

*Dendrolagus bennettianus*
*(ben'-et-ee-ah'-nus)*

PLATE. 19:1

DERIVATION. *bennettianus*—after G. Bennett, first curator of the
Australian Museum.

LENGTH. 1590 mm.

HABITAT. Tropical rainforest.

NOTES. Sleeps by day, crouched on tree branch. Similar in behaviour to
Lumholtz's Tree-kangaroo. Feeds mainly on leaves, supplemented by
fruits. Solitary. Males much larger than females.
Details of reproduction and development not known.

STATUS. Range reduced by logging of rainforests. Sparse in remaining
habitat.

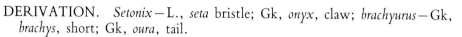

# Quokka

*Setonix brachyurus*
*(see'-ton-ix brak'-ee-yue'-rus)*

PLATE. 20:3

DERIVATION. *Setonix* — L., *seta* bristle; Gk, *onyx*, claw; *brachyurus* — Gk, *brachys*, short; Gk, *oura*, tail.

LENGTH. 695–850 mm.

HABITAT. From wet sclerophyll forest to dry sclerophyll forest, woodland and heath.

NOTES. Sleeps by day in dense vegetation. At night, moves along established runways and pathways to open areas where it grazes on native grasses. Requires access to water. Gregarious, sleeping and moving in groups of up to 150. Males larger than females.

    Breeding continuous on mainland but restricted to a single mating between January and March on Rottnest Island, which is arid in summer. Young vacates the pouch at about 30 weeks and is suckled to about 40 weeks. Embryonic diapause.

STATUS. Mainland population declined severely following European settlement but has shown slight recent recovery. Abundant on Rottnest Island, where it is the largest mammal.

# Red-legged Pademelon

*Thylogale stigmatica*
*(thie'-lo-gah'-lay stig-mat'-ik-ah)*

PLATE. 20:4 and 8

DERIVATION. *Thylogale* — Gk, *thylakos*, pouch; Gk, *gale*, weasel: *stigmatica* — Gk, *stigmatikos*, punctured, pricked.

LENGTH. 840–1010 mm.

HABITAT. Rainforest to wet sclerophyll forest.

NOTES. Sleeps from mid-morning to mid-afternoon, supported by tree or rock. Forages from late afternoon to early morning for fallen leaves of trees; also eats leaves and berries of shrubs, and native grasses. Males larger than females.

    Nothing known of reproduction.

STATUS. One subspecies in New Guinea; three along eastern coast of mainland: *T. s. stigmatica*, Cairns region; *T. s. coxenii*, Cape York; *T. s. wilcoxi*, southern Queensland and New South Wales. All common.

# Tasmanian Pademelon

*Thylogale billardierii*
*(bil-ard'-ee-air'-ee-ee)*

PLATE.   20:6

DERIVATION.   *billardieri* — after J. J. H. La Billardière,
French naturalist who collected first specimen.

LENGTH.   970–1200 mm.

HABITAT.   Rainforest, wet sclerophyll forest and damp areas of dry
sclerophyll forest.

NOTES.   Sleeps by day in dense vegetation. At night, moves along
established paths into more open vegetation to graze on native grasses
and, to a lesser extent, to browse on shrubs. Solitary. Males much larger
than females.

Sexually mature early in second year. Breeding continuous with peak
of births from April to June. Young remain in pouch until about 28
weeks old.

STATUS.   Has become extinct on southern mainland since European
settlement but is common in Tasmania and some Bass Strait islands.

# Red-necked Pademelon

*Thylogale thetis*
*(the'-tis)*

PLATE.   20:2

DERIVATION.   *thetis* — after French research vessel *Thétis.*

LENGTH.   570–1130 mm.

HABITAT.   Rainforest and wet sclerophyll forest, particularly where
adjoining grassland.

NOTES.   Sleeps by day in shallow scrape in dense vegetation. At night
moves along established runways to more open areas to graze on grasses
and herbs and, to a lesser degree, to browse on shrubs. Solitary.

Sexually mature about eighteen months. Mating in January and
February. Young leave pouch at about 26 weeks.

STATUS.   Common.

# Swamp Wallaby

*Wallabia bicolor*
*(wol-ah'-bee-ah bie'-kol-or)*

PLATE.   20:1

DERIVATION.   *Wallabia*—Aborig., *wolabi*, wallaby: *bicolor*—L., *bi-*, two; L., *color*, colour.

LENGTH.   1410–1710 mm.

HABITAT.   Rainforest, sclerophyll forest, woodland with dense understorey; from tropical to cool-temperate climate.

NOTES.   Sleeps by day in dense vegetation. Moves out at night to browse on native shrubs but will eat pastures and crops and pine seedlings. Solitary but may form feeding aggregations. Males larger than females.
    Sexually mature at 15 to 18 months. Breeding continuous, with peak from May to August. Young vacates pouch at about 36 weeks and is suckled to age of about 15 months. Embryonic diapause.

STATUS.   Four poorly defined subspecies along eastern coast of Australia. All common.

# Parma Wallaby

*Macropus parma*
*(mak'-roh-poos par'-mah)*

PLATE.   20:7

DERIVATION.   *macropus*—Gk, *makros*, great; Gk, *pous*, foot: *parma*—Aborig., *pama*, name of species in Illawarra region.

LENGTH.   970–1075 mm.

HABITAT.   Wet sclerophyll forest with dense understorey and grassed areas. Now mainly montane.

NOTES.   Sleeps by day in dense vegetation. Emerges at night along established runways to graze in more open areas. Solitary, but may form small feeding aggregates. Males larger than females.
    Females sexually mature at 12 months; males at 20–24 months. Breeding continuous with most births from February to June. Young leaves pouch at about 30 weeks and is weaned at about 42 weeks. Embryonic diapause.

STATUS.   First described from Illawarra region of New South Wales and assumed to be extinct by twentieth century, but numerous small populations remain in relatively undisturbed valleys of Great Dividing Range. Rare.

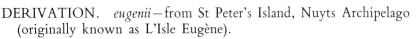

# Tammar Wallaby

*Macropus eugenii*
*(yue-zhay'-nee-ee)*

PLATE. 20:5

DERIVATION. *eugenii*—from St Peter's Island, Nuyts Archipelago (originally known as L'Isle Eugène).

LENGTH. 970–1130 mm.

HABITAT. Dry sclerophyll to woodland and shrubland.

NOTES. Sleeps by day in dense vegetation. At night moves along established runways or paths to graze in more open areas. At least some populations in arid coastal areas drink seawater. Size varies considerably between isolated populations but males always notably larger than females. Solitary.

Females sexually mature at nine months, males at about 22 months. Mating in December and February. Young remain in pouch to age of about 36 weeks and continue suckling to age of about 40 weeks. Embryonic diapause.

STATUS. In addition to Western Australian and South Australian populations there are at least 10 island populations, each differing in some degree. Common over most of its limited range.

# Toolache Wallaby

*Macropus greyi*
*(gray'-ee)*

PLATE. 21:3

DERIVATION. *greyi*—after George Grey, explorer, who collected specimens of the species.

LENGTH. 1540 mm.

HABITAT. Heathland with associated tussock grassland.

NOTES. Common name is pronounced toh-lay'-chee. Slept by day in cover of casuarina thickets. Emerged at dusk to graze on native grasses. Social: resting, moving and grazing in groups. Males and females similar in size. Nothing known of reproduction or development.

STATUS. Abundant at the time of European settlement but extinct by the 1920s, apparently owing to removal of habitat, exacerbated by hunting.

# Whiptail Wallaby

*Macropus parryi*
*(pa'-ree-ee)*

PLATE.  21:1

DERIVATION.  *parryi*—after Edward Parry, explorer, who brought a live specimen to England.

LENGTH.  1400–2000 mm.

HABITAT.  Wet and dry sclerophyll forest with grassy understorey or adjacent grassy areas. Usually on hillsides.

NOTES.  Sleeps much of the night and middle of the day in shelter of a shrub or low tree. From before dawn into early morning and from late afternoon to early night grazes on native grasses, herbs and ferns. Seldom drinks. Gregarious, moving in groups of up to 50. Males up to twice weight of females.

Females sexually mature towards end of second year; males begin mating at age of two or three years. Breeding continuous. Young vacates pouch at about 40 weeks but continues to suckle to about 64 weeks. Embryonic diapause.

STATUS.  Common.

# Black-striped Wallaby

*Macropus dorsalis*
*(dor-sah'-lis)*

PLATE.  21:6

DERIVATION.  *dorsalis*—L., *dorsum*, back.

LENGTH.  2160–2420 mm.

HABITAT.  Wet and dry sclerophyll forest to woodland with dense understorey and associated grassy areas.

NOTES.  Sleeps by day under cover of dense vegetation. At night moves along established pathways to grazing areas, seldom distant from cover. Gregarious: moving, feeding and sleeping in groups of about 20. Males up to nearly three times weight of females.

Females sexually mature at 14 months, males at 20 months. Breeding continuous. Young vacates pouch at 30 weeks. Embryonic diapause.

STATUS.  Common.

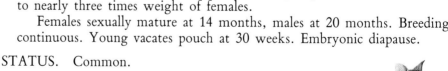

# Red-necked Wallaby

*Macropus rufogriseus*
*(rue'-foh-griz-ay'-us)*

PLATE.   21:5

DERIVATION.   *rufogriseus*—L., *rufus*, red; L., *griseus*, grey.

LENGTH.   1370–1800 mm.

HABITAT.   Wet and dry sclerophyll forests to woodland, all with dense understorey and associated grassy areas.

NOTES.   Sleeps most of day in dense vegetation. In late afternoon grazes close to forest edge; after dark moves into more open areas. Solitary but may form feeding aggregations. Males notably larger than females. Embryonic diapause.

   Females sexually mature early in second year; males late in second year. Breeding continuous on mainland but from January to July in Tasmania, with peaks in February and March. Young leaves pouch at 40 weeks but suckled to 50–70 weeks.

STATUS.   Common.

# Agile Wallaby

*Macropus agilis*
*(a-jil'-is)*

PLATE.   21:4

DERIVATION.   *agilis*—L., *agilis*, agile.

LENGTH.   1400–1700 mm.

HABITAT.   Tropical to subtropical sclerophyll forest and woodland with adjacent grassy areas.

NOTES.   Sleeps most of day in dense vegetation. In late afternoon and through most of night grazes on native grasses, browses, and eats native fruits. Males up to twice weight of females. Sociable, moving in groups of about 10 and forming larger feeding aggregations.

   Females sexually mature at about 14 months, males at about 16 months. Breeding continuous. Young vacates pouch at about 30 weeks and is weaned at about 48 weeks. Embryonic diapause.

STATUS.   Three ill-defined subspecies in Australia: *M. a. agilis* in Northern Territory, *M. a. nigrescens* in Western Australia; *M. a. jardinii* in Queensland. Also *M. a. papuanus* in New Guinea. All common.

# Western Brush Wallaby

*Macropus irma*
*(er'-mah)*

PLATE.   21:2

DERIVATION.   *irma* — significance unknown.

LENGTH.   1500–2500 mm.

HABITAT.   Dry sclerophyll (Jarrah) forest to woodland with associated grassy areas.

NOTES.   Sleeps most of night and middle of day in clump of vegetation. Moves into open areas in early morning and late afternoon to graze on native grasses. Males and females similar in size. Gregarious, fast, agile.

   Little known of reproduction or development. Most young born in April and May. Young leave pouch at age of about 26 weeks.

STATUS.   Common.

# Antilopine Wallaroo

*Macropus antilopinus*
*(an'-til-oh-pee'-nus)*

PLATE.   22:4

DERIVATION.   *antilopinus* — sci., *Antilope*, antelope.

LENGTH.   1700–2100 mm.

HABITAT.   Tropical woodland.

NOTES.   The name of this species refers to its supposedly antelope-like fur. Sleeps most of day under shrubs or rock shelter. In late afternoon and night moves into open country to graze. Much more dependent upon water than Common Wallaroo. Social, moving in groups of up to 10. Males can be more than twice weight of females.

   Breeding continuous but most births from February to June. Young vacate pouch at about 38 weeks. No embryonic diapause.

STATUS.   Common over much of range.

# Black Wallaroo

*Macropus bernardus*
*(ber-nar'-dus)*

PLATE.   22:1

DERIVATION.   *bernardus* — after Bernard Woodward, first curator of the Western Australian Museum.

LENGTH.   1100–1400 mm.

HABITAT.   Tropical woodland with grassy understorey on steep rocky slopes.

NOTES.   Sleeps by day in the shelter of a low tree or rock shelf. At night moves out to graze, often at foot of escarpment. Requires access to fresh water. Agility comparable to that of rock-wallaby. Solitary. Males up to 1.5 times weight of females.
   Nothing known of reproduction or development.

STATUS.   Common in parts of range.

# Red Kangaroo

*Macropus rufus*
*(rue'-fus)*

PLATE.   22:5 and 6

DERIVATION.   *rufus* — L., *rufus*, red.

LENGTH.   1645–2400 mm.

HABITAT.   From woodland, shrubland, grassland to desert, and from cool temperate to tropical.

NOTES.   Although almost all males are notably reddish, females in the eastern part of the range tend to be blue-grey. Sleeps most of the day in the shade of a tree. Usually obtains sufficient water from food to make drinking unnecessary but will drink when water is available. Males more than twice weight of females. Gregarious, moving in groups of up to 200 or more.
   Females sexually mature at about 18 months, males at two years. Breeding continuous. Young vacates pouch at about 33 weeks but continues to suckle until about one year old. Embryonic diapause.

STATUS.   Common over most of range.

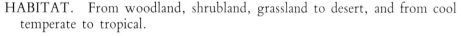
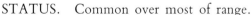

# Western Grey Kangaroo

*Macropus fuliginosus*
*(foo-lij'-in-oh'-sus)*

PLATE. 22:2

DERIVATION. *fuliginosus* — L., *fuliginosus*, sooty.

LENGTH. 950–2300 mm.

HABITAT. Dry sclerophyll forest to woodland and grassland.

NOTES. Sleeps by day in shelter of low tree or shrub. At night grazes on native grasses. Sociable, moving in groups of variable size. Males up to twice weight of females.
 Females sexually mature at 18 months, males at two years. Breeding continuous. Young vacates pouch at about 42 weeks. No embryonic diapause.

STATUS. Mainland population incorrectly attributed to *Macropus giganteus* until 1971. Two subspecies: *M. f. fuliginosus*, Kangaroo Island; and *M. f. melanops*, mainland. Both common.

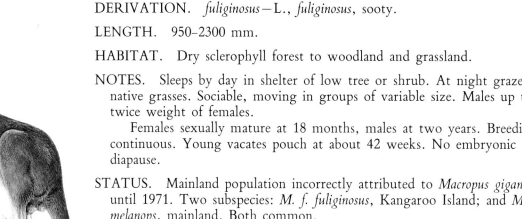

# Eastern Grey Kangaroo

*Macropus giganteus*
*(jee'-gan-tay'-us or jie'-gan-tay-us)*

PLATE. 22:3

DERIVATION. *giganteus* — L., *giganteus*, giant.

LENGTH. 900–2300 mm.

HABITAT. Dry sclerophyll forest to woodland and scrubland in association with grassy areas.

NOTES. Sleeps by day under a shrub or low tree. From late afternoon to early morning moves into open areas to graze on native grasses and shrubs. Gregarious, moving in groups. Males about twice weight of females.
 Females sexually mature at 18 months, males at two years. Breeding continuous. Young vacates pouch at about 44 weeks but continues suckling to about 18 months. Embryonic diapause.

STATUS. Two subspecies: *M. g. giganteus* on mainland; and *M. g. tasmaniensis* in Tasmania. Both common.

# Common Wallaroo

*Macropus robustus*
*(roh-bus'-tus)*

PLATE.  23:1–5

DERIVATION.  *robustus*—L., *robustus*, robust.

LENGTH.  1600–3000 mm.

HABITAT.  Extremely varied: from wet sclerophyll forest to arid grassland and from subalpine to tropical. Usually associated with stony slopes with caves or rock shelves.

NOTES.  Sleeps by day in a cave or under a rocky shelf, usually towards the top of a slope. At night descends to graze on native grasses. Usually obtains sufficient water from food to make drinking unnecessary. Solitary. Males up to twice weight of females.

    Sexually mature at 18 months to two years. Breeding continuous. Embryonic diapause. Young remains in pouch until age of 36 weeks.

STATUS.  Four subspecies: *M. r. robustus*, the typical wallaroo from eastern Australia, has long grey fur; *M. r. erubescens*, occupying most of rest of the continent, has short reddish fur and is known as the Euro; *M. r. woodwardi*, Kimberleys and Northern Territory; and *M. r. isabellinus*, Barrow Island. All abundant.

# PLACENTAL MAMMALS

*SUBCLASS EUTHERIA*
*(yue-thee'-ree-ah)*

DERIVATION.   Eutheria—Gk, *eus*, good, perfect; Gk, *therion*, beast.

Most of the characteristics of these mammals have been mentioned or implied in the introductory accounts of the monotremes and marsupials. Eutherians can be defined as mammals that have separate external apertures for voiding urine and faeces and (in the female) a third aperture for copulation and birth. Young are born with fully developed hindlimbs. There is a prolonged placental connection between the embryo and the wall of its mother's uterus and for this reason, eutherians are commonly referred to as placental mammals. The name is appropriate but not exclusive: some marsupials have placentas. Eutherians are the familiar mammals—familiar because, on the whole, they have proved to be more successful than other groups of mammals and, indeed, other groups of vertebrate animals.

Eutherians range from polar regions to the equator, from rainforests to deserts, from treetops to below the surface of the ground and from the air to the deep oceans. It is because they are so widespread and diverse and because the group includes humans and all our domestic mammals that we often regard them as the pinnacle of the evolutionary process—as though all the changes that ever took place in the fauna of the earth over billions of years led (whether by accident or design) to the eventual production of eutherian mammals and ourselves (the icing on the cake!). A modest and realistic view is that the eutherians merely happen to be the dominant terrestrial animals at the present stage of evolution of life on earth.

The Australian native eutherians include members of the orders Chiroptera (bats), Rodentia (rodents), Sirenia (Dugong) and Pinnipedia (seals).

# ORDER CHIROPTERA

*(kie-rop'-ter-ah)*

DERIVATION.   Chiroptera—Gk, *kheir*, hand; Gk, *pteron*, wing.

The bats are a very successful group of mammals, second only to rodents in number of living species. They fly by means of wings of thin skin, each extending from the side of the body, backwards from the thumb, between the elongated fingers and thence to the ankle. There is usually also a web, the interfemoral membrane, between the hindlimbs and extending for a variable length along the tail. All bats have a claw on the first finger (thumb); fruit-bats and their relatives also have a claw on the second finger: these are employed in crawling. The five toes, all of about the same length, lie alongside each other, each with a curved claw. Together, they make a hook by which a bat suspends itself when roosting; a comb, for grooming the fur; and, in fishing bats, a rake—for capturing fishes or aquatic invertebrates.

Some fruit-bats have a wingspan of a metre or so and a weight of around 1.5 kilograms but the majority of bats are small—between five and 50 grams and mostly towards the lower end of that range. Any mammal of such size has difficulty in maintaining a constant high temperature and the relatively enormous area of the naked wings vastly increases this problem in bats. To obtain the energy necessary for their particularly strenuous mode of locomotion, to maintain their body temperature in flight and to keep warm when resting, small bats must consume large quantities of food.

Warm surroundings reduce the rate of heat loss. It is undoubtedly for this reason that the majority of bats live in tropical or subtropical regions. Yet quite a few species exist in cool temperate regions. Most of these roost communally in caves or similar shelters where the heat lost from their bodies tends to warm the surrounding air rather than being totally dissipated. Another stratagem, employed by all but the largest bats, is to become torpid when they rest or sleep during the day, permitting the body temperature to drop to about that of the surrounding air. Thus very little energy is expended in heat-production but the bat's responses are then sluggish. In regions where the winter is cold and food is correspondingly scarce, neither of these strategies works. Bats must either migrate to warmer regions or hibernate through the winter, lowering the rate of metabolism until they come close to a state of suspended animation.

Most animals living in temperate regions find it advantageous to hatch or bear their young early in spring, a time of increasing warmth and food supply: this is generally true of bats. However, bats have relatively long gestation periods (a minimum of seven weeks) and, if mating were to take place at the end of hibernation, births would be delayed until the end of spring or well into summer. To overcome this difficulty, many bats mate prior to hibernation. In some species, the female stores the sperm that she receives at the end of summer and, without further assistance from the male, fertilises one or two eggs towards the end of hibernation. In others, copulation leads directly to fertilisation but development of the embryo(s) is halted at an early stage, resuming at a time appropriate for birth in spring.

The functional teats lie in each armpit but many bats also possess a pair of false (non-milk-producing) teats in the groin. In bats which carry their young when flying, the young bite firmly onto the false teats to secure their attachment. More commonly, the young are left in creches, closely packed together to conserve body heat and to reduce loss of water by evaporation.

Bats fall into two distinct groups. Megachiropterans are characterised by having large eyes, a rather pointed snout, and a diet of fruit, nectar or pollen, while Microchiropterans have small eyes, short snouts, large ears, and the ability to locate small objects by echo-location.

# FLYING-FOXES AND BARE-BACKED FRUIT-BAT

PLATE 24

*1*

2

3

4

5

# VARIOUS BATS

*1*

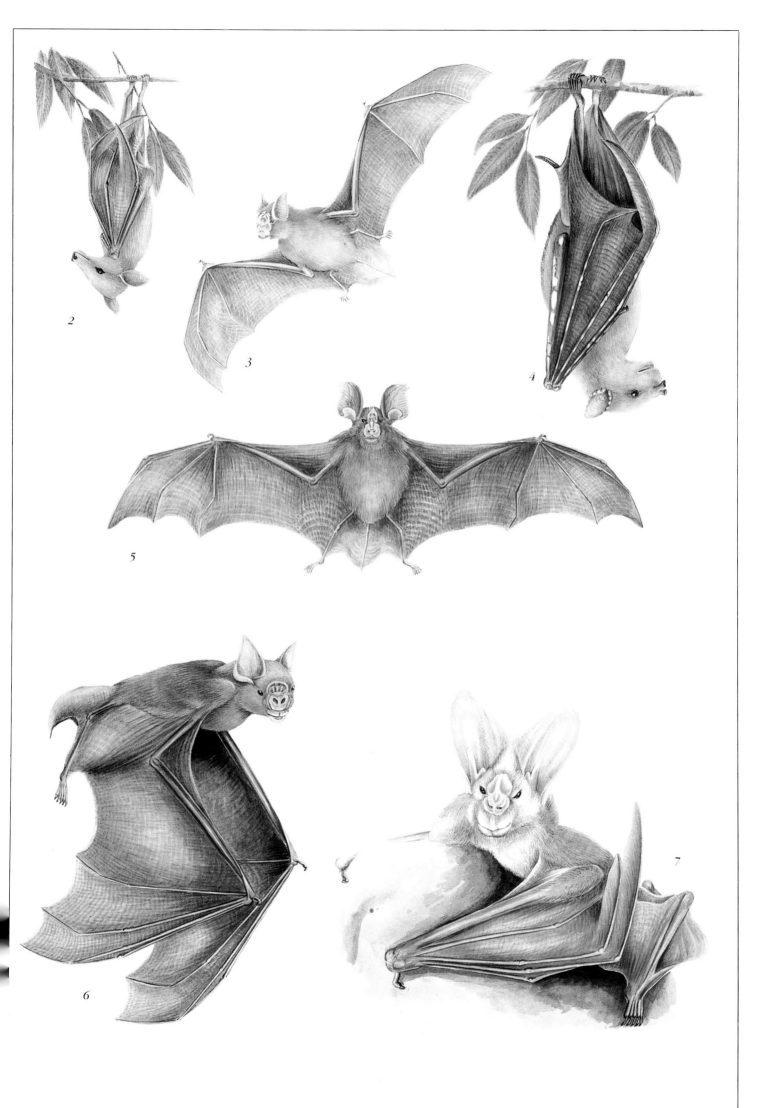

# HORSESHOE-BATS

PLATE 26

*1*

# SHEATHTAIL-BATS

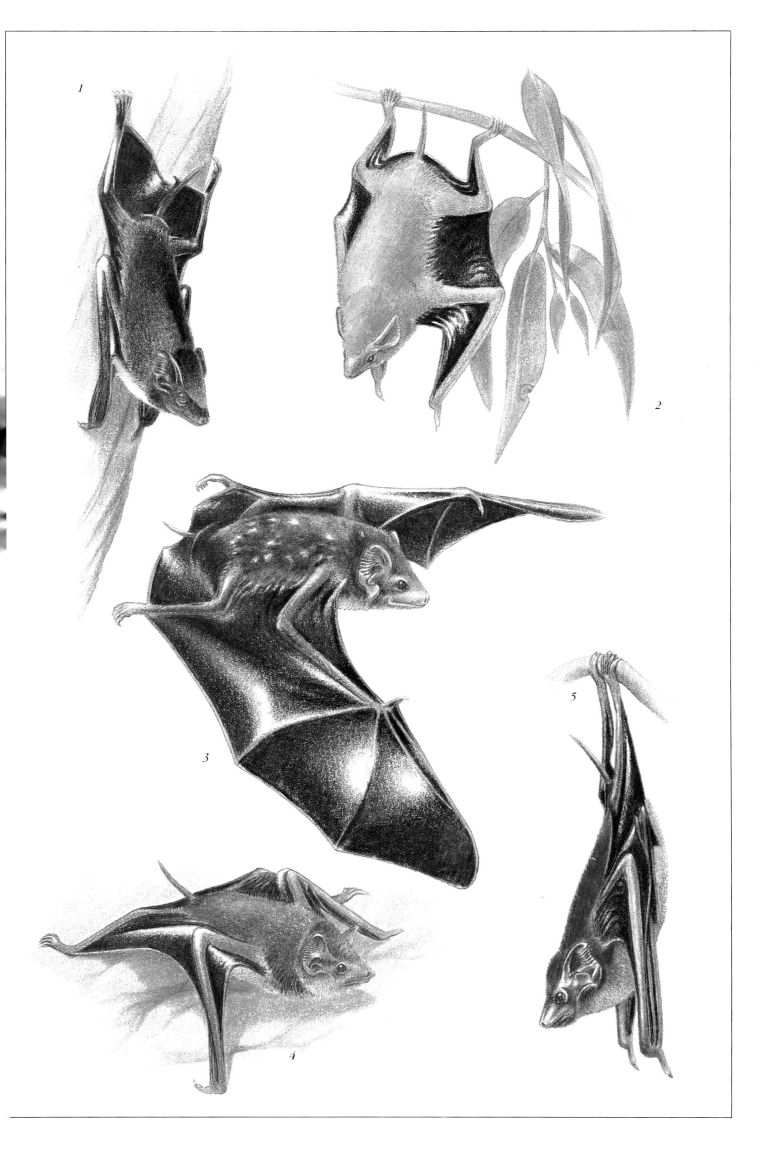

# SHEATHTAIL-BATS AND MASTIFF-BATS

PLATE 28

1 NORTH-EASTERN SHEATHTAIL-BAT *Taphozous australis* (see page 184)

2 YELLOW-BELLIED SHEATHTAIL-BAT *Taphozous flaviventris* (see page 184)

3 NORTHERN MASTIFF-BAT *Chaerophon jobensis* (see page 186)

4 WHITE-STRIPED MASTIFF-BAT *Tadarida australis* (see page 185)

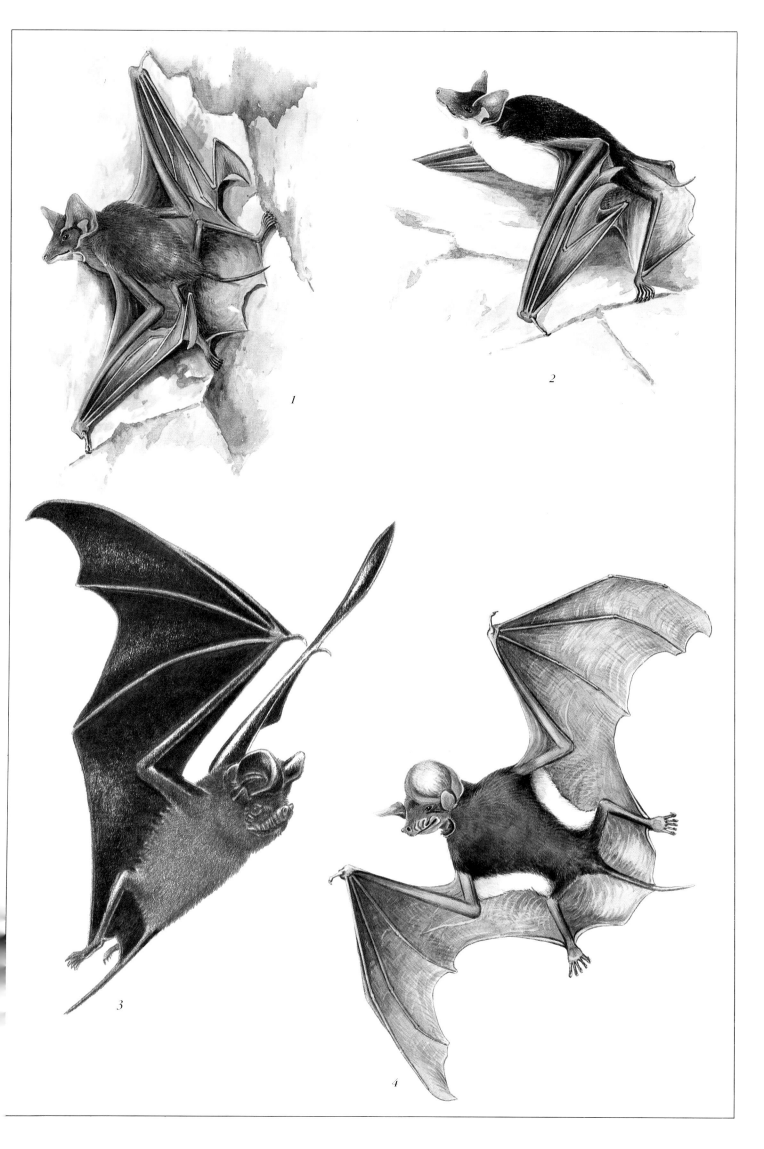

# MASTIFF-BATS AND BENT-WING BATS

PLATE 29

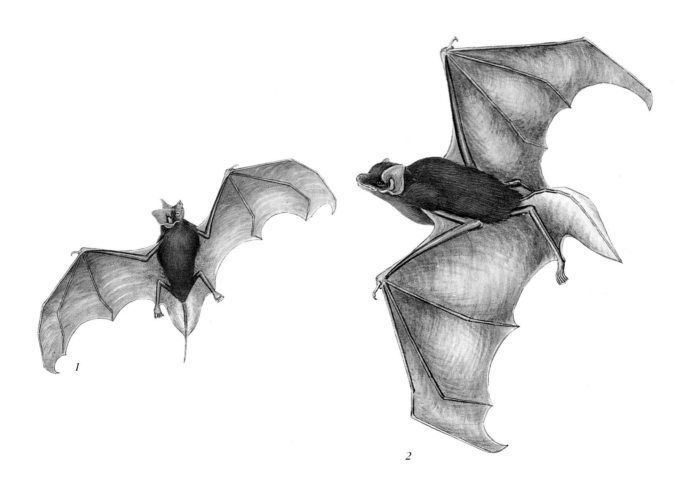

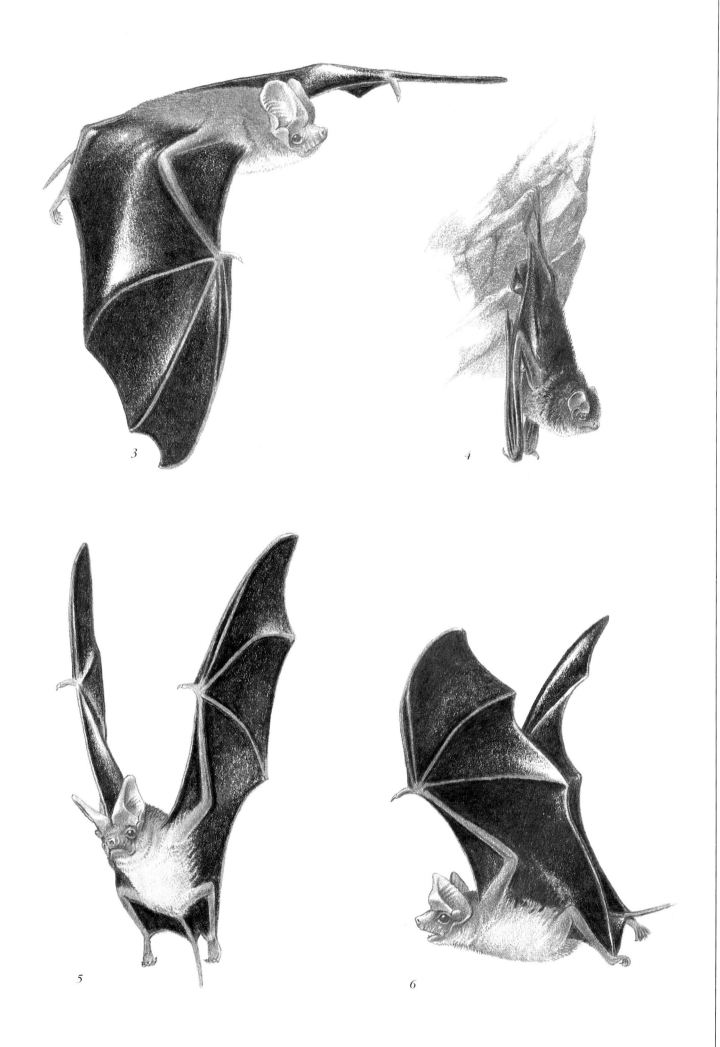

# LONG-EARED BATS

PLATE 30

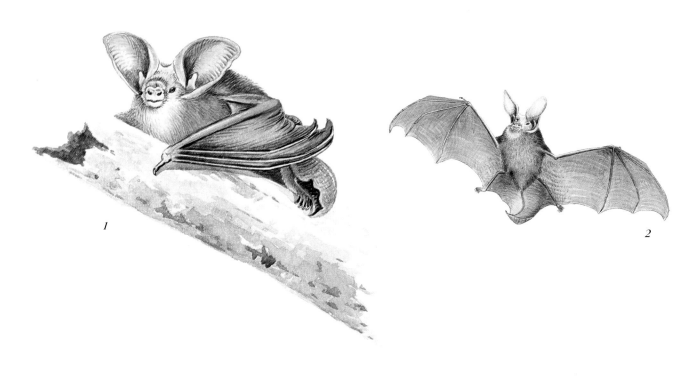

3

4

5

6

# VARIOUS VESPERTILIONID BATS

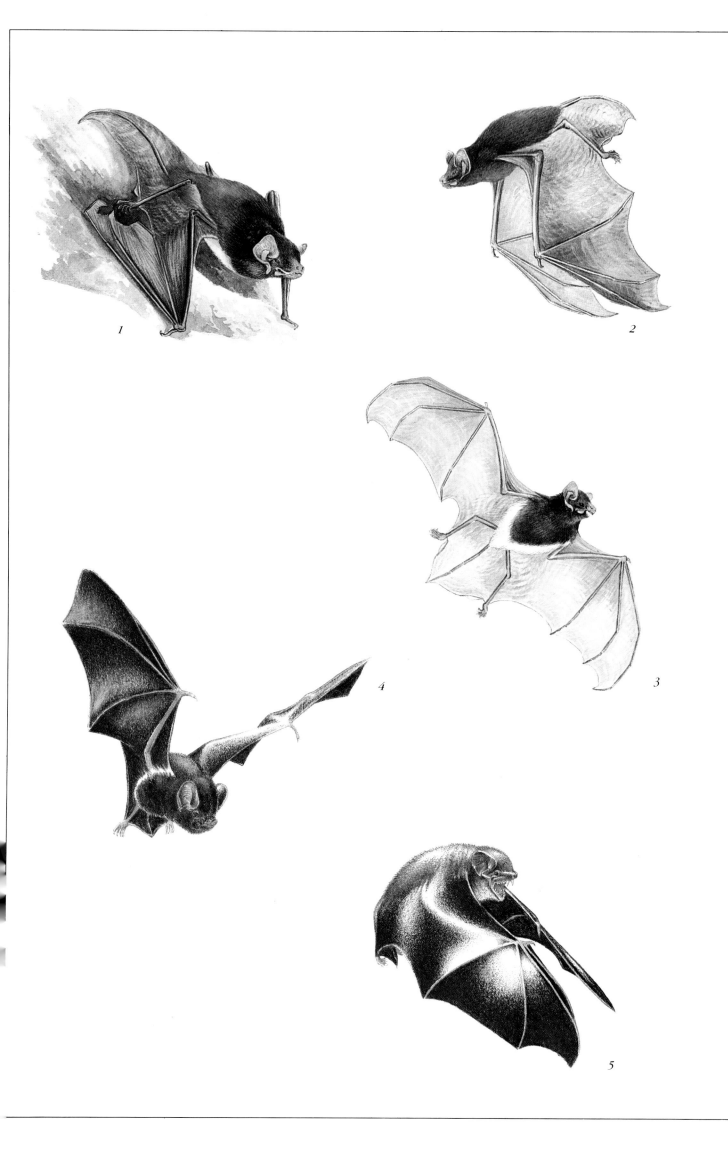

*1*

*2*

*3*

*4*

*5*

# VARIOUS VESPERTILIONID BATS

PLATE 32

*1*

2

3

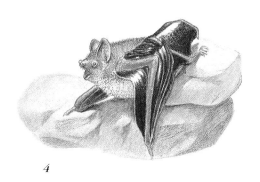

4

5

6

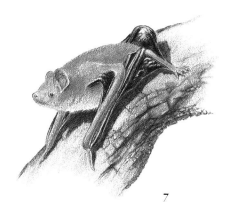

7

# Various Vespertilionid Bats

PLATE 33

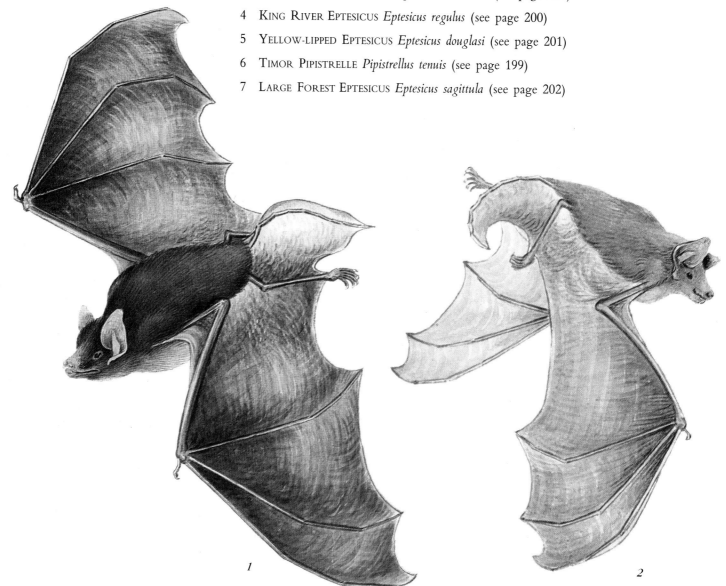

*1*

*2*

# SUBORDER Megachiroptera
*(meg'-ah-kie-rop'-ter-ah)*

DERIVATION.  Megachiroptera—Gk, *megas*, great; sci., Chiroptera, bats.

Bats in this group are distinguished by possession of claws on the first and (usually) second fingers, a long snout, large eyes, and ears of "normal" size and shape. When roosting, they fold the wings around the body and hold the head at a right angle to the chest (as in humans). The tail is short or absent and the interfemoral membrane is correspondingly reduced.

Typical megachiropterans feed on the juices of fruits. Pieces of fruit are bitten off, crushed between the molars and squeezed between the tongue and the palate. The juice (together with small seeds) is swallowed through a remarkably narrow oesophagus and the fibrous remainder is spat out. Food passes through the gut in a matter of hours and seeds are defecated without being digested: these bats thus provide a very effective means of seed dispersal and play an important role in the maintenance of forest diversity.

Since fruit-bats require daily access to food throughout the year, they are commonest in tropical and subtropical rainforests. The few species that exploit the spring and summer fruits of temperate regions migrate towards the equator in winter. Megachiropterans do not hibernate and the larger species do not become torpid when roosting. Some species have specialised in a diet of nectar and pollen. These have long, brush-tipped tongues with which to probe into flowers and some are able to hover like a humming-bird when feeding. They appear to be the major pollinators of some rainforest trees.

The senses of sight, smell and hearing are well developed in megachiropterans. Navigation appears to be primarily by visual clues; food is located and selected on the basis of its appearance and odour; communication is largely by sound and odour. Megachiropterans lack the highly developed ultrasonic echo-location capacity of the microchiropterans but a few cave-roosting species echo-locate by means of audible clicks.

Megachiropterans are restricted to Africa, Asia, Melanesia and Australia: the Australian species are closely related to those of Asia. The suborder comprises only one family, the Pteropodidae.

FAMILY

# Pteropodidae
*(te'-roh-poh'-did-ee)*

DERIVATION. sci., *Pteropus*, flying-fox; *-idae*, familial suffix.

This family includes all species of the suborder Megachiroptera: its characteristics are therefore those of the suborder. Typical members are the fruit-bats, known in Australia as flying-foxes. These have a predominantly tropical distribution but two species migrate southward as far as Victoria in the warmer months.

Many bats aggregate for mutual benefit in common roosts but flying-foxes have a more complex social organisation, coordinated by scent signals and an elaborate code of vocalisations. Camps of tens or even hundreds of thousands of individuals are formed in forested areas, with older members acting as sentinels on the perimeter. At night, adults and juvenile bats move out in enormous feeding flocks.

One of the Australian pteropodids, the Bare-backed Fruit-bat (also occurring from Sulawesi to the Philippines), is unusual in having the wing membranes originating from the middle of the back rather than from the sides of the body, an arrangement which permits it to fly very slowly and even to hover. Because the hairless wings met in the mid-line, the back of the bat appears to be naked.

Two small Australian pteropodids feed on nectar and pollen. The Queensland Tube-nosed Bat has nostrils on the summit of cylindrical stumps but the significance of this arrangement is unknown. The Queensland Blossom-bat is similar in appearance to a flying-fox but considerably smaller: it can hover when lapping nectar or pollen with its long tongue.

# Grey-headed Flying-fox

*Pteropus poliocephalus*
*(te'-roh-poos poh'-lee-oh-sef'-al-us)*

PLATE. 24:3

DERIVATION. *Pteropus* — Gk, *pteryx*, wing; Gk, *pous*, foot: *poliocephalus* — Gk, *polios*, grey; Gk, *kephale*, head.

LENGTH. 230–280 mm.

HABITAT. Wet and dry sclerophyll forest; mangroves.

NOTES. Roosts by day in large groups, hanging by hind feet from branch of a tree, usually with wings wrapped around body. Flock flies at night to feeding grounds to eat nectar, flowers and fruits of native trees, occasionally cultivated fruits.

Mating occurs in March or April. Pregnant females form maternity camp in September and bear single young in October. Young remains attached to mother until five weeks old, thereafter left in camp and suckled daily until about 10 weeks old; independent at 12 weeks. Males rejoin female camp, establish pairs and eventually mate.

STATUS. Common in many parts of range.

# Little Red Flying-fox

*Pteropus scapulatus*
*(skap'-yue-lah'-tus)*

PLATE.   24:5

DERIVATION.   *scapulatus*—L., *scapula*, shoulder.

LENGTH.   195–235 mm.

HABITAT.   Tropical and temperate rainforest, wet and dry sclerophyll
forest, woodland.

NOTES.   Roosts by day, usually in immense numbers, hanging by feet
from tree branches. At night colonies disperse in search of nectar, flowers
and fruits of native trees; may also feed on soft cultivated fruits. Flies
deliberately with slow wing-beats.

Sexually mature at eighteen months. Young born in March or April,
after which females congregate in maternity camp. Shortly after single
young born in April or May, animals disperse. Camps form again in
November or December, with six-month-old animals segregated from
adults.

STATUS.   Common over most of range.

# Black Flying-fox

*Pteropus alecto*
*(ah-lek'-toh)*

PLATE.   24:4

DERIVATION.   *alecto*—Gk, *Alekto*, one of the mythical Furies.

LENGTH.   240–260 mm.

HABITAT.   Tropical and subtropical rainforest, monsoon forest, wet
sclerophyll forest and mangroves.

NOTES.   Roosts by day in large numbers in rather dense foliage, hanging
from tree branch by hind feet. At night feeds on flowers of native trees;
also eats cultivated soft fruits. Flies fast with rapid wing-beats.

Mating occurs from March to April. Single young born between
August and November, with most births in October. Young remains
attached to mother until four weeks old; thereafter left in camp while
mother forages. Independent at age of 13 weeks.

STATUS.   Species widespread through eastern Indonesia and New Guinea.
Australian population is outlying subspecies *P. a. gouldii*. Common.

# Spectacled Flying-fox

*Pteropus conspicillatus*
*(kon-spis'-il-ah'-tus)*

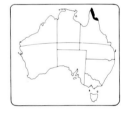

PLATE. 24:2

DERIVATION. *conspicillatus* — N.L., *conspicillus*, spectacles.

LENGTH. 220–240 mm.

HABITAT. Tropical rainforest, wet sclerophyll forest, mangroves.

NOTES. Roosts during the day in large numbers, usually in tall rainforest. Groups disperse at night to feed on flowers of native trees and fruits of palms; cultivated fruits also eaten.

Sexually mature at age of two years, mating from March to May. Females bear single young from October to November. Young remains attached to mother for one to two weeks, thereafter left in roost while mother forages. Independent at about 12 weeks.

STATUS. Widespread in New Guinea and surrounding islands. Australian population is referable to *P. c. conspicillatus*. Common.

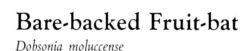

# Bare-backed Fruit-bat

*Dobsonia moluccense*
*(dob-soh'-nee-ah mol'-uk-en'-say)*

PLATE. 24:1

DERIVATION. *Dobsonia* — after G. E. Dobson, British authority on bats: *moluccense* — from Molucca.

LENGTH. 320–330 mm.

HABITAT. Tropical rainforest.

NOTES. Uniquely among Australian bats, wings meet along midline of back. Roosts by day in caves, crevices among rocks, or very dense foliage. Feeds at night on flowers and fruits of native trees and banana flowers. Flies slowly and with good manoeuvrability.

Sexually mature at two years. Mating in May or June. Between September and November, female bears single young which clings to mother for four weeks; thereafter it is suckled in roost to age of 22–26 weeks.

STATUS. Species widely distributed in New Guinea and surrounding islands. Australian population is an outlying subspecies, *D. m. magna*. Common over most of range; rare in Australia.

# Queensland Tube-nosed Bat

*Nyctimene robinsoni*
*(nik'-tee-may'-nay rob'-in-sun-ee)*

PLATE. 25:4

DERIVATION. *Nyctimene*—Gk, *nyx*, night; Gk, *mene*, moon: *robinsoni*—after H. C. Robinson, who collected first specimen.

LENGTH. 120–135 mm.

HABITAT. Rainforest to wet and dry sclerophyll forest and woodland.

NOTES. Distinctive among Australian bats for its protruding tubular nostrils and yellow-spotted wings. Roosts by day in dense vegetation. At night flies along habitual pathways to more open country to feed on fruits, nectar and pollen. Solitary, nomadic, may form relatively large feeding aggregations. Young born from October to November.

STATUS. Common, regarded as an orchard pest in some parts of its range.

# Queensland Blossom-bat

*Syconycteris australis*
*(sie'-koh-nik'-te-ris os-trah'-lis)*

PLATE. 25:2

DERIVATION. *Syconycteris*—Gk, *sykon*, fig tree; Gk, *nykteris*, bat: *australis*—L., *australis*, southern.

LENGTH. *c.* 40–50 mm.

HABITAT. Rainforest to wet sclerophyll forest.

NOTES. One of the smallest of the Australian megachiropterans (about 15 grams).
   Roosts by day in dense vegetation. At night moves along habitual flyways to feed with long, brushy tongue on nectar of a variety of native trees. Can hover while feeding from a flower. Mating occurs in October or November; single young born about a year later.

STATUS. Common over much of its range.

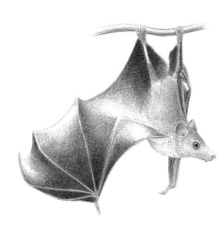

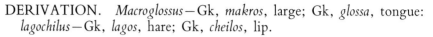

# Northern Blossom-bat

*Macroglossus lagochilus*
*(mak'-roh-glos'-us  lah'-goh-kee'-lus)*

PLATE.   25:1

DERIVATION.   *Macroglossus* — Gk, *makros*, large; Gk, *glossa*, tongue:
 *lagochilus* — Gk, *lagos*, hare; Gk, *cheilos*, lip.

LENGTH.   *c.* 55–60 mm.

HABITAT.   Monsoon forest and woodland, paperbark and bamboo thickets
in wet areas.

NOTES.   Very small, about the same size as Queensland Blossom-bat.
Roosts by day, singly or in small groups, in dense vegetation including
canopies of palmtrees and in rolled banana leaves. At night feeds on nectar
of a variety of trees. Can hover while feeding from a flower. Solitary.
   Births known to occur in August and September but breeding season
could be much longer.

STATUS.   It is possible that this bat is, in fact, an outlier of a South-East
Asian species, *M. minimus*. Common in parts of its Australian range.

# SUBORDER Microchiroptera
*(mike'-roh-kie-rop'-ter-ah)*

DERIVATION.   Microchiroptera—Gk, *mikros*, small; sci., Chiroptera, bats

This group includes the vast majority of bats and a significant proportion—about one in five—of all the living mammal species. Most microchiropterans are small, insectivorous species but a few prey upon other vertebrates; some catch fishes and a small number (the vampires of South and Central America) lap blood. Allied to the vampires and occurring in much the same area, is a subfamily of fruit-eating bats which presumably evolved because of the absence of megachiropterans from the Americas.

Microchiropterans are characterised by having only one clawed digit—the thumb—on the forelimb, large and often elaborately sculptured ears, a short snout and very small eyes. In those which roost hanging downwards (some cling crabwise to the wall of a cave) the wings are usually folded against the sides of the body and the head is directed either downwards or at a right angle to the back (as if, in a human, the head were facing to the rear). The tail is usually of moderate length and helps to support the interfemoral membrane between the hindlegs.

Probably the most remarkable feature of microchiropterans is their capacity for echo-location. Like dolphins, they can locate an object in their surroundings by emitting pulses of high-pitched sound or ultrasound and perceiving the direction of the echo reflected from it. To say this, however, is rather like saying that humans have "visual location" and can determine the position of an object by the light reflected from it. Sight enables us to locate *all* the light-reflecting or light-emitting objects in our field of view—to form a picture of what is in front of us—and it seems that a bat does much the same with vibrations in the air. It "hears a picture" of the trees, foliage, rocks and ground, the insects that are flying in the vicinity or resting upon leaves, the birds that may prey upon it and the other bats in its vicinity ("lit up" by *their* ultrasonic emissions). It is highly probable that the ultrasonic "picture" also includes something akin to colour and texture, for most bats emit a spectrum of vibrations and reflecting objects differ in their absorption and reflection of various wavelengths. Ultrasonic calls are emitted through the mouth, except in the horseshoe-bats, which employ the nostrils: it is apparently in relation to this that horseshoe-bats have an elaborate system of baffles (the noseleaf) on the snout.

Of the 15 or so families of the Microchiroptera, five are represented in Australia: the Megadermatidae with one species; the Rhinolophidae, or horseshoe-bats; the Emballonuridae, or sheathtail-bats; the Molossidae or mastiff-bats; and the Vespertilionidae, perhaps best referred to as "ordinary" bats.

FAMILY
# Megadermatidae
*(meg'-ah-der-mat'-id-ee)*

DERIVATION. Megadermatidae—sci., *Megaderma*, False Vampire; *-idae*, familial suffix.

Sometimes known as "false vampires", this family has only one Australian representative, the Ghost Bat, which is the largest living microchiropteran. In addition to their relatively large size, megadermatids are unusual in having large eyes and a noseleaf similar to that of a horseshoe-bat: the enormous ears are fused together at their bases. The Ghost Bat navigates and hunts both by sight and by echo-location, preying upon smaller bats, birds and large flying insects. It also pounces upon terrestrial mammals, reptiles and frogs, enfolding them in its wings while it delivers killing bites.

# Ghost Bat
*Macroderma gigas*
*(mak'-roh-der'-mah jee'-gas)*

PLATE. 25:7

DERIVATION. *Macroderma*—Gk, *makros*, large; Gk, *derma*, skin: *gigas*— L., *gigas*, giant.

LENGTH. 200–240 mm.

HABITAT. Rainforest, wet and dry sclerophyll forest and arid woodland.

NOTES. Largest of the world's microchiropterans (150 grams), and the only carnivorous Australian species. Roosts communally by day in caves. At night forages on a range of small vertebrates, mostly caught on the ground and enveloped in the wings. Also catches smaller bats in flight. Unusual among bats in having good vision as well as echo-location.

　Mating in July and August. Single young born from September to November. Young segregated in nursery colonies.

STATUS. Two subspecies: *M. g. gigas* over most of range; and *M. g. saturata* in Pilbara region of Western Australia. Range and numbers probably diminished by disturbance. Sparse over much of range, possibly vulnerable.

FAMILY
# Rhinolophidae
*(rie'-noh-loh'-fid-ee)*

DERIVATION.   sci., *Rhinolophus*, horseshoe-bat; *-idae*, familial suffix.

The most characteristic feature of members of this family is the elaborate noseleaf surrounding the nostrils, sometimes based on a ridge in the shape of a horseshoe. Rhinolophids emit their ultrasonic calls through the nostrils and can do so even when engaged in eating: the noseleaf apparently serves to direct the vibrations forward. The ears are large and tail is short, often not extending to the trailing edge of the interfemoral membrane.

Horseshoe-bats are slow fliers, feeding on flying insects in the lower storey of forests, often among dense undergrowth. They are able to hover before darting on slow-moving prey. Unlike other microchiropterans, a roosting horseshoe-bat wraps its wings around its body.

# Eastern Horseshoe-bat
*Rhinolophus megaphyllus*
*(rie'-noh-loh'-fus meg'-ah-fil'-us)*

PLATE   25:5

DERIVATION.   *Rhinolophus*—Gk, *rhis*, snout; Gk, *lophos*, crest: *megaphyllus*—Gk, *megas*, great; Gk, *phyllon*, leaf.

LENGTH.   80–100 mm.

HABITAT.   Wet and dry tropical to cool temperate sclerophyll forests.

NOTES.   Roosts by day in small, humid caves, hanging from ceiling. At night flies slowly among understorey in pursuit of large insects. Can hover. In tropics and subtropics may form large colonies that are active throughout year; in cooler parts of range colonies are small and bats hibernate from about April to July.

Females sexually mature in second or third year; males in second year. Mating usually occurs between April and June: the single young is born around November and weaned in January or February.

STATUS.   Two subspecies. *R. m. megaphyllus* in northern part of range is common; *R. m. ignifer* in southern part of range is sparse.

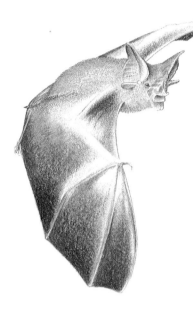

# Large-eared Horseshoe-bat

*Rhinolophus philippinensis*
*(fil'-ip-in-en'-sis)*

PLATE. 26:4

DERIVATION. *philippinensis* — from the Philippines.

LENGTH. 90–110 mm.

HABITAT. Tropical rainforest and vine thickets to open forest.

NOTES. Roosts by day in small, humid caves, hanging individually from ceiling. At night cruises slowly among dense vegetation of the understorey, hovering and then darting at its prey of large insects.
Nothing known of reproduction in Australia.

STATUS. Australian population, *R. p. robertsi*, is an outlier of a tropical species that is widespread from Sulawesi to the Philippines. Rare in Australia; common elsewhere.

# Orange Horseshoe-bat

*Rhinonicteris aurantius*
*(rie'-noh-nik'-te-ris or-an'-tee-us)*

PLATE. 25:3

DERIVATION. *Rhinonicteris* — Gk, *rhis*, snout; Gk, *nykteris* bar: *aurantius* — L., *aurantium*, orange.

LENGTH. 70–80 mm.

HABITAT. Monsoon forest, dry sclerophyll forest to woodland.

NOTES. Characterised by golden fur (but note that some individuals of other rhinolophid species are also golden or reddish). Roosts by day in deep caves, hanging individually from ceiling. At night flies slowly among understorey of forest in vicinity of cave, feeding on medium-sized insects.
Nothing known of breeding biology.

STATUS. Endemic and the only member of its genus. Sparse.

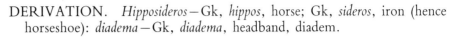

# Diadem Horseshoe-bat

*Hipposideros diadema*
*(hip'-oh-sid-air'-os die'-eh-dem'-ah)*

PLATE.   25:6

DERIVATION.   *Hipposideros* — Gk, *hippos*, horse; Gk, *sideros*, iron (hence horseshoe): *diadema* — Gk, *diadema*, headband, diadem.

LENGTH.   105–125 mm.

HABITAT.   Monsoon forest, tropical rainforest.

NOTES.   A very large bat, three to five times the weight of other Australian rhinolophids. Roosts by day in almost any available shelter — cave, crevice, hollow tree, tree canopy, human constructions. At night flies to foraging area, often some kilometres from roost, to hunt for large insects. May patrol an area or hang from a branch, dropping from it to pursue prey. Flight more direct, less fluttery, than in most horseshoe-bats.
Single young born about November.

STATUS.   Species common and widespread from South-East Asia to Philippines. Two subspecies in Australia: *H. d. inornatus* in Northern Territory; and *H. d. reginae* in Queensland. Both sparse.

# Fawn Horseshoe-bat

*Hipposideros cervinus*
*(ser-vee'-nus)*

PLATE.   26:1

DERIVATION.   *cervinus* — L., *cervinus*, fawn-coloured.

LENGTH.   75–85 mm.

HABITAT.   Tropical rainforest and vine thicket.

NOTES.   Roosts by day in warm cave, hanging individually from ceiling. At night flies slowly and close to the ground among dense understorey vegetation and over water, preying upon medium-sized insects.
Little known of reproduction.

STATUS.   Australian population is an outlier of a species that is common from South-East Asia to the Philippines. The Australian subspecies, *H. c. cervinus*, is sparse to rare.

# Dusky Horseshoe-bat

*Hipposideros ater*
*(ah'-ter)*

PLATE. 26:2

DERIVATION. *ater*—L., *ater*, black.

LENGTH. *c.* 65–75 mm.

HABITAT. Tropical vine thickets and open forest to rainforest.

NOTES. Roosts by day in small caves or crevices, hanging individually from the ceiling, often in company of other species. At night flies slowly among dense understorey vegetation, feeding upon small to medium-sized insects.

 Mating occurs in April; young born in November and weaned in late December or January.

STATUS. Australian population is outlier of common tropical species centred on New Guinea. Two Australian subspecies: *H. a. albanensis*, Northern Queensland; and *H. a. gilberti*, Kimberleys and Northern Territory. Both sparse in Australia.

# Greater Wart-nosed Horseshoe-bat

*Hipposideros semoni*
*(se-moh'-nee)*

PLATE. 26:3

DERIVATION. *semoni*—after R. W. Semon, German zoologist.

LENGTH. 50–70 mm.

HABITAT. Tropical rainforest to woodland.

NOTES. Roosts by day in cave or crevice, hanging individually from ceiling. At night flies deliberately among understorey, foraging for slow-flying insects.

 Nothing known of reproduction or development.

STATUS. Australian population is outlier of species centred on New Guinea. Rare in Australia.

# Lesser Wart-nosed Horseshoe-bat

*Hipposideros stenotis*
*(sten-oh'-tis)*

PLATE.  26:5

DERIVATION.  *stenotis* — Gk, *stenos*, narrow; Gk, *otous*, ear.

LENGTH.  65–75 mm.

HABITAT.  Tropical woodland, sclerophyll and monsoon forest.

NOTES.  Roosts by day in rock crevices and small caves, hanging individually from ceiling or wall. At night, flies slowly among the understorey, darting to capture small to medium-sized insects.
Nothing known of breeding or development.

STATUS.  This is the only species of *Hipposideros* endemic to Australia. Sparse to rare over large range.

FAMILY
# Emballonuridae
*(em-bal'-on-yue'-rid-ee)*

DERIVATION.  sci., *Emballonura*, genus of Old World sheathtail-bats; *-idae*, familial suffix.

The most recognisable characteristic of members of this family is the manner in which the tail is connected to the interfemoral membrane. It gives the impression of piercing the membrane from below but, in fact, is joined to it by an elastic, tubular sheath. This arrangement frees the legs for independent walking movements and contributes to the ease with which these bats move over, and roost on, the walls of caves or the bark of trees. Their rapid movement over a rock face has been likened to that of a spider.

# Common Sheathtail-bat

*Taphozous georgianus*
*(taf'-oh-zoh'-us jor'-jee-ah'-nus)*

PLATE.  27:4

DERIVATION.  *Taphozous*—Gk, *taphos*, grave, tomb; Gk, *zoos*, life, dwelling place: *georgianus*—from King George Sound, WA.

LENGTH.  95–115 mm.

HABITAT.  Warm to tropical wet and dry sclerophyll forest to woodland.

NOTES.  Roosts by day in cave, crevice or abandoned mine; usually individually but forming small clusters in response to cold. Roosting bats hold to wall with feet and wings. At night, flies swiftly in search of small insects. Smallest of the Australian sheathtail-bats.

STATUS.  Widespread, common.

# Naked-rumped Sheathtail-bat
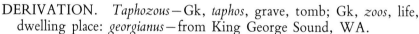

*Taphozous saccolaimus*
*(sak'-oh-lay'-mus)*

PLATE.  27:3

DERIVATION.  *Saccolaimus*—Gk, *sakka*, bag; Gk, *laimos*, throat.

LENGTH.  115–135 mm.

HABITAT.  Tropical rainforest, vine forest, sclerophyll forest, woodland.

NOTES.  Roosts by day in cave, crevice or human constructions, usually in large colonies with individuals some distance from each other. Clings to wall of cave or shelter with feet and wings and moves quite fast on four limbs. At night flies swiftly and directly above the canopy, hunting small insects.
    Little known of breeding or development.

STATUS.  Widely distributed from India to New Guinea. Common over much of range but sparse in Australia.

# Papuan Sheathtail-bat

*Taphozous mixtus*
*(mix'-tus)*

PLATE.  27:1

DERIVATION.  *mixtus*—L., *mixtus*, mixed, intermediate.

LENGTH.  95–105 mm.

HABITAT.  Tropical sclerophyll forest.

NOTES.  Roosts by day in a cave. At night flies swiftly and directly above the canopy, hunting insects. Virtually nothing known of biology.

STATUS.  Not known. Rare in Australia, possibly also rare in New Guinea.

# White-striped Sheathtail-bat

*Taphozous kapalgensis*
*(kap'-al-gen'-sis)*

PLATE.  27:2

DERIVATION.  *kapalgensis*—from Kapalga, NT.

LENGTH.  95–110 mm.

HABITAT.  Woodland and monsoon forest, often close to fresh water.

NOTES.  Reported to roost on pandanus trees, in crevices where leaves adjoin trunks. At night flies fast and directly above canopy, hunting insects. May forage low over water.
  Reproduction and development unknown.

STATUS.  Uncertain, but apparently sparse in restricted area.

# Hill's Sheathtail-bat

*Taphozous hilli*
*(hil'-ee)*

PLATE.  27:5

DERIVATION.  *hilli*—after J. E. Hill, British authority on bats.

LENGTH.  80–110 mm.

HABITAT.  Warm temperate to tropical arid woodland.

NOTES.  One of the smaller of the Australian sheathtail-bats (about 20 grams). Roosts by day in caves. At night flies swiftly and directly around and above trees.
  Single young born between December and March.

STATUS.  Common in parts of range.

# North-eastern Sheathtail-bat

*Taphozous australis*
*(os-trah'-lis)*

PLATE.   28:1

DERIVATION.   *australis*—L., *australis*, southern.

LENGTH.   100–115 mm.

HABITAT.   Tropical rainforest, wet sclerophyll forest.

NOTES.   Roosts by day, usually in a cave but occasionally in more exposed shelter; usually singly, but small clusters may form in response to cold. At night, flies swiftly in pursuit of medium-sized insects. Possibly hibernates in winter.
   Probably mates in April. Single young born in October or November.

STATUS.   Also occurs in New Guinea, where rare. Sparse in Australia.

# Yellow-bellied Sheathtail-bat

*Taphozous flaviventris*
*(flah'-vee-vent'-ris)*

PLATE.   28:2

DERIVATION.   *flaviventris*—L., *flavus*, yellow; L., *venter*, belly.

LENGTH.   95–120 mm.

HABITAT.   Temperate to tropical woodland, sclerophyll forest and rainforest.

NOTES.   Largest of the Australian sheathtail-bats (up to 60 grams). Sleeps singly by day in hollow trees, tree-holes or human constructions. At night flies swiftly above the canopy, hunting insects. Southern populations may migrate northward in winter.
   Reproduction and development unknown.

STATUS.   Sparsely distributed over large range.

FAMILY
# Molossidae
*(mol-os'-id-ee)*

DERIVATION.   sci., *Molossus*, genus of Old World mastiff-bats; *-idae*, familial suffix.

The name of this family refers to the rather blunt and slightly upturned snout, bearing some resemblance to that of a mastiff. The molossids are also known as "freetail bats", in reference to the protrusion of the tip of the tail beyond the interfemoral membrane. They are fast-flying bats which usually hunt small insects above the forest canopy but also descend to the forest floor in search of terrestrial insects. Supporting themselves on thumbs and hindlegs, they can move over the ground with surprising agility, for which reason they are sometimes called "scurrying bats".

# White-striped Mastiff-bat
*Tadarida australis*
*(tah'-dah-ree'-dah os-trah'-lis)*

PLATE.   28:4

DERIVATION.   *Tadarida* — significance unknown: *australis* — L., *australis*, southern.

LENGTH.   125–155 mm.

HABITAT.   Temperate wet and dry sclerophyll forest to arid woodland.

NOTES.   Largest of Australian mastiff-bats (about 35 grams). Roosts by day in small groups in tree-holes, hollow trees or human constructions. At night flies swiftly and directly above the canopy in search of flying insects; also descends to ground, where it chases and catches medium-sized insects.
Single young born in November or December.

STATUS.   Two subspecies: *T. a. australis* over greater part of southern half of continent; and *T. a. atratus* in the central desert. Former common, latter sparse.

# Northern Mastiff-bat

*Chaerophon jobensis*
*(kee'-roh-fon joh-ben'-sis)*

PLATE.   28:3

DERIVATION.   *Chaerophon* — Gk, *khoiros*, pig; Gk, *phonos*, sound:
   *jobensis* — from Jobi Island.

LENGTH.   115–135 mm.

HABITAT.   Tropical dry sclerophyll forest to woodland.

NOTES.   Roosts by day in colonies of up to hundreds in hollow trees or
   human constructions; rarely in caves. Flies swiftly and directly above the
   canopy in search of flying insects. Probably also hunts insects on the
   ground.
      Single young probably born towards end of year.

STATUS.   Species has wide distribution through Melanesia. Sparse over
   large area in Australia.

# Little Mastiff-bat

*Mormopterus planiceps*
*(mor-mop'-ter-us plan'-i-seps)*

PLATE.   29:3

DERIVATION.   *Mormopterus* — Gk, *Mormo*, a monster; Gk, *pteron*, wing:
   *planiceps* — L., *planus*, flat; L., *ceps* head.

LENGTH.   80–105 mm.

HABITAT.   Dry sclerophyll to woodland and desert.

NOTES.   Roosts by day in tree-holes or cracks and in human constructions.
   At night forages above the tree canopy for small flying insects. Also
   alights to take non-flying insects from trees or on the ground. Flight fast
   and direct.
      Single young probably born in December.

STATUS.   Common over much of range.

# Eastern Little Mastiff-bat

*Mormopterus norfolkensis*
*(nor'-foh-ken'-sis)*

PLATE. 29:1

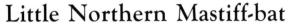

DERIVATION. *norfolkensis* — (mistakenly) from Norfolk Island.

LENGTH. 75–95 mm.

HABITAT. Temperate to subtropical wet sclerophyll forest and woodland.

NOTES. Named in error. This species has never been found on Norfolk Island. Roosts by day in tree-holes and cracks. At night hunts above the canopy for small flying insects. Probably also alights to take non-flying insects. Flight fast and direct.
Reproduction unknown.

STATUS. Sparse to rare.

# Little Northern Mastiff-bat

*Mormopterus loriae*
*(lor'-ee-ee)*

PLATE. 29:5

DERIVATION. *loriae* — after L. Loria, Italian naturalist.

LENGTH. 65–90 mm.

HABITAT. Temperate to tropical dry sclerophyll forest and woodland.

NOTES. Roosts by day in tree-holes or cracks and in human constructions. At night forages above the canopy for flying insects and alights to take non-flying insects. Flight fast and direct.
Single young born in December or January.

STATUS. Two subspecies in Australia: *M. l. coburgensis* in NT; and *M. l. ridei* on eastern coast. Both common.

# Beccari's Mastiff-bat

*Mormopterus beccarii*
*(bek-ah'-ree-ee)*

PLATE. 29:6

DERIVATION. *beccarii* — after O. Beccari, Italian naturalist.

LENGTH. 80–100 mm.

HABITAT. Subtropical to tropical woodland to dry and wet sclerophyll forests and rainforests. Found in urban areas.

NOTES. Roosts by day in tree-holes, cracks and human constructions. At night hunts above the canopy and over water for flying insects. Flight fast and direct.

One young, probably born around December.

STATUS. Species extends from eastern Indonesia through Melanesia. Common over much of range, including Australia.

FAMILY
# Vespertilionidae
*(ves'-per-til'-ee-on'-id-ee)*

DERIVATION.   L., *vespertilio*, bat; sci., *-idae*, familial suffix.

More than five per cent of all the living mammals on earth are members of this highly successful family, which is represented in every continent. The group is so large and diverse that it is difficult to diagnose its members on externally visible features. About half of the Australian bats are vespertilionids.

Of all the families of bats, none is better represented in the cool temperate regions than the Vespertilionidae: in adaptation to this distribution, many vespertilionids are able to hibernate. Slightly more than half of the species native to Australia have a distribution wholly or partly south of the tropic of Capricorn.

# Common Bent-wing Bat
*Miniopterus schreibersii*
*(min'-ee-op'-ter-us shrie'-ber-zee-ee)*

PLATE.   29:2

DERIVATION.   *Miniopterus* — Gk, *minys*, small; Gk, *pteryx*, wing:
*schreibersii* — after K. F. A. von Schreibers, Austrian zoologist.

LENGTH.   105–115 mm.

HABITAT.   Cool to tropical wet and dry sclerophyll forest, monsoon forest.

NOTES.   Roosts communally in caves, mines and human constructions. At night hunts above the tree canopy for flying insects. Flight is swift and direct. In southern part of range hibernates during the coldest months.

Mating occurs from May to June in the southern part of the range; in September in the tropics. Pregnant females congregate in nursery caves around September. Single young born in December. Caves may contain thousands of young, closely packed to conserve heat and humidity.

STATUS.   Species is cosmopolitan and one of the world's most widely distributed mammals. The two subspecies in Australia are *M. s. oceanensis*, eastern coastal mainland; and *M. s. orianae*, Northern Territory and Kimberleys. Both common.

# Little Bent-wing Bat

*Miniopterus australis*
*(os-trah'-lis)*

PLATE. 29:4

DERIVATION. *australis*—L., *australis*, southern.

LENGTH. 85–95 mm.

HABITAT. Warm wet and dry sclerophyll forest to tropical rainforest.

NOTES. Similar to, but about half the size of, the Common Bent-wing Bat. Roosts by day in caves, mines or tunnels. At night hunts flying insects below the forest canopy. Flight slower and less direct than that of its larger relative.

  Mating occurs mostly in August. Pregnant females congregate in nursery caves, single young born in December.

STATUS. Species extends from South-East Asia through Indonesia and Melanesia to the Philippines. The Australian population, *M. a. australis*, is common.

# Greater Long-eared Bat

*Nyctophilus timoriensis*
*(Nik'-toh-fil'-us tee-mor'-ee-en'-sis)*

PLATE. 30:1

DERIVATION. *Nyctophilus*—Gk, *nyktos*, night; Gk, *philos*, loving: *timoriensis*—from Timor.

LENGTH. 100–125 mm.

HABITAT. Mostly arid to semi-arid temperate woodland, extending to dry and wet sclerophyll forest.

NOTES. Roosts by day, in tree-holes and under loose bark. At night forages for large insects, often over water. Very manoeuvrable in flight.

  Reproduction unknown. Young probably born between January and March.

STATUS. Sparse.

# Lesser Long-eared Bat

*Nyctophilus geoffroyi*
*(jef-roy'-ee)*

PLATE. 30:2

DERIVATION. *geoffroyi*—after E. Geoffroy St.-Hilaire, French zoologist.

LENGTH. 40–50 mm.

HABITAT. All Australian environments except tropical and subtropical rainforest.

NOTES. Roosts by day in tree-holes and under bark, in caves and in human constructions: extremely adaptable. At night forages for small flying insects, often close to the ground. In the southern part of the range animals may become torpid in winter but do not hibernate.

    Pregnant females segregate into maternity colonies and give birth, usually to two young, from about September to about November. Weaned at about eight weeks.

STATUS. Three subspecies: *N. g. geoffroyi* mainly in Western Australia; *N. g. pallescens* in the northern part of South Australia; *N. g. pacificus* in eastern Australia and Tasmania.

# Gould's Long-eared Bat

*Nyctophilus gouldi*
*(gule'-dee)*

PLATE. 30:5

DERIVATION. *gouldi*—after J. Gould, British naturalist.

LENGTH. 100–120 mm.

HABITAT. Temperate dry and wet sclerophyll forest, extending to woodland.

NOTES. Roosts by day in tree-holes, under bark, or in human constructions. At night forages for flying insects and also descends to take insects from leaves. Very manoeuvrable in flight.

    Animals in the southern part of the range hibernate during the coldest months.

    Usually two young, born in summer.

STATUS. Common.

# Queensland Long-eared Bat

*Nyctophilus bifax*
*(bie'-fax)*

PLATE. 30:3

DERIVATION. *bifax* — L., *bi-*, two; L., *facies*, face.

LENGTH. 85–100 mm.

HABITAT. Tropical rainforest to woodland.

NOTES. Roosts by day in tree-holes and in human constructions. At night hunts flying insects, often close to the ground. Is able to hover while gleaning insects from leaves and can alight on, and take off from, the ground.
    Two young born, probably around December.

STATUS. Common.

# Arnhem Land Long-eared Bat

*Nyctophilus arnhemensis*
*(ar'-nem-en'-sis)*

PLATE. 30:4

DERIVATION. *arnhemensis* — from Arnhem Land.

LENGTH. 75–95 mm.

HABITAT. Monsoon forest, tropical woodland.

NOTES. Roosts by day in tree-hole, under bark, or in human constructions. At night hunts deliberately in the understorey or over water. Flight very manoeuvrable.
    One or two young, born between October and February.

STATUS. Common over much of range.

# Pygmy Long-eared Bat

*Nyctophilus walkeri*
*(waw'-ker-ee)*

PLATE. 30:6

DERIVATION. *walkeri* — after J. J. Walker, who collected first specimen.

LENGTH. 70–80 mm.

HABITAT. Fringing vegetation around tropical waterbodies.

NOTES. Smallest of the long-eared bats (about 45 grams), and least known. Probably roosts in tree-holes or under bark.
    Two young, probably born in early summer.

STATUS. Probably rare.

# Gould's Wattled Bat

*Chalinolobus gouldii*
*(kal'-in-oh-loh'-bus gule'-dee-ee)*

PLATE.  31:1

DERIVATION.  *Chalinolobus*—Gk, *chalinos*, bridle; Gk, *lobos*, lobe: *gouldii*—after J. Gould, British naturalist.

LENGTH.  105–125 mm.

HABITAT.  Cool temperate to tropical, rainforest to desert.

NOTES.  Roosts by day in tree-holes, under bark and in almost any natural or man-made cavity. At night forages below the canopy and often close to the ground, hunting for flying beetles and moths and gleaning some insects from foliage. In southern part of range bats may become torpid in the colder months but do not hibernate. Flight rather slow and manoeuvrable.

   Mating occurs around May and sperm is stored by female for fertilisation around July. Two young usually born around November. All breeding events earlier in northern part of range.

STATUS.  Two subspecies: *C. g. gouldii* in southern part of range; and *C. g. venatoris* in northern part. Both common.

# Chocolate Wattled Bat

*Chalinolobus morio*
*(mo'-ree-oh)*

PLATE.  31:2

DERIVATION.  *morio*—Gk, *Moros*, son of night.

LENGTH.  95–110 mm.

HABITAT.  Cool temperate to subtropical, from wet and dry sclerophyll forest to woodland and desert. Roosts in warm dry microclimate.

NOTES.  Much smaller than the related Gould's Wattled Bat. Roosts by day, typically in tree-holes or similar cavities, but occupies caves in Nullarbor Plain. At night forages below tree canopy for small moths. Flight rather slow and very manoeuvrable. In southern part of range, bats hibernate for the coldest months (but for a lesser period than other resident species).

   Two young born in December or January; up two months earlier at northern extreme of range.

STATUS.  Common over much of range.

# Hoary Bat

*Chalinolobus nigrogriseus*
*(nig'-roh-griz-ay'-us)*

PLATE.  31:5

DERIVATION.  *nigrogriseus* — L., *niger,* black; L., *griseus,* grey.

LENGTH.  80–100 mm.

HABITAT.  Subtropical to tropical wet sclerophyll forest to woodland and heath.

NOTES.  Roosts by day in rock crevices, probably also in tree-holes. At night forages below the canopy for small flying insects and others which it gleans from foliage. Probably alights to catch some non-flying insects (in same manner as mastiff-bats). Flight speed moderate; highly manoeuvrable.
Probably two young born towards middle of summer.

STATUS.  Two supposed subspecies: *C. n. nigrogriseus,* New Guinea and eastern Australia; and *C. n. rogersi,* northern Australia to the west of Cape York. Both common over much of range.

# Little Pied Bat

*Chalinolobus picatus*
*(pik-ah'-tus)*

PLATE.  31:3

DERIVATION.  *picatus* — L., *picatus,* black and white.

LENGTH.  75–85 mm.

HABITAT.  Temperate to tropical semi-arid to arid woodland.

NOTES.  Smallest Australian member of genus. Roosts by day, mainly in caves or mines but also in tree-holes, under bark and in human constructions. At night forages for small flying insects. Flies low at moderate speed; very manoeuvrable.
Two young born, probably between November and January.

STATUS.  Sparsely distributed.

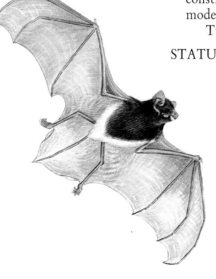

# Large Pied Bat

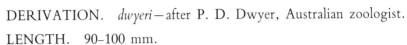

*Chalinolobus dwyeri*
*(dwie'-er-ee)*

PLATE. 31:4

DERIVATION.   *dwyeri*—after P. D. Dwyer, Australian zoologist.

LENGTH.   90–100 mm.

HABITAT.   Warm temperate to subtropical dry sclerophyll forest to woodland.

NOTES.   Despite common name, is only marginally larger on average than Little Pied Bat. Roosts by day in caves or abandoned mines. At night forages below canopy for small flying insects. Flight speed moderate, highly manoeuvrable. In southern part of range probably hibernates.
   Usually two young born in November or December.

STATUS.   Sparse to rare.

# Large-footed Myotis

*Myotis adversus*
*(my-oh'-tis ad-ver'-sus)*

PLATE.   32:2

DERIVATION.   *Myotis*—Gk, *mys*, mouse; Gk, *otous*, ear: *adversus*—L., *adversus*, opposed.

LENGTH.   80–100 mm.

HABITAT.   Cool temperate to tropical wet sclerophyll forest and rainforest, usually close to open fresh water.

NOTES.   Roosts by day in caves or abandoned mines, or in dense rainforest foliage. At night, flies over bodies of water, dipping claws of hindfeet just below surface to catch aquatic insects that are sensed by echo-location. Also takes flying insects on the wing. Only Australian bat to take food from the water. Flight fast and direct.
   Males establish and defend harems of several females. Pattern of breeding varies with latitude. In cool temperate part of range, one young is born in November or December. In subtropics, breeding is continuous and three young may be born in a year.

STATUS.   Species is widespread from eastern Indonesia through Melanesia and western Pacific islands. Two subspecies in Australia: *M. a. macropus* in the south-east; and *M. a. moluccarum* in the north. Both sparse.

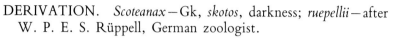

# Greater Broad-nosed Bat

*Scoteanax rueppellii*
*(skoh'-tay-an'-ax rue-pel'-ee-ee)*

PLATE. 32:1

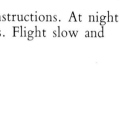

DERIVATION. *Scoteanax*—Gk, *skotos*, darkness; *ruepellii*—after W. P. E. S. Rüppell, German zoologist.

LENGTH. 120–150 mm.

HABITAT. Cool temperate to tropical wet sclerophyll forest and rainforest.

NOTES. Roosts by day in tree hollows or human constructions. At night forages among the understorey for large flying insects. Flight slow and direct, often low over water.

Single young born in January.

STATUS. Sparse to rare.

# Little Broad-nosed Bat

*Scotorepens greyii*
*(skoh'-toh'-rep-enz gray'-ee-ee)*

PLATE. 32:3

DERIVATION. *Scotorepens*—Gk, *skotos*, darkness; L., *repens*, to creep: *greyii*—after G. Grey, British explorer of Australia.

LENGTH. 70–95 mm.

HABITAT. Cool temperate to tropical, deserts and woodland to dry and wet sclerophyll forests.

NOTES. Roosts by day in tree hollows and other crevices, also in human constructions. At night forages for small flying insects. Flight fast and darting. Often skims surface of water to drink.

In southern part of range mating probably occurs in April. Usually two young born in December.

STATUS. Common.

# Inland Broad-nosed Bat

*Scotorepens balstoni*
*(bawl'-ston-ee)*

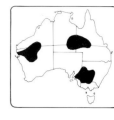

PLATE.  32:5

DERIVATION.  *balstoni*—after W. E. Balston, who funded expedition by G. C. Shortridge to south-western Australia in 1904.

LENGTH.  80–90 mm.

HABITAT.  Tropical to cool temperate arid woodland, near permanent water.

NOTES.  Sleeps by day in tree-hole or crevice, sometimes in man-made structures. Feeds from dusk on small flying insects, particularly mosquitoes. A fast and agile flier.
    Mating occurs around early May. One or two young born in November. Carried by mother until about 10 days old, then left in creche. Independent at about five weeks.

STATUS.  Common.

# Little Northern Broad-nosed Bat

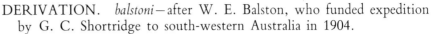

*Scotorepens sanborni*
*(san'-born-ee)*

PLATE.  32:7

DERIVATION.  *sanborni*—after C. S. Sanborn, American zoologist.

LENGTH.  65–90 mm.

HABITAT.  Tropical rainforest and monsoon forest to woodland, usually near permanent water.

NOTES.  Sleeps by day in tree-hole or crevice, sometimes in man-made structures. Feeds from sunset on mayflies, midges and mosquitoes. An agile, swift flier in understorey of forest. Females larger than males.
    Mating probably occurs around May. Young probably born around November.

STATUS.  Common.

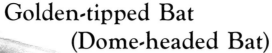

# Golden-tipped Bat (Dome-headed Bat)

*Phoniscus papuensis*
*(foh-nis'-kus pah'-pue-en'-sis)*

PLATE. 32:6

DERIVATION. *Phoniscus*—Gk, *phonos*, murder; Gk, *-iskos*, diminutive suffix: *papuensis*—from Papua.

LENGTH. 90–110 mm.

HABITAT. Cool temperate to tropical rainforest.

NOTES. Roosts by day under dead, hanging fronds of palms and in human constructions, probably also in tree-holes or cracks. At night forages below canopy for small flying insects. Flight fast or slow, including hovering. Winter behaviour of southern populations unknown. Details of reproduction unknown.

STATUS. Sparse in Australia.

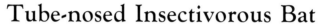

# Tube-nosed Insectivorous Bat

*Murina florium*
*(mue-ree'-nah flor-ee-um)*

PLATE. 32:4

DERIVATION. *Murina*—L., *murinus*, mouse-like: *florium*—L., *flos*, flower.

LENGTH. *c.* 80 mm.

HABITAT. Tropical misty rainforests.

NOTES. Roosts by day among foliage with the wings overlapping in front of the chest but held away from the body and with the tail membrane curled forward to cover it. This arrangement acts as an umbrella: water falling or condensing on the wings drains away via the wing tips. At night, flies slowly in search of insects. When feeding, hangs by its feet and thumbs so that the tail-membrane forms a cup into which any insect fragments or faeces fall. Scraps are checked to ensure that nothing edible remains, then, hanging only by the claws on its wings, the bat shakes away the residue. Nostrils lie at the end of short lateral projections, as in *Nyctimene*, but the significance of this arrangement is unknown.

STATUS. One specimen, trapped on the Atherton Tablelands, is the only record from Australia. Rare.

# Timor Pipistrelle

*Pipistrellus tenuis*
*(pip'-is-trell'-us ten'-ue-is)*

PLATE.  33:6

DERIVATION.  *Pipistrellus*—Ital., *pipistrello*, bat: *tenuis*—L., tenuis, narrow.

LENGTH.  60–85 mm.

HABITAT.  Tropical rainforest and monsoon forest.

NOTES.  Roosts by day in tree hollows and under dead, hanging fronds of palm trees; also in human constructions. At night hunts between understorey and canopy for flying insects. Flight fast and with sudden changes of direction.
    One young, time of birth unknown.

STATUS.  Species extends through Indonesia and Melanesia. Australian population is *P. t. papuanus*. Common.

# Tasmanian Pipistrelle

*Falsistrellus tasmaniensis*
*(fol'-sis-trell'-us taz-may'-nee-en'-sis)*

PLATE.  33:1

DERIVATION.  *Falsistrellus*—L., *falsus*, false; sci., *Pipistrellus*, another genus of bats to which this species was previously thought to belong: *tasmaniensis*—from Tasmania.

LENGTH.  95–120 mm.

HABITAT.  Cool temperate to subtropical wet and dry sclerophyll forest.

NOTES.  Roosts by day, usually in tree hollows, but also in caves and human constructions. At night hunts medium-sized insects below the forest canopy. Flight swift with sharp changes of direction. Southern populations may hibernate.
    Nothing known of reproduction.

STATUS.  Sparse.

# Little Cave Eptesicus

*Eptesicus pumilus*
*(ep'-te-see'-kus poom'-il-us)*

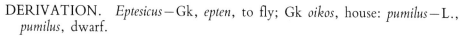

PLATE. 33:2

DERIVATION. *Eptesicus*—Gk, *epten*, to fly; Gk *oikos*, house: *pumilus*—L., *pumilus*, dwarf.

LENGTH. 70–90 mm.

HABITAT. Warm temperate to tropical woodland, sclerophyll forest and rainforest.

NOTES. Roosts by day in caves, rock crevices or abandoned mines. At night hunts between the understorey and the canopy for very small flying insects. Flies at moderate speed with sharp changes of direction.
   One or two young born, time of birth variable.

STATUS. Two subspecies: *E. p. pumilus* on east coast; and *E. p. caurinus*, north-western and central Australia. Both common.

# King River Eptesicus

*Eptesicus regulus*
*(reg'-yue-lus)*

PLATE. 33:4

DERIVATION. *regulus*—L., *regulus*, little king.

LENGTH. 80–100 mm.

HABITAT. Cool temperate sclerophyll forest to subarid woodland.

NOTES. Roosts by day in tree-holes and cracks. Probably hunts below the canopy for small flying insects. Flight fast with rapid changes of direction.
   Mating occurs around May; single young born around November.

STATUS. Common.

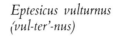

# Little Forest Eptesicus

*Eptesicus vulturnus*
*('vul-ter'-nus)*

PLATE. 33:3

DERIVATION. *vulturnus* — L., *vulturinus*, vulture-like.

LENGTH. 70–90 mm.

HABITAT. Cool temperate to subtropical sclerophyll forest to arid woodland.

NOTES. Roosts by day in tree-holes, cracks and human construction. At night hunts between the understorey and the canopy for flying insects. Flight fast with rapid changes of direction.
   Females form maternity colonies. Single young born in November or December.

STATUS. Common over much of range.

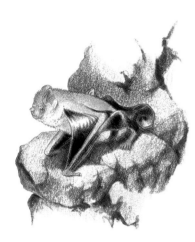

# Yellow-lipped Eptesicus

*Eptesicus douglasi*
*(dug'-las-ee)*

PLATE. 33:5

DERIVATION. *douglasi* — after A. Douglas, Australian naturalist.

LENGTH. 65–85 mm.

HABITAT. Tropical monsoon forest and woodland.

NOTES. Roosts by day in a cave. At night hunts over water for flying insects. Flight fast, with rapid changes of direction.
   Females form maternity colonies. Single young born between October and January.

STATUS. Sparse.

# Large Forest Eptesicus

*Eptesicus sagittula*
*(sa-jit'-yue-lah)*

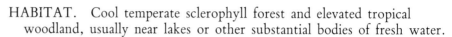

PLATE.  33:7

DERIVATION.  *sagittula* — L., *sagittula*, little arrow.

LENGTH.  80–100 mm.

HABITAT.  Cool temperate sclerophyll forest and elevated tropical woodland, usually near lakes or other substantial bodies of fresh water.

NOTES.  Roosts by day in tree-holes or cracks. At night hunts for small insects. Flight fast, with rapid changes of direction. Bats in southern populations become torpid in coldest months but on warmer days emerge from torpor and feed.
    Single young born around November.

STATUS.  Common.

# ORDER RODENTIA

(roh-dent'-ee-ah)

DERIVATION.   *rodentia* — L., *rodens*, gnawing.

The name of this order of mammals draws attention to its most obvious characteristic, a pair of chisel-like, gnawing incisors in the upper and lower jaws. Faced with a thick layer of enamel on the front and with softer dentine behind, these teeth retain their sharp cutting edges as they are worn away. The teeth grow continuously throughout life.

Rodents are the outstanding gnawers among the mammals — beavers can even fell substantial trees. Most rodents are less concerned with engineering and use their teeth to gnaw nuts, seeds and tough grasses. Surprisingly, in view of such great dental specialisation, a number of rodents have become secondarily insectivorous, and a few even prey upon small vertebrates.

Rodents are an extremely widespread and diverse group. Although many species probably remain to be described, those that are known (over 2000) constitute more than half the known mammals. Four suborders comprise some two dozen families but only one family is represented in Australia.

Indeed, apart from the so-called "new endemic" rats of the genus *Rattus*, which probably have been in Australia for less than a million years, all the Australian rodents are members of a single subfamily, though evolution within this subfamily has led to a number of quite distinct types. *Hydromys* and *Xeromys* are amphibious predators which find most of their prey — crabs, mussels and frogs — underwater. The mosaic-tailed rats of the genera *Uromys* and *Melomys* are primarily arboreal feeders on tropical rainforest fruits and seeds, although the Grassland Melomys feeds more on grasses. Tree-rats of the genera *Conilurus* and *Mesembriomys* are also tropical and arboreal. Rock-rats of the genus *Zyzomys* are terrestrial, feeding on fallen seeds, fruits, fungi and insects. The Prehensile-tailed Rat (*Pogonomys*) is an arboreal genus, widespread in the rainforests of New Guinea and sparsely represented in northern Queensland.

Two species of stick-nest rats (*Zyzomys*) have declined severely since European settlement. One is almost certainly extinct and the other now limited to an offshore island. These arid-adapted rodents fed upon succulent desert plants and built large shelters out of sticks and branches.

The Broad-toothed Rat, which feeds on grasses, sedges and seeds, requires a damp, cool climate and is restricted to subalpine country with dense ground cover. It is capable of living below the snow in winter.

Most distinctive in appearance of all the Australian rodents are the hopping-mice of the genus *Notomys*. They have long hindlegs and feet reminiscent of those of a kangaroo or a Jerboa, and long, slender, flexible tails which act as balancers. Hopping-mice, which are largely creatures of the arid interior, construct deep burrows in which to shelter during the day. They have efficient mechanisms for water conservation and most species do not need to drink.

The paucity of names is confusing because, quite apart from the introduced Brown and Black Rats, there are seven native rodents of the genus *Rattus*, which merit the common name "rat". It is interesting that these species, relatively recently descended from one or more New Guinean ancestors, remain restricted to fairly wet forested areas and have not been able to adapt to the arid interior of the continent. The Long-haired Rat, which periodically erupts in plague proportions in inland Australia is not really an exception to this generalisation, for it is able to do so only when unusually heavy and prolonged rainfall provides widespread vegetation and drinking water in areas where these resources are infrequently available.

# VARIOUS RODENTS

PLATE 34

*1*

2

3

4

# MELOMYSES AND WHITE-TAILED RAT

PLATE 35

*1*

# HOPPING-MICE

PLATE 36

# ROCK-RATS, STICK-NEST RATS AND TREE-RATS

PLATE 37

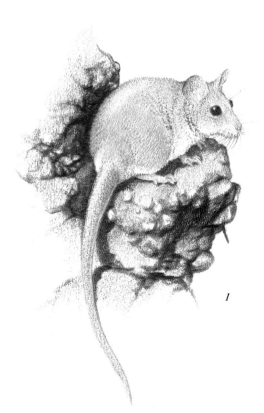

*1*

*2*

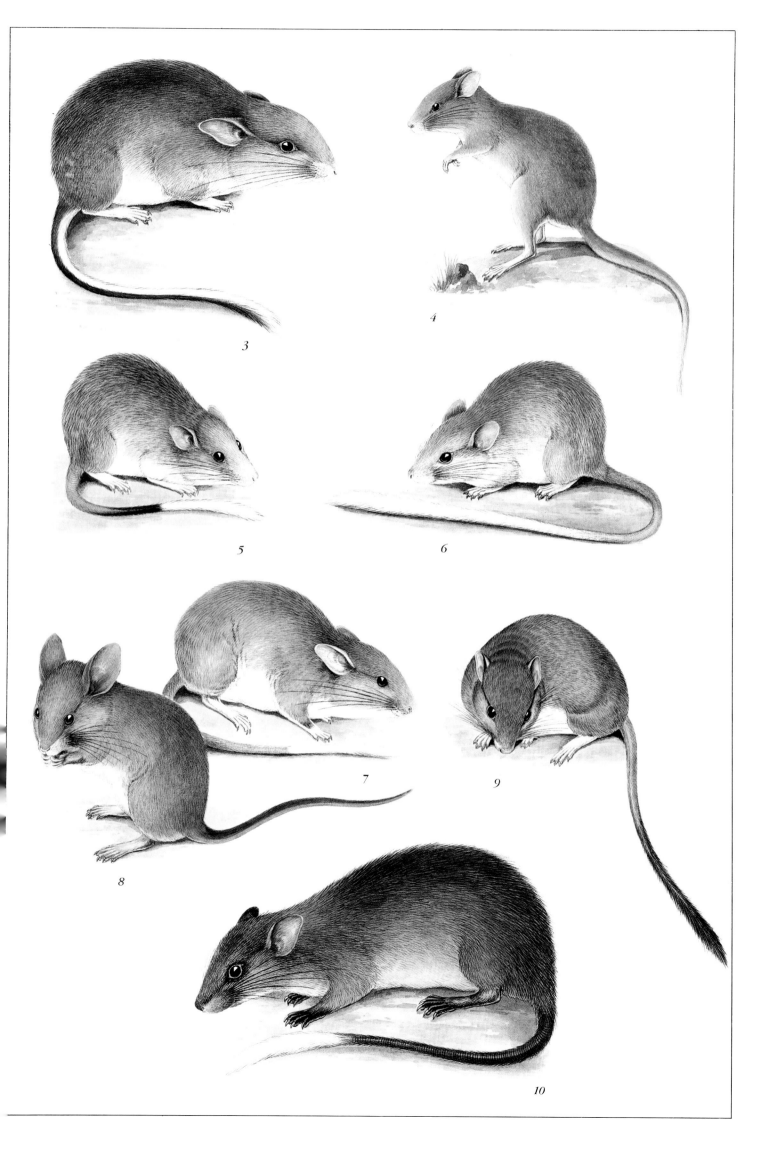

# NATIVE MICE

PLATE 38

*1*

*2*

*3*

*4*

*5*

*6*

*7*

*8*

# NATIVE MICE

PLATE 39

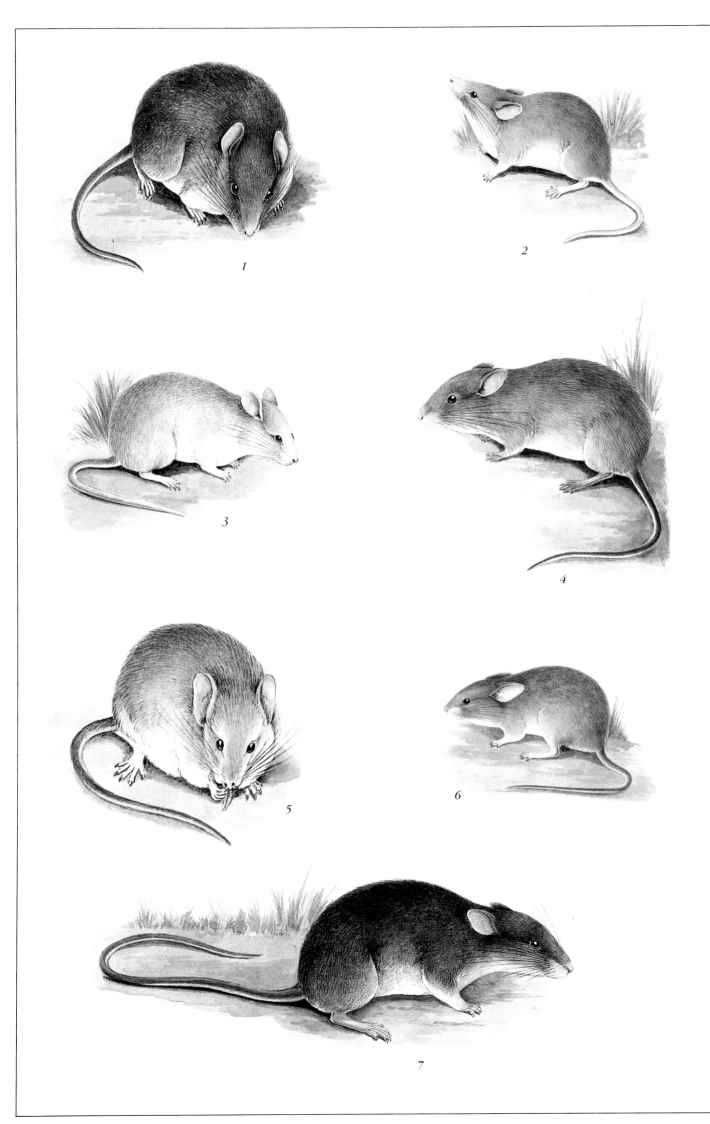

# NATIVE MICE

# BROAD-TOOTHED RAT, PREHENSILE-TAILED RAT AND "NEW ENDEMIC" RATS

3

4

5

6

# "NEW ENDEMIC" RATS

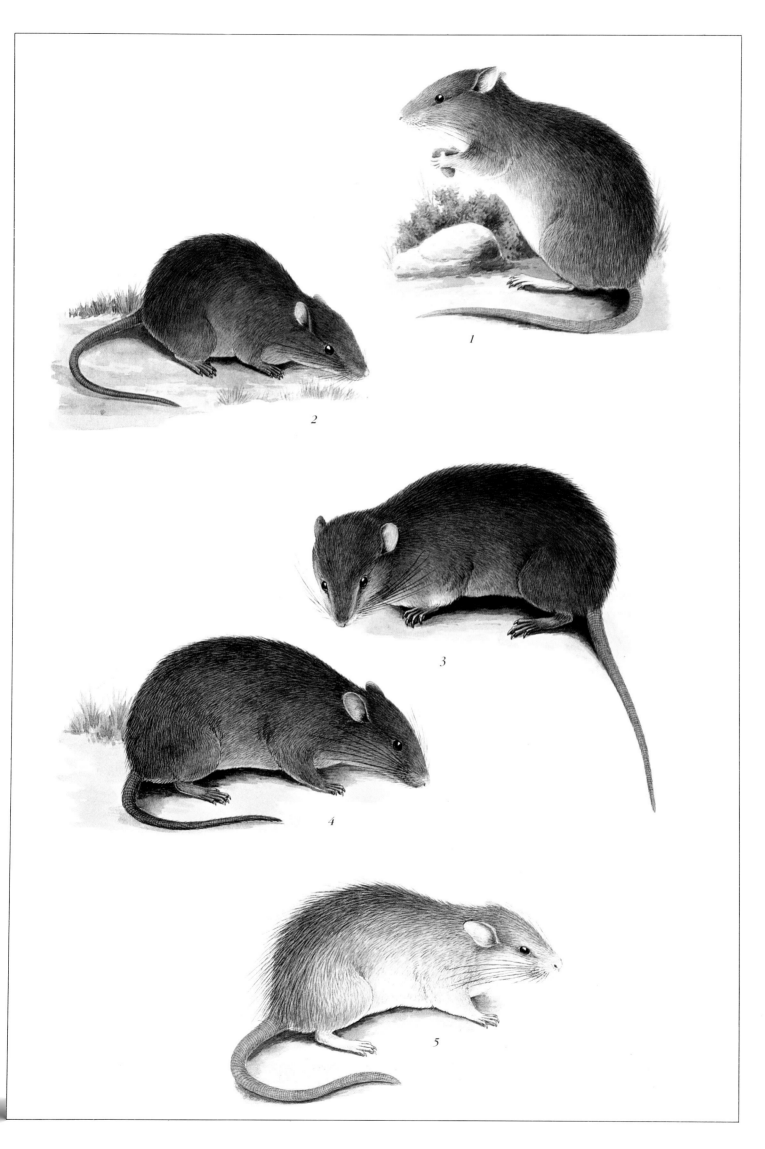

SUBORDER **Myomorpha**

*(mie'-oh-mor'-fah)*

DERIVATION.   Gk, *mys*, mouse; *morphos*, form.

Rodents fall into three suborders: the Sciuromorpha, including the squirrel-like forms; the Caviomorpha, including the cavies and porcupines; and the Myomorpha—the rats, mice, dormice, jerboas and jumping-mice. The Myomorpha is by far the largest suborder in the class Mammalia.

FAMILY
# Muridae
*(myue'-rid-ee)*

DERIVATION.   L., *mus*, mouse; sci., *-idae*, familial suffix.

This family includes no less than a thousand species, spread over almost the entire land surface of the earth. Some eighteen subfamilies of murids are currently recognised but only two of these are represented in Australia. The Hydromyinae includes all the native Australian rodents except the rats of the genus *Rattus*, which belong to the Murinae.

# Water-rat

*Hydromys chrysogaster*
*(hie'-droh-mis kris'-oh-gas'-ter)*

PLATE.   34:2 and 4

DERIVATION.   *Hydromys*—Gk, *hydor*, water; Gk, *mys*, mouse: *chrysogaster*—Gk, *chrysos*, gold; Gk, *gaster*, belly.

LENGTH.   460–665 mm.

HABITAT.   From tropical rainforest to cool temperate dry sclerophyll forest, always close to fresh water.

NOTES.   Sleeps through much of the night in a tunnel in the bank of a stream, swamp or beach. During the twilight hours, and even during the day, feeds on crabs, crayfishes, fishes, young birds and large insects: an opportunistic predator. Aided by partially webbed hindfeet, it swims with ease below the water surface. Fur dense and water-repellent, moulted twice a year. Despite aquatic adaptations, also hunts on land.

Sexually mature at about one year. Breeds throughout year, with a peak from September to March. Female has four teats and usually rears three to four young, suckled for four weeks and remain with mother for further four weeks. Several litters may be reared in a year.

STATUS.   Distribution also includes New Guinea and some nearby islands. Numbers have declined since European settlement in Australia, partly because of extensive hunting for pelt. Common to sparse over large range.

# False Water-rat

*Xeromys myoides*
*(zee'-roh-mis mie-oy'-dayz)*

PLATE.   34:1

>DERIVATION.   *Xeromys*—Gk, *xeros*, dry; Gk, *mys*, mouse:
>*myoides*—Gk, *mys*, mouse; Gk, *-eides*, resembling.

LENGTH.   210–230 mm.

HABITAT.   Tropical rainforest and mangroves, always close to water.

NOTES.   Related to Water-rat, but somewhat less aquatic and without
>webs on hindfeet. Habits little known, but probably crepuscular and
>occasionally diurnal. Range of shelter unknown, but has been observed to
>make burrows in mud of mangrove swamp, sometimes in a mound of
>clay above high tide level. Known to eat crabs and probably an
>opportunistic predator. Lives near shallow water.
>   Female has four teats. Nothing known of breeding.

STATUS.   Rare.

# Fawn-footed Melomys

*Melomys cervinipes*
*(mel'-oh-mis ser-vin'-i-pez)*

PLATE.   34:3

DERIVATION.   *Melomys*—Melanesia; Gk, *mys*, mouse: *cervinipes*—L.,
>*cervinus*, tawny; L., *pes*, foot.

LENGTH.   200–400 mm.

HABITAT.   Subtropical to tropical wet sclerophyll forest and rainforest.

NOTES.   Sleeps by day, probably in nest in tree. Known to feed on seeds,
>fruits and sugar cane, but diet may be more extensive.
>   Breeding throughout the year but mostly from September to June.
>Females have four long teats and usually rear two young, which remain
>attached to teats if female flees nest. Young weaned at age of three weeks.
>Up to five litters in a year.

STATUS.   Common over range wherever rainforest remains.

# Cape York Melomys

*Melomys capensis.*
*(kay-pen'-sis)*

PLATE.   35:2

DERIVATION.   *capensis* — Cape York Peninsula; L., *-ensis*, from the vicinity of.

LENGTH.   225–320 mm.

HABITAT.   Edges of wet sclerophyll forest and rainforest.

NOTES.   Externally identical with Fawn-footed Melomys, but genetically and biochemically distinct. Sleeps by day, possibly in a nest in a tree. Feeds by night on seeds of trees, perhaps mainly on those that fall to the ground.
    Breeding unknown.

STATUS.   Rare.

# Bramble Cay Melomys

*Melomys rubicola*
*(rue-bik'-oh-lah)*

PLATE.   35:4

DERIVATION.   *rubicola* — L., *rubus*, blackberry bush, bramble; L., *colo*, I inhabit.

LENGTH.   230–430 mm.

HABITAT.   High grass near beach of low coral cay.

NOTES.   Sleeps by day under cover of logs. Feeds at night, probably on vegetation, possibly also on insects. Almost nothing known of biology.

STATUS.   May be a subspecies of *M. capensis*. Endangered because cay is disintegrating.

# Grassland Melomys

*Melomys burtoni*
*(ber'-tun-ee)*

PLATE.  35:5

DERIVATION.  *burtoni* — after W. Burton, taxidermist.

LENGTH.  260–280 mm.

HABITAT.  Subtropical to tropical grasslands.

NOTES.  Sleeps by day in a globular nest of leaves, typically attached to several stout grass stems and well clear of ground; also in trees, rarely in burrows. Feeds on grasses and seeds and has become a major pest of sugar cane.

Breeding possible throughout year, but peaks of mating probably determined by pattern of rainfall. Female has four long teats and normally rears two to three young, weaned at three to four weeks. Young remain attached to teats if female flees nest.

STATUS.  Abundant (to pest proportions) in sugar cane areas in Queensland. Sparse to rare elsewhere.

# Thornton Peak Melomys

*Melomys hadrourus*
*(had-rue'-rus)*

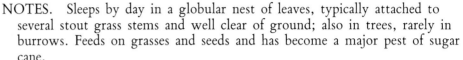

PLATE.  35:3

DERIVATION.  *hadrourus* — Gk, *hadros*, strong; Gk, *oura*, tail.

LENGTH.  355–375 mm.

HABITAT.  Rainforest.

NOTES.  Extremely limited distribution, apparently confined to upper level of Thornton Peak, north-eastern Queensland. Very few specimens taken and little known of biology. Probably feeds mainly on large seeds of rainforest trees.

Slight indication of breeding in autumn.

STATUS.  Rare.

# White-tailed Rat

*Uromys caudimaculatus*
*(yue'-roh-mis kaw'-dee-mak-yue-lah'-tus)*

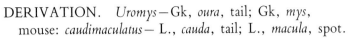

PLATE. 35:1

DERIVATION. *Uromys* — Gk, *oura*, tail; Gk, *mys*,
mouse: *caudimaculatus* — L., *cauda*, tail; L., *macula*, spot.

LENGTH. 570–700 mm.

HABITAT. Tropical wet sclerophyll forest and rainforest.

NOTES. Sleeps by day in a nest in a tree, possibly also in burrows or
caves. Feeds by night, mostly on seeds, fruits and bark plus fungi, insects
and small vertebrates. Excellent climber. Enters houses in search of food.
Is a pest of coconut plantations, where it damages young nuts.

Sexually mature at about 10 months. Mating occurs in October or
November. Female has four long teats and usually rears two to three
young which attach to teats if female changes nest or flees from it.
Suckled for about five weeks, independent at about eight weeks.

STATUS. Common.

# Mitchell's Hopping-mouse

*Notomys mitchelli*
*(noh'-to-mis mit'-chel-ee)*

PLATE. 36:1

DERIVATION. *Notomys* — Gk, *notos*, south; Gk, *mys*, mouse: *mitchelli* —
after Sir Thomas Mitchell, Australian explorer.

LENGTH. 240–280 mm.

HABITAT. Cool to warm temperate semi-arid mallee woodland.

NOTES. Sleeps by day in a nest of vegetable fibre in a deep burrow.
Gregarious when not breeding. Feeds at night on seeds, leaves, roots and
insects. Requires some drinking water.

Probably capable of breeding at any favourable time of the year.
Female usually raises litter of three to four which become independent at
about five weeks.

STATUS. Some decline in range since European settlement but still
common.

# Fawn Hopping-mouse

*Notomys cervinus*
*(ser-vee'-nus)*

PLATE. 36:2

DERIVATION. *cervinus* — L., *cervinus*, tawny, fawn.

LENGTH. 200–280 mm.

HABITAT. Arid gibber plains.

NOTES. Sleeps by day in burrow in hard gibber soil. At night feeds on seeds, other parts of tough desert plants, and insects. Does not need to drink. Gregarious.

Probably capable of breeding throughout year, but mating stimulated by rainfall. Female usually raises litter of one to five young which become independent at about four weeks.

STATUS. Common.

# Big-eared Hopping-mouse

*Notomys macrotis*
*(mak-roh'-tis)*

PLATE. 36:3

DERIVATION. *macrotis* — Gk, *makros*, big; Gk, *otous*, ear.

LENGTH. 245–255 mm.

HABITAT. Semi-arid woodland.

NOTES. Known only from two specimens collected in first half of nineteenth century. Nothing known of biology.

STATUS. Most of original habitat has been cleared for agriculture. Extinct.

# Long-tailed Hopping-mouse

*Notomys longicaudatus*
*(lon'-jee-kaw-dah'-tus)*

PLATE. 36:4

DERIVATION. *longicaudatus* — L., *longus*, long; L., *cauda*, tail.

LENGTH. Up to 305 mm.

HABITAT. Inhabited arid to semi-arid woodland, heath and hummock grassland, usually on clayey soil.

NOTES. Nothing known of biology.

STATUS. No reports of living animals for more than eighty years. Extinct.

# Short-tailed Hopping-mouse

*Notomys amplus*
*(am'-plus)*

PLATE.   36:5

DERIVATION.   *amplus*—L., *amplus*, large.

LENGTH.   Up to 300 mm.

HABITAT.   Inhabited desert dune or gibber country.

NOTES.   Nothing known of biology.

STATUS.   Known from only two specimens collected towards end of nineteenth century. Extinct.

# Dusky Hopping-mouse

*Notomys fuscus*
*(fus'-kus)*

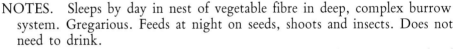

PLATE.   36:6

DERIVATION.   *fuscus*—L., *fuscus*, dusky.

LENGTH.   195–270 mm.

HABITAT.   Desert dunes.

NOTES.   Sleeps by day in nest of vegetable fibre in deep, complex burrow system. Gregarious. Feeds at night on seeds, shoots and insects. Does not need to drink.
   Probably capable of breeding throughout year, with mating stimulated by rainfall. Female raises litter of one to five young which become independent at four to five weeks.

STATUS.   Range has declined severely since European settlement. Rare.

# Northern Hopping-mouse

*Notomys aquilo*
*(ak-wil'-oh)*

PLATE.   36:7

DERIVATION.   *aquilo*—L., *aquilo*, the North (Wind).

LENGTH.   250–285 mm.

HABITAT.   Tropical coastal dunes with acacia scrub over spinifex hummock grass.

NOTES.   Sleeps by day in long burrow. Little known of biology.

STATUS.   Apparently rare.

# Spinifex Hopping-mouse

*Notomys alexis*
*(ah-lek'-sis)*

PLATE. 36:8

DERIVATION. *alexis* — refers to Alexandria Downs Station, NT.

LENGTH. 225–260 mm.

HABITAT. Arid cool temperate to tropical spinifex (*Triodia*) hummock grassland on sand, including desert dunes.

NOTES. Sleeps most of day in nest within complex, deep burrow system. Feeds at evening and night on seeds, shoots, roots and insects. Does not need to drink. Gregarious.

Capable of reproduction throughout year, but mating probably stimulated by rainfall. Sexually mature at about nine weeks. Female usually raises three to four in litter and may rear successive litters.

STATUS. Three supposed subspecies: *N. a. alexis*, western part of range; *N. a. everardensis*, central part of range; *N. a. reginae*, eastern part of range. Common over much of range.

# Black-footed Tree-rat

*Mesembriomys gouldii*
*(mez-em'-bree-oh-mis' gule'-dee-ee)*

PLATE. 37:10

DERIVATION. *Mesembriomys* — Gk, *mesembria*, south; Gk, *mys*, mouse: *gouldii* — after J. Gould, British naturalist.

LENGTH. 585–720 mm.

HABITAT. Tropical sclerophyll forest and woodland.

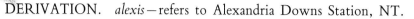

NOTES. Sleeps by day in tree-holes, also crevices in buildings. Excellent climber. Feeds at night on fruits, flowers and large seeds, supplemented by insects and snails. One of the largest Australian rodents (males up to 870 grams and 720 millimetres total length).

Most breeding probably from about June to August. Gestation period unusually long: a little more than six weeks; young born partly furred. Litter one to three. Young remain attached to nipples as mother moves about.

STATUS. Common to rare over range.

# Golden-backed Tree-rat

*Mesembriomys macrurus*
*(mak-rue'-rus)*

PLATE.   37:6

DERIVATION.   *macrurus*—Gk, *makros*, large; Gk, *oura*, tail.

LENGTH.   480–605 mm.

HABITAT.   Inhabits a variety of tropical habitats including woodlands, tussock grasslands, pandanus scrub and vine-thickets.

NOTES.   Sleeps by day in a nest in a tree-hole or crevice. Feeds at night on foliage and ground plants, possibly supplemented by insects. Recorded as eating oysters at an oyster farm in north-western Australia. Enters houses and known to eat rice and flour.
    Breeding season unknown. Female has four teats and rears one to two young.

STATUS.   Distribution has declined since European settlement. Sparse to rare.

# Brush-tailed Tree-rat

*Conilurus penicillatus*
*(kon'-il-yue'-rus pen'-i-sil-ah'-tus)*

PLATE.   37:5 and 9

DERIVATION.   *Conilurus*—Gk, *konilos*, rabbit, cony; Gk, *oura*, tail: *penicillatus*—L., *penicillus*, brush.

LENGTH.   330–415 mm.

HABITAT.   From monsoon forest through dry sclerophyll forest to woodland and pandanus scrub.

NOTES.   Sleeps by day in tree-holes or crevices. At night feeds on plant material, including seeds and fruits, in trees and on the ground. Little known of general biology.
    Probably breeds throughout the year, with peaks determined by variable rainfall. Female has four teats and normally rears one to three young, weaned and independent at three weeks. Likely that several litters reared in rapid succession.

STATUS.   Also occurs in New Guinea. Sparse in Australia.

# Rabbit-eared Tree-rat

*Conilurus albipes*
*(al'-bi-pez)*

PLATE. 37:3

DERIVATION. *albipes*—L., *albus*, white; L., *pes*, foot.

LENGTH. 450–600 mm.

HABITAT. Subtropical to cool temperate wet and dry sclerophyll forest.

NOTES. Slept by day in nest of leaves in tree-hole. Diet unrecorded.
Female had four teats and reared as many as three young. Young attached themselves to teats in times of danger.

STATUS. Extinct.

# Greater Stick-nest Rat

*Leporillus conditor*
*(lep'or-ill'-us kon'-dit-or)*

PLATE. 37:8

DERIVATION. *Leporillus*—L., *lepus*, hare; L., *-illus*, diminutive suffix: *conditor*—L., *conditor*, builder.

LENGTH. 315–440 mm.

HABITAT. Warm temperate to cool temperate arid woodland.

NOTES. Sleeps by day in a grass-lined nest within a pile of tangled branches and sticks which, over several generations, may exceed one cubic metre. Ten to 20 individuals may inhabit such a structure. At night feeds on leaves of succulent plants.
Mating probably from March to June. One or two young which attach to mother's four teats and are dragged with her; independent at about four weeks.

STATUS. Immense reduction in range since European settlement. Now exists only on Franklin Island. Rare, vulnerable.

# Lesser Stick-nest Rat

*Leporillus apicalis*
*(ah'-pik-ah'-lis)*

PLATE.   37:7

DERIVATION.   *apicalis* — L., *apex*, point, tip.

LENGTH.   390–440 mm.

HABITAT.   Arid woodland and shrubland.

NOTES.   Little known of biology but probably similar to Greater Stick-nest Rat.

STATUS.   Has disappeared from extensive range (more than a quarter of the continent). Probably extinct.

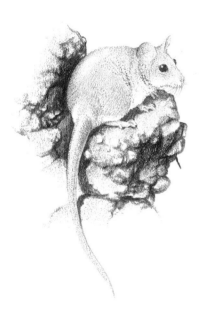

# Common Rock-rat

*Zyzomys argurus*
*(ziz'-oh-mis ar-gue'-rus)*

PLATE.   37:1

DERIVATION.   *Zyzomys* — *zyzo*, significance unknown; Gk, *mys*, mouse: *argurus* — Gk, *argyros*, silver; Gk, *oura*, tail.

LENGTH.   Up to 225 mm.

HABITAT.   Widely distributed over non-arid parts of tropical Australia, always on rocky outcrops.

NOTES.   Sleeps by day in nest in narrow rock cleft. At night feeds on seeds, mostly of native grasses, supplemented by fungi and insects.

Males and females sexually mature at five to six months. Breeding throughout year but mostly from March to May, in early part of the dry season. Female has four teats and rears one to four young, which are left in the nest while the mother forages. Young independent at about four to five weeks.

STATUS.   Common.

# Large Rock-rat

*Zyzomys woodwardi*
*(wood'-war-dee)*

PLATE. 37:2

DERIVATION. *woodwardi* — after B. M. Woodward, first curator of the Western Australian Museum.

LENGTH. Up to 320 mm.

HABITAT. Similar to that of Common Rock-rat, but somewhat wetter and with denser cover.

NOTES. Sleeps by day in a nest in a cleft among rocks. Feeds at night on seeds and fruits of rainforest trees. Seeds in faeces of fruit-pigeons are eaten when other food is scarce.

    Males and females sexually mature at five to six months. Breeding throughout the year, but mostly in the early part of the dry season (March, April). Female has four teats, normally rears two to three young, independent at three to four weeks.

STATUS. Common in parts of range.

# Central Rock-rat

*Zyzomys pedunculatus*
*(ped-unk'-yue-lah'-tus)*

PLATE. 37:4

DERIVATION. *pedunculatus* — L., *pendunculus*, little foot, swelling at end of stalk.

LENGTH. 220–280 mm.

HABITAT. Tropical arid woodland and shrubland.

NOTES. Scientific name refers to a swelling of fatty tissue near to, but not quite at, the base of the tail, possibly giving it greater freedom of movement than if the tail were thickened at its base. Is adapted to very arid central Australian habitat, but habits unknown.

STATUS. Known from only six specimens since discovery in 1896. Last confirmed sighting in 1960. Rare.

# Forrest's Mouse

*Leggadina forresti*
*(leg'-ah-dee'-na fo'-res-tee)*

PLATE.   38:7

DERIVATION.   *Leggadina* — sci., *Leggada*, genus of mice from India; L.,
   *-ina*, diminutive suffix: *forresti* — after Sir John Forrest, Australian explorer.

LENGTH.   130–170 mm.

HABITAT.   Temperate to tropical arid tussock grassland.

NOTES.   Sleeps by day in burrow. Feeds at night on seeds and vegetation.
   Probably does not need to drink.
      Probably capable of breeding throughout year, known to breed after
   winter rain. Female has four teats; usually rears three to four young in
   litter.

STATUS.   Sparse, widespread.

# Lakeland Downs Mouse

*Leggadina lakedownensis*
*(lake'-down-en'-sis)*

PLATE.   38:4

DERIVATION.   *lakedownensis* — after Lakeland Downs Station, north
   Queensland.

LENGTH.   100–120 mm.

HABITAT.   Wet tropical grassland and savannah.

NOTES.   Sleeps by day. Feeds at night, probably mainly on seeds. Little
   known of biology.
      Probably capable of breeding throughout year. Litter two to four.

STATUS.   Usually very rare. Occasionally irrupts in plague proportions in
   relatively small areas.

# Delicate Mouse

*Pseudomys delicatulus*
*(sue'-doh-mis del'-i-kat'-yue-lus)*

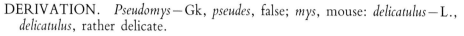

PLATE. 38:6

DERIVATION. *Pseudomys*—Gk, *pseudes*, false; *mys*, mouse: *delicatulus*—L., *delicatulus*, rather delicate.

LENGTH. 110–155 mm.

HABITAT. Tropical grasslands and, to a lesser extent, woodland and dry sclerophyll forest.

NOTES. Sleeps by day in nest in confined space above ground or at end of burrow. At night feeds on seeds, mostly those of native grasses.
　　Males and females sexually mature at 10–11 months. Mating in June and July. Female normally rears two to four young which are independent at three to four weeks.

STATUS. Two subspecies: *P. d. delicatulus* on mainland; and *P. d. mimula* on Groote Eylandt. Both sparse and seasonally variable.

# Silky Mouse

*Pseudomys apodemoides*
*(ap'-oh-dem-oy'-dayz)*

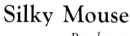

PLATE. 38:2

DERIVATION. *apodemoides*—sci., *Apodemus*, a European field-mouse; Gk, *-eides*, resembling.

LENGTH. 155–190 mm.

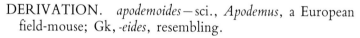

HABITAT. Cool temperate semi-arid mallee heathland, particularly around Desert Banksia shrubs.

NOTES. Sleeps by day in a nest in a complex burrow system as much as three metres below surface and extending laterally up to four metres from a Desert Banksia. Gregarious. Feeds at night on seeds, supplemented by insects and by nectar of Desert Banksia in winter. Population density highest in regenerating vegetation two to three years after bushfire.
　　In optimal conditions breeds throughout year, female producing successive litters of about four young. When food is limited, breeding is restricted: some populations breed in winter, others in spring and summer.

STATUS. Common.

# Smoky Mouse

*Pseudomys fumeus*
*(fue-may'-us)*

PLATE.  38:1

DERIVATION.  *fumeus*—L., *fumeus*, smoky.

LENGTH.  195–245 mm.

HABITAT.  Subalpine sclerophyll forest and woodland with heath understorey, often on mountain ridges, sometimes lower.

NOTES.  Sleeps by day. Food varies with season: predominantly seeds and berries in summer and underground fungi in winter. Bogong Moths provide significant food in spring. Population density highest in vegetation regenerating after bushfire.
   Female produces one or two litters a year, usually of three to four young.

STATUS.  Range has decreased since European settlement. Now restricted to several small areas. Sparse to rare. Vulnerable.

# Western Mouse

*Pseudomys occidentalis*
*(ok'-sid-ent-ah'-lis)*

PLATE.  38:3

DERIVATION.  *occidentalis*—L., *occidentalis*, western.

LENGTH.  210–250 mm.

HABITAT.  Cool temperate semi-arid woodland and shrubland on sandy clay or loam.

NOTES.  Sleeps by day. Feeds at night on seeds, stems and leaves. Biology little known.
   Mating probably in August and September.

STATUS.  Common, limited. Vulnerable.

# Shark Bay Mouse

*Pseudomys praeconis*
*(pree-koh'-nis)*

PLATE.  38:5

DERIVATION.  *praeconis* — L., *praeco*, herald.

LENGTH.  200–240 mm.

HABITAT.  Coastal dunes.

NOTES.  Sleeps by day in tunnel made in dense vegetation. Feeds by night on flowers, leaves and stems.
 Breeding season unknown. Female has four teats and rears up to four young which are independent at about four weeks. Young remain attached to teats while mother forages.

STATUS.  First reported from Shark Bay, but now extinct on mainland and restricted to Bernier Island. Sparse to rare.

# Gould's Mouse

*Pseudomys gouldii*
*(gule'-dee-ee)*

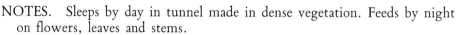

PLATE.  38:8

DERIVATION.  *gouldii* — after J. Gould, British naturalist.

LENGTH.  190–230 mm.

HABITAT.  Sandhills and grassy plains.

NOTES.  Little known of biology. Constructed extensive burrow systems with terminal grassy nests. Gregarious.

STATUS.  Extinct.

# Sandy Inland Mouse

*Pseudomys hermannsburgensis*
*(her'-mans-berg-en'-sis)*

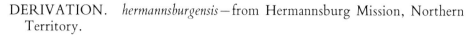

PLATE.   39:2

DERIVATION.   *hermannsburgensis* — from Hermannsburg Mission, Northern
   Territory.

LENGTH.   135–175 mm.

HABITAT.   Arid tropical to cool temperate hummock grassland and mulga
   woodland.

NOTES.   Sleeps by day in a nest in a deep burrow. Gregarious. Feeds at
   night on seeds and other vegetable material. Probably does not need to
   drink.
      Probably capable of breeding throughout year, but mating stimulated
   by rainfall. Female usually rears litter of three to four, independent at four
   to five weeks.

STATUS.   Common.

# New Holland Mouse

*Pseudomys novaehollandiae*
*(no'-vee-hol-and'-ee-ee)*

PLATE.   39:5

DERIVATION.   *novaehollandiae* — N.L., *Nova Hollandia,* New
   Holland = Australia.

LENGTH.   145–195 mm.

HABITAT.   Low heath on sandy soil.

NOTES.   Sleeps by day in burrow up to five metres long. At night feeds
   on seeds, other parts of plants, fungi and insects. Most abundant in areas
   regenerating after bushfire.
      Sexually mature at seven weeks or more. Mating from August to
   December. Female normally rears litter of three to four young which
   become independent at three to four weeks. Females mating in the year of
   birth produce one litter in that year; three to four successive litters in the
   following year.

STATUS.   Thought to have become extinct in mid-nineteenth century.
   Since rediscovery in 1967, has been shown to be common over
   considerable area.

# Ash-grey Mouse

*Pseudomys albocinereus*
*(al'-boh-sin-er-ay'-us)*

PLATE.   39:3

DERIVATION.   *albocinereus* — L., *albus*, white: L., *cinereus*, ashy.

LENGTH.   160–200 mm.

HABITAT.   Semi-arid subtropical to cool temperate woodland and heath on sandy soil.

NOTES.   Sleeps by day in a complex burrow system up to four metres long. Feeds at night on seeds and other plant material (winter), supplemented by insects (summer). Probably does not need to drink.
   Mating from February to October. Female produces litter of two to six young.

STATUS.   Two subspecies: *P. a. albocinereus*, mainland; and *P. a. squalorum*, Bernier Island, Western Australia. Both common over much of range.

# Plains Mouse

*Pseudomys australis*
*(os-trah'-lis)*

PLATE.   39:1 and 6

DERIVATION.   *australis* — L., *australis*, southern.

LENGTH.   180–260 mm.

HABITAT.   Arid gibber plains.

NOTES.   Gregarious, constructing large and complex systems of colonial burrows, connected by runways on the surface. Sleeps by day in burrow. When not breeding, up to 20 animals may inhabit a single burrow system; when breeding, group is reduced to a male and two or three females. Feeds at night, mostly upon seeds; does not need to drink. A population can vary considerably in density and may suddenly disappear.
   Females sexually mature at nine to ten weeks. Breeding possible throughout the year, but mostly in winter and spring, after rain. Female has four teats and usually rears three to four young, suckled for about four weeks. Several litters probably reared in rapid succession when conditions are favourable.

STATUS.   Common.

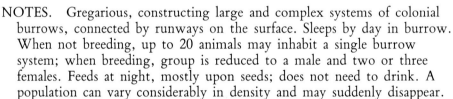

# Long-tailed Mouse

*Pseudomys higginsi*
*(hig'-in-zee)*

PLATE. 39:7

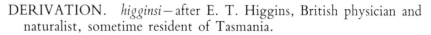

DERIVATION. *higginsi*—after E. T. Higgins, British physician and naturalist, sometime resident of Tasmania.

LENGTH. 260–350 mm.

HABITAT. The very wet Southern Beech rainforests of Tasmania.

NOTES. Sleeps by day in a nest of shredded plant fibre at the end of a short burrow. Feeds by night (sometimes by day in the winter) on a wide variety of plant material, plus insects and spiders. Male and female form a permanent pair which defends a common territory.

    Mating occurs from October to February. Female has four teats and normally rears three to four young which are suckled for about four weeks but remain with parents until about 13 weeks old. One or two litters reared each year.

STATUS. Common.

# Desert Mouse

*Pseudomys desertor*
*(dez-er'-tor)*

PLATE. 39:4

DERIVATION. *desertor*—erroneous formation from L., *desertum*, wilderness.

LENGTH. 160–195 mm.

HABITAT. Generally found in arid dunes of central Australia, but possibly enters driest areas only when climatic conditions are favourable.

NOTES. Sleeps by day in globular nest under vegetation at the end of a burrow. Solitary. Feeds at night on all parts of sedges and grasses. Probably does not drink. Males and females inhabit separate nests and defend territories, coming together only for brief periods of mating.

    Males and females sexually mature at about 10 weeks. Mating at least from June to December. Females normally rear about three young which are independent at about three weeks. Under favourable conditions, several litters may be reared in rapid succession.

STATUS. Rare, probably with great oscillations in range and density.

# Hastings River Mouse

*Pseudomys oralis*
*(o-rah'-lis)*

PLATE.  40:7

DERIVATION.  *oralis* — L., *oralis*, pertaining to the mouth.

LENGTH.  240–320 mm.

HABITAT.  Dry sclerophyll forest, often with bracken understorey.

NOTES.  Sleeps by day, probably in nest at end of burrow, and probably feeds mainly on seeds.
  Details of breeding unknown.

STATUS.  Only two specimens of uncertain provenance known until 1969. Investigations since then reveal species to be present in scattered populations from southern Queensland to region of Hastings River. Sparse to rare.

# Heath Rat

*Pseudomys shortridgei*
*(short'-rid-jee)*

PLATE.  40:2

DERIVATION.  *shortridgei* — after G. C. Shortridge, British naturalist.

LENGTH.  170–230 mm.

HABITAT.  Inhabits cool temperate dry heathlands and is abundant only in areas of early regeneration after bushfire.

NOTES.  Sleeps by day in a nest among vegetation or in a burrow. At night feeds on seeds, grasses and fungi.
  Through most of autumn, diet is meagre, restricted largely to grass stems and leaves; subterranean fungi are eaten in winter and early spring; seeds, berries and fruits in late spring and summer.
  Sexually mature at about 11 months. Mating occurs from October to January. Females normally rear about three young in a litter. One or two litters a year are reared for up to four years.

STATUS.  Extinct in Western Australia; range reduced in south-eastern Australia. Rare and vulnerable.

# Eastern Chestnut Mouse

*Pseudomys gracilicaudatus*
*(gras'-il-i-kaw-dah'-tus)*

PLATE.  40:1

DERIVATION.  *gracilicaudatus* — L., *gracilis*, slender; L., *cauda*, tail.

LENGTH.  195–265 mm.

HABITAT.  Swamps, wet heathland and grassy woodland.

NOTES.  Sleeps by day in a nest of grass at ground level or within a
burrow. At night feeds on grass, seeds and stems. Population density
varies, being highest in the period of vigorous plant growth following an
intense bushfire.

    Males and females sexually mature at about six months. Mating occurs
from August or September to March. Female usually rears three young in
a litter; newborn are partly furred and young are weaned at four weeks.
Up to three successive litters may be reared in breeding season.

STATUS.  Sparse.

# Western Chestnut Mouse

*Pseudomys nanus*
*(nah'-nus)*

PLATE.  40:6

DERIVATION.  *nanus* — L., *nanus*, dwarf.

LENGTH.  150–260 mm.

HABITAT.  Lives among tropical tussock grasses, often with eucalypt
woodland cover.

NOTES.  In captivity constructs nests, but normal resting places unknown.
Feeds by night on grasses and probably seeds. May not need to drink.

    Breeds throughout year except September–November. Female has four
teats and normally rears three young which are weaned at three to four
weeks. Several litters are probably reared in rapid succession during
favourable climatic conditions.

STATUS.  Two subspecies: *P. n. nanus* on mainland; and *P. n. ferculinus* on
Barrow Island. Both abundant.

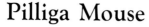

# Pilliga Mouse

*Pseudomys pilligaensis*
*(pil'-i-gah-en'-sis)*

PLATE. 40:3

DERIVATION. *pilligaensis* — from the Pilliga Scrub, NSW.

LENGTH. 130–160 mm.

HABITAT. Inhabits very limited area of cypress pine forest with heath understorey on sandy soil.

NOTES. Probably sleeps by day in burrow. Diet unknown but probably includes seeds and insects.
Breeding at least from October to February.

STATUS. Rare, possibly vulnerable.

# Western Pebble-mound Mouse

*Pseudomys chapmani*
*(chap'-man-ee)*

PLATE. 40:8

DERIVATION. *chapmani* — after G. Chapman, Australian zoologist.

LENGTH. 125–145 mm.

HABITAT. Arid tropical spinifex grassland and acacia woodland on pebbly soil in Pilbara region of Western Australia.

NOTES. Sleeps by day in nest of vegetable fibre in tunnel made in mound of pebbles constructed by successive generations. Pebbles weighing about five grams are collected by mouse and carried to mound, which, over generations, may cover up to nine square metres. Providing thermal insulation, and probably moist microclimate, mound is a practical alternative to burrowing in very hard soil. Diet unknown but probably includes seeds and insects. Breeding unknown.

STATUS. Range has contracted since European settlement. Rare.

# Central Pebble-mound Mouse

*Pseudomys johnsoni*
*(jon'-sun-ee)*

> PLATE.  40:4
>
> DERIVATION.  *johnsoni* — after K. Johnson, Australian zoologist.
>
> LENGTH.  150–170 mm.

HABITAT.  Arid tropical acacia woodland and hummock grassland on stony ridges and plains.

NOTES.  Probably sleeps by day in a nest in a tunnel made in a mound of pebbles constructed by successive generations of the species, but no direct observations of this behaviour. Nothing known of biology.

STATUS.  Described in 1985 from twelve specimens. Rare.

# Bolam's Mouse

> *Pseudomys bolami*
> *(boh'-lam-ee)*
>
> PLATE.  40:5
>
> DERIVATION.  *bolami* — after A. J. Bolam, Australian naturalist.
>
> LENGTH.  140–170 mm.
>
> HABITAT.  Temperate arid woodland with sparse scrub cover.

NOTES.  Long regarded as subspecies of Hermannsburg Mouse but separated in 1984. Biology little known but probably similar to *P. hermannsburgensis.*

STATUS.  Sparse (?).

# Prehensile-tailed Rat

*Pogonomys mollipilosus*
*(poh-gon'-oh-mis mol'-ee-pil-oh'-sus)*

PLATE.  41:5

DERIVATION.  *Pogonomys* — Gk, *pogon*, beard; Gk, *mys*, mouse: *mollipilosus* — L., *mollis*, soft; L., *pilosus*, haired.

LENGTH.  290–360 mm.

HABITAT.  Tropical rainforest and monsoon forest.

NOTES.  Sleeps by day in nest in burrow. Gregarious. At night feeds on leaves and nuts on ground or in trees. An excellent climber with long, strongly prehensile tail.
   Breeding pattern in Australia unknown; from October to January in New Guinea.

STATUS.  A predominantly Melanesian species, first recorded from Australia in 1974. Common in New Guinea, apparently rare in Australia.

# Broad-toothed Rat

*Mastacomys fuscus*
*(mas'-tah-koh-mis fus'-kus)*

PLATE.   41:6

DERIVATION.   *Mastacomys* — Gk, *mastax*, jaw; Gk, *mys*, mouse: *fuscus* — L., *fuscus*, dusky.

LENGTH.   240–300 mm.

HABITAT.   Cold wet alpine grassland, sedge rush and shrubland, often near permanent water.

NOTES.   In summer, sleeps by day in nest in dense vegetation or under fallen logs or other solid shelter. During winter, is active by day in runways and other spaces under snow-covered vegetation. Thanks to very large molars, is able to feed on tough grasses, supplemented by seeds and other vegetable material.
    Sexually mature at about one year. Mating from November to February on mainland; September to January in Tasmania. Female has four teats, usually rears two young, independent at five to six weeks.

STATUS.   Common to sparse over range.

# Dusky Rat

*Rattus colletti*
*(rat'-us col'-et-ee)*

PLATE.   41:3

DERIVATION.   *Rattus* — L., *rattus*, rat: *colletti* — after R. Collett, Norwegian zoologist.

LENGTH.   145–360 mm.

HABITAT.   Tropical flood plains and grassy borders.

NOTES.   Sleeps by day in burrow or under shelter of log, roots or rocks. Feeds at night, mainly on roots of grasses and corms of sedges.
    Females sexually mature from age of about six weeks. Female has 12 teats, usually rears about nine young in litter, independent at three to four weeks. Capable of breeding througout year but major peak is May–June. Heavy mortality in the dry season.

STATUS.   Usually common but local populations vary from sparse to abundant in response to rainfall and flooding.

# Cape York Rat

*Rattus leucopus*
*(lue'-koh-poos)*

PLATE.   41:4

DERIVATION.   *leucopus* — Gk, *leukos*, white; Gk, *pous*, foot.

LENGTH.   300–420 mm.

HABITAT.   Tropical rainforest.

NOTES.   Probably sleeps by day under logs or among buttress roots. At night feeds on fruits and nuts of rainforest trees, supplemented by insects. Not arboreal. Probably solitary.
   Sexually mature at about 12 weeks. Breeding apparently throughout year except winter. Female has six teats and usually rears two to four young, independent at about four weeks.

STATUS.   Australian population is an outlier of a New Guinea species. Two Australian subspecies: *R. l. leucopus*, northern Cape York Peninsula; and *R. l. cooktownensis*, southern Cape York Peninsula. Both common.


# Canefield Rat

*Rattus sordidus*
*(sor'-did-us)*

PLATE.   41:1

DERIVATION.   *sordidus* — L., *sordidus*, dirty.

LENGTH.   *c.* 260–410 mm.

HABITAT.   Tropical grassland and grassed patches within and at edges of rainforest; abundant and a pest in sugar cane plantations.

NOTES.   Sleeps by day in nest in a burrow. Gregarious. Feeds at night (occasionally by day) on grasses, supplemented by insects; also upon sugar cane stems.
   Sexually mature at nine to ten weeks. Capable of breeding throughout year, but most births from March to May. Female has 12 teats and usually rears about six young, independent at about three weeks. Extremely fecund.

STATUS.   Common in northern part of range, rare in the southern part.

# Pale Field-rat

*Rattus tunneyi*
*(tun'-ee-ee)*

PLATE.  41:2

DERIVATION.  *tunneyi* — after J. T. Tunney, collector of first specimen.

LENGTH.  185–345 mm.

HABITAT.  Tall grassland close to water.

NOTES.  Sleeps by day in short, shallow burrow. Feeds at night on all parts of grasses. Enters camps and houses in search of food.
   Sexually mature at about five weeks. Female has 10 teats, usually rears litter of four, independent at about three weeks. Several litters may be raised successively. Breeding extends from May to August in the Northern Territory, possibly from March to May in Queensland.

STATUS.  Two subspecies: *R. t. tunneyi*, north and north-western Australia; and *R. t. culmorum*, eastern Australia. Both common.

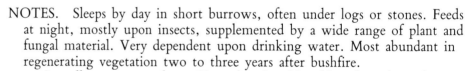

# Bush Rat

*Rattus fuscipes*
*(fus'-ki-pez)*

PLATE.  42:1 and 3

DERIVATION.  *fuscipes* — L., *fuscus*, dusky; L., *pes*, foot.

LENGTH.  175–390 mm.

HABITAT.  Tropical to cool temperate coastal rainforest to sclerophyll forest with ground cover of shrubs and ferns.

NOTES.  Sleeps by day in short burrows, often under logs or stones. Feeds at night, mostly upon insects, supplemented by a wide range of plant and fungal material. Very dependent upon drinking water. Most abundant in regenerating vegetation two to three years after bushfire.
   Sexually mature at about 17 weeks. Capable of breeding throughout year but more births in summer than in winter. Female has eight teats and usually rears about five young, independent at four to five weeks.

STATUS.  Four subspecies: *R. f. fuscipes*, Western Australia; *R. f. greyii*, South Australia to western Victoria; *R. f. assimilis*, most of eastern Australia; and *R. f. coracius*, southern Cape York Peninsula. All abundant to common.

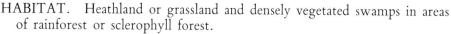

# Swamp Rat

*Rattus lutreolus*
*(lue'-tree-oh'-lus)*

PLATE. 42:2 and 4

DERIVATION. *lutreolus*—L., *lutra*, otter.

LENGTH. 210–340 mm.

HABITAT. Heathland or grassland and densely vegetated swamps in areas of rainforest or sclerophyll forest.

NOTES. Sleeps by day or night in nest in burrow or in tunnel in dense vegetation. Feeds by night (often also by day) on grasses, sedges, seeds and insects. Solitary.

    Sexually mature at 12 weeks. Female has 10 teats and usually rears three to four young, independent at three to four weeks. Capable of breeding throughout year, but most births in spring and summer.

STATUS. Three subspecies: *R. l. lutreolus*, south-eastern Australia; *R. l. lacus*, Queensland; and *R. l. velutinus*, Tasmania. All common.

# Long-haired Rat

*Rattus villosissimus*
*(vil'-o-sis'-i-mus)*

PLATE. 42:5

DERIVATION. *villosissimus*—L., *villosus*, hairy; L., *-issimus*, superlative suffix.

LENGTH. 275–400 mm.

HABITAT. Inhabits almost all arid to semi-arid areas of inland Australia.

NOTES. The only Australian *Rattus* living in deserts, but retains need for access to drinking water. Sleeps by day in short burrow in warren system. Gregarious. Feeds at night on grasses, seeds, succulent plants and insects. When population density is high and normal food is exhausted, will attempt to eat almost any organic material, including leather and rubber.

    Sexually mature at about 10 weeks. Female has 12 teats, normally rears about seven young, independent at about three weeks.

STATUS. Characterised by immense variations in numbers. Usually rare but occasionally irrupting in "plague" proportions following several years of unusually high rainfall.

# ORDER SIRENIA

*(sie-ree'-nee-ah)*

DERIVATION.  *Sirenia* — Gk, *seiren*, mythical half-human creatures who lured seamen to their doom.

This small group, aptly called "Sea-cows", comprises only four living species. Among many other peculiarities, its members are distinguished from all other aquatic mammals by being herbivorous. Grazing upon sea-grasses, they are largely restricted to shallow tropical or subtropical rivers or coastal waters.

Like whales, sirenians have lost their hindlimbs. They have paddle-like forelimbs and a horizontal tail-fluke. Two families are recognised: the Trichechidae, or manatees, of the warmer estuaries and rivers of the Atlantic; and the Dugongidae, or dugongs, from the warmer coastal waters of the Indian and western Pacific oceans.

Dugongs and manatees are superficially similar but differ in their anatomy and habits. Manatees chew their food with molar teeth that erupt from the rear of each tooth-row as those in the front wear down and are shed. The vestigial molar teeth of dugongs appear to play little part in chewing, a function that is largely relegated to horny pads on the upper and lower palates.

FAMILY
# Dugongidae
*(dyue-gong'-id-ee)*

DERIVATION.  sci., *Dugong*—Dugong; *-idae*, familial suffix.

This family includes only one species, the Dugong. Its major characteristics are described above.

# Dugong

*Dugong dugon*
*(dyue'-gong dyue'-gon)*

PLATE.  43:4

DERIVATION.  Generic and specific names derive from Malay, *duyong*, Dugong.

LENGTH.  2.5–4.5 m.

HABITAT.  Calm, shallow tropical waters of the continental shelf and estuaries where sea-grasses grow abundantly.

NOTES.  Sleeps or rests in deeper water at low tide. At high tide, moves into sea-grass "meadows" to feed on the leaves of this marine plant. Gregarious, occurring in herds of several hundred animals. Sexes similar in size.

   Sexually mature at 10–15 years. Mating from May to November. Gestation period about 12 months, single young, dependent for one to two years. Births three to six years apart. Very low fecundity.

STATUS.  Low fecundity probably appropriate to a long-lived species with few natural enemies. With the advent of heavy mortality from humans (killing for meat and accidental capture in fishing nets) slow reproduction is disastrous. Rare over much of range in Indian Ocean. Sparse to locally common in Australian waters. Vulnerable.

# ORDER PINNIPEDIA

*(pin'-i-pee'-dee-ah)*

DERIVATION.  *Pinnipedia*—L., *pinna*, feather, wing, fin; L., *pes*, foot.

This group of mammals, generally referred to as seals, comprises two distinct types of marine mammal which have probably evolved independently from the Carnivora. Indeed, some authorities regard the pinnipeds as no more than a sub-group of the Carnivora. The true seals (family Phocidae), have their fin-like hindlimbs directed permanently backwards (creating the equivalent of a tail-fin) and lack external ears. The other pinnipeds—eared seals (family Otariidae) and the Walrus (family Odobenidae)—have much more mobile hindlimbs that can be employed in clumsy walking (even running) movements; the otariids retain vestiges of an external ear.

Phocids swim with a horizontal undulatory motion, the webs of the hindlimbs providing the propulsory surface; otariids propel themselves by powerful movements of the paddle-shaped forelimbs, "rowing" or "flying" through the sea in much the same way as a penguin.

The phocids mentioned in this book occur in Australian antarctic or subantarctic territories but are only rare or accidental visitors to continental Australia.

# DUGONG AND VARIOUS PINNIPEDS

PLATE 43

1   NEW ZEALAND FUR-SEAL *Arctocephalus forsteri* (left) male, (right) female (see page 259)

2   AUSTRALIAN FUR-SEAL *Arctocephalus pusillus* (see page 259)

3   AUSTRALIAN SEA-LION *Neophoca cinerea* (see page 258)

4   DUGONG *Dugong dugon* (see page 252)

*1*

2

3

4

# VARIOUS PINNIPEDS

PLATE 44

*1*

2

3

4

FAMILY
# Otariidae
*(oh'-tah-ree'-id-ee)*

DERIVATION.   sci., *Otaria*, a genus of sea-lions; L., *-idae*, familial suffix.

This group, including the sea-lions and fur-seals, is represented in both hemispheres. Otariids are well adapted to life in the oceans but move with reasonable agility on land, being able to rotate the hindlimbs in front of and behind the hip. Short ears remain as a reminder of their terrestrial ancestry, probably from a group related to the canids.

Although several species are found on Australian coasts, only one, the Australian Fur-seal, is restricted to Australia.

# Australian Sea-lion

*Neophoca cinerea*
*(nee'-oh-foh'-kah sin'-er-ay'-ah)*

PLATE.   43:3

DERIVATION.   *Neophoca*—Gk, *neos*, new; Gk, *phoke* seal: *cinerea*—L., *cinereus*, ash-coloured.

LENGTH.   1.7–2.4 m.

HABITAT.   Cool temperate coastal seas. When on land, occupies sandy beaches; breeds in rocky areas.

NOTES.   Feeds on squids, and possibly other marine animals. Males much larger than females.
   Births from October or earlier to January. Some evidence of a very unusual 18-month breeding cycle. Young independent at 12–14 months.

STATUS.   Only phocid endemic to Australia. Exterminated in Bass Strait by hunting. Elsewhere sparse, possibly increasing. Not endangered.

# Australian Fur-seal

*Arctocephalus pusillus*
*(ark'-to-sef'-al-us pue-sil'-us)*

PLATE.   43:2

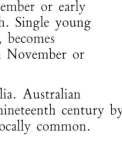

DERIVATION.   *Arctocephalus*—Gk, *arktos*, bear; Gk, *kephale*, head: *pusillus*—L., *pusillus*, small, weak.

LENGTH.   1.2–2.2 m.

HABITAT.   Cool temperate coastal seas; may enter estuaries. Comes ashore on rocky or pebbly beaches, rock platforms and reefs.

NOTES.   Feeds mainly on squids and octopuses, also on fishes and rock-lobsters. Males much larger than females. Can dive to at least 150 m.
   Sexually mature at four to five years, but breeding restricted to largest and most aggressive males. Mating occurs in late November or early December, about a week after a female has given birth. Single young from previous mating suckled for about eight months, becomes independent at about 11 months. Next young born in November or December, about twelve months after mating.

STATUS.   Species occurs in southern Africa and Australia. Australian subspecies is *A. p. doriferus*. Severely reduced in early nineteenth century by hunting. Population has recovered to about 20,000. Locally common.

# New Zealand Fur-seal

*Arctocephalus forsteri*
*(for'-ster-ee)*

PLATE.   43:1

DERIVATION.   *forsteri*—after G. Forster, natural history illustrator.

LENGTH.   1.5–2.5 m.

HABITAT.   Cool temperate coastal seas. Comes ashore on rocky coasts or beaches. When breeding, seeks shade of boulders or vegetation.

NOTES.   Feeds on squids, fishes and rock lobsters; occasionally takes penguins. Males larger than females.
   Sexually mature at four to five years but males seldom able to mate until about 10 years old. Mating occurs about one week after female has given birth, male inseminating about six females under his domination. Single young from previous mating suckled for about eight months, becomes independent at about 10 months. Next young born from late November to early January.

STATUS.   Australian population is outlier of much larger New Zealand population. Sparse in Australia, common in New Zealand.

FAMILY
# Phocidae
*(foh'-sid-ee)*

DERIVATION.   sci., *Phoca*, a genus of seals; L., *-idae*, familial suffix.

These are the "true" seals, lacking external ears and with hindlimbs turned backwards to make a propulsive tail-fin. Phocids cannot walk on land but are able to propel themselves by a caterpillar-like undulation. It appears that phocids have evolved from the same ancestors as otters.

Phocids occur in both hemispheres but no species is resident in Australian coastal waters. Some come ashore to breed on Australian antarctic or subantarctic territories and occasional vagrants from these stocks become stranded on Tasmanian and mainland beaches or reefs.

# Southern Elephant-seal

*Mirounga leonina*
*(mi-roong'-gah lay'-oh-nee'-nah)*

PLATE.   44:4

DERIVATION.   *Mirounga*—Aborig., *miouroung*, elephant-seal: *leonina*—L., *leoninus*, lion-like.

LENGTH.   2.5–5 m.

HABITAT.   Cold subantarctic seas. Comes ashore on rocky beaches.

NOTES.   Feeds on squids, cuttlefishes and fishes. Males very much larger than females; possess proboscis which acts as resonator for aggressive roar.
Females sexually mature at about five years; males seldom have opportunity to mate until about 14 years old. Mating occurs in late October or November, about three weeks after female has given birth, male inseminating a number of females under his domination. Single young from previous mating suckled for three weeks, becomes independent at about 10 weeks.

STATUS.   Tasmanian and Bass Strait population, which was outlier of essentially subantarctic species, now extinct. Populations on subantarctic islands severely reduced by hunting but now recovering. Locally common.

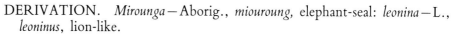

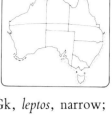

# Leopard Seal

*Hydrurga leptonyx*
*(hie-drer'-gah lep-ton'-ix)*

PLATE.   44:1

DERIVATION.   *Hydrurga*—Gk, *hydor*, water: *leptonyx*—Gk, *leptos*, narrow; Gk, *onyx*, claw.

LENGTH.   2.5–3 m.

HABITAT.   Antarctic and subantarctic seas.

NOTES.   Not strictly an Australian species, but stranded animals are not uncommon on Australian beaches. Feeds on krill and, to a considerable extent, on Adelie Penguins, other seabirds, young seals of other species, and carrion. Females slightly larger than males.

    Reproductive biology not well known. Mating possibly from November to March, two to three months after female has given birth. The single young from previous mating may be suckled for no more than two to three weeks.

STATUS.   Common.

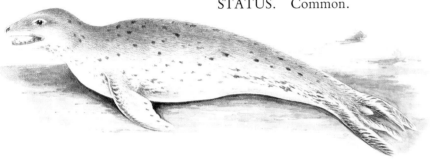

# Weddell Seal

*Leptonychotes weddellii*
*(lep-ton'-ik-oh'-tayz wed'-el-ee-ee)*

PLATE.   44:3

DERIVATION.   *Leptonychotes*—Gk, *leptos*, slender; Gk, *onyx*, claw: *weddellii*—after J. Weddell, antarctic navigator.

LENGTH.   2.5–3 m.

HABITAT.   Cold antarctic seas.

NOTES.   Spends much of its time under ice, remaining submerged for up to an hour. Feeds at night on fishes, squids and shrimps. Sexes similar in size. Only one record from the Australian coast.

    Mating occurs between October and December, about six weeks after female has given birth. Single young from previous mating suckled for about four weeks but swims with mother from age of two to three weeks.

STATUS.   Common.

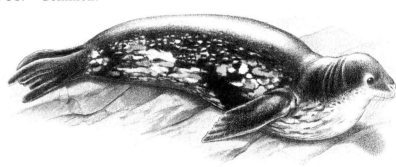

# Crab-eater Seal

*Lobodon carcinophagus*
*(loh'-boh-don kar'-sin-oh-fah'-gus)*

PLATE. 44:2

DERIVATION. *Lobodon*—Gk, *lobos*, lobe; Gk, *odous*, tooth:
*carcinophagus*—Gk, *karkinos*, crab; Gk, *phagein*, to eat.

LENGTH. *c.* 2.6 m.

HABITAT. Antarctic pack-ice.

NOTES. Very occasionally stranded upon Australian coast. Feeds at night on krill, taking in a mouthful of water and crustaceans and expelling the water through its clenched teeth, which act as a sieve. Sexes similar in size.

Females mature at three to four years, males somewhat later. Mating occurs on pack ice in November or December, about five weeks after the female has given birth. Single young from previous mating is weaned and independent at about four weeks.

STATUS. Common. By far the most abundant of the antarctic pinnipeds.

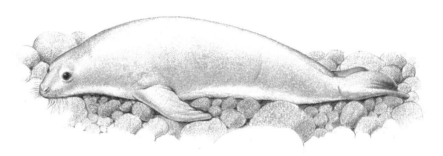

# FURTHER READING

Archer, M. (ed.). *Carnivorous Marsupials*, 2 vols. Royal Zoological Society of New South Wales, Sydney, 1982.

Covacevich, J. and A. Easton. *Rats and Mice in Queensland*. Queensland Museum, Brisbane, 1974.

Frith, H. J. and J. H. Calaby. *Kangaroos*. Cheshire, Melbourne, 1969.

Grant, T. *The Platypus*. New South Wales University Press, Sydney, 1984.

Gould, J. (with modern commentaries by J. Dixon). *Kangaroos*, 1973; *Marsupials and Monotremes*, 1974; *Placental Mammals of Australia*, 1976. Macmillan, Melbourne.

Green, R. H. *The Mammals of Australia*. Tasmanian Museum and Art Gallery, Hobart, 1960.

Griffiths, M. *The Biology of Monotremes*. Academic Press, New York, 1978.

Hall, L. S. and G. C. Richards. *Bats of Eastern Australia*. Queensland Museum, Brisbane, 1979.

Hume, I. *Digestive Physiology and Nutrition of Marsupials*. Cambridge University Press, Cambridge, 1985.

Hyett, J. and N. Shaw. *Australian Mammals: a Field Guide for New South Wales, Victoria, South Australia and Tasmania*. Nelson, Melbourne, 1980.

Jones, F. W. *The Mammals of South Australia*. Australian Government Printer, Adelaide, 1923-25 (reprinted 1968).

King, J. E. *Seals of the World*. British Museum (Natural History), London, 1983.

Lee, A. K. and A. Cockburn. *Evolutionary Ecology of Marsupials*. Cambridge University Press, Cambridge, 1985.

Le Souef, A. S. and H. Burrell. *The Wild Animals of Australasia*. Harrap, London, 1926.

Lyne, A. G. *Marsupials and Monotremes of Australia*. Angus & Robertson, Sydney, 1967.

Marlow, B. J. *Marsupials of Australia*. Jacaranda Press, Brisbane, 1962.

Ovington, D. *Australia's Endangered Species*. Cassell, Sydney, 1978.

Ride, W. D. L. *A Guide to the Native Mammals of Australia*. Oxford University Press, Melbourne, 1970.

Smith, A. and I. Hume (ed.). *Possums and Gliders*. Surrey Beatty, Sydney, 1984.

Strahan, R. *A Dictionary of Australian Mammal Names*. Angus & Robertson, Sydney, 1981.

Strahan, R. (ed.). *The Australian Museum Complete Book of Australian Mammals*. Angus & Robertson, Sydney, 1983.

Triggs, B. *Mammal Tracks and Signs: a Fieldguide for South-eastern Australia*. Oxford University Press, Melbourne, 1984.

Troughton, E. *Furred Animals of Australia*. Angus & Robertson, Sydney, 1941.

Tyndale-Biscoe, H. *The Life of Marsupials*. Arnold, London, 1973.

Watts, C. H. S. and H. J. Aslin. *The Rodents of Australia*. Angus & Robertson, Sydney, 1981.

# INDEX